ORDER TO KILL

Center Point
Large Print

Also by Vince Flynn with Kyle Mills
and available from Center Point Large Print:

The Survivor

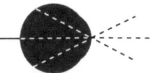

**This Large Print Book carries the
Seal of Approval of N.A.V.H.**

VINCE FLYNN

ORDER TO KILL

A MITCH RAPP NOVEL
by Kyle Mills

CENTER POINT LARGE PRINT
THORNDIKE, MAINE

This Center Point Large Print edition is published in the year 2016 by arrangement with Atria Books, a division of Simon & Schuster, Inc.

The text of this Large Print edition is unabridged. In other aspects, this book may vary from the original edition. Printed in the United States of America on permanent paper. Set in 16-point Times New Roman type.

ISBN: 978-1-68324-194-2

Library of Congress Cataloging-in-Publication Data

Names: Mills, Kyle, 1966– author. | Flynn, Vince, 1966–2013.
Title: Order to kill : a Mitch Rapp novel / by Kyle Mills.
Other titles: At head of title: Vince Flynn
Description: Center Point Large Print edition. | Thorndike, Maine : Center Point Large Print, 2016.
Identifiers: LCCN 2016041255 | ISBN 9781683241942 (hardcover : alk. paper)
Subjects: LCSH: United States. Central Intelligence Agency—Fiction. | Rapp, Mitch (Fictitious character)—Fiction. | Intelligence officers—Fiction. | Terrorism—Prevention—Fiction. | Large type books. | GSAFD: Spy stories. | Adventure fiction.
Classification: LCC PS3563.I42322 O73 2016 | DDC 813/.54—dc23
LC record available at https://lccn.loc.gov/2016041255

Acknowledgments

I again owe a great debt to the people who helped me get *Order to Kill* from blank page to finished novel. Simon Lipskar, Sloan Harris, and Emily Bestler, of course. My mother, who has the keen eye of a true fan of the genre. Rod Gregg for keeping me from making any embarrassing firearms errors and for tolerating my political musings. Ryan Steck for lending me his encyclopedic knowledge of the Rappverse. And finally, my wife, Kim, who has to live with my occasional spasms of doubt as well as the general moping that inevitably follows.

Prelude

Central Siberia

Grisha Azarov steered clear of the main street, taking a random path as he walked through what had once been one of Russia's many oil boomtowns. The satellite photos provided to him had been out of date, depicting prosperity and activity that had disappeared so completely it was hard to believe either ever existed.

Wood buildings constructed in better times were jumbled together on both sides of him. Peeling and soot stained, most were now abandoned. Curtains, wet from the recent rain, fluttered through broken windows, slapping audibly against the frames.

The population of this particular company town had dropped by more than eighty percent as the collapse in oil prices made extraction unprofitable. The most capable workers had moved on to more viable fields. Many others had returned home or gone in search of opportunities outside the energy sector. The men who had stayed—those he occasionally passed on the narrow street—were the ones with nowhere to go. Trapped in this forsaken corner of Siberia, they were now beset by deepening poverty, alcoholism, and drug addiction. When the winter cold descended, some would finally move on. Others would die.

Despite the worsening decay, the Russian oligarch he was there to meet—a billionaire many times over—remained. He had grown up in towns like this and his father had died in a Soviet-era mining accident only a few hundred kilometers away.

Dmitry Utkin worked hard to maintain the legend of his meager beginnings. He wore the frayed work clothes still admired by the Russian masses and made no effort to hide the literal and figurative scars left by a childhood of hard labor. Into this working-class persona, he skillfully weaved a beautiful wife, Italian sports cars, and watches worth more than some of his country-men would make over their lifetimes.

And they loved him for it. He provided the illusion that Russia's path to greatness was still accepting travelers. That they too could rise from squalor to become one of the country's great men.

Azarov turned down a muddy alleyway and slowed his pace as he approached the edge of town. Overhead photographs had depicted a disorienting change from gray and black to green and white. He'd expected the reality on the ground to be less stark but if anything it was even more so.

The opulent mansion had been completed

almost ten years ago and now jutted up behind massive trees flown in beneath cargo helicopters borrowed from the military. Rumors were that the structure consisted of nearly a hundred rooms. According to the architectural plans Azarov had been provided, the actual number was higher. One hundred and six.

Photos of the façade were surprisingly hard to come by, so Azarov stopped to examine it through the swaying leaves of imported landscaping. It was a typically grand and tasteless attempt to resurrect the past. To emulate the long-dead royalty with whom men like Utkin felt such kinship.

Security men began to appear as he closed in. Not surprisingly, they seemed confused. While he was precisely on time, they would have been told to watch for a man in an expensive European suit driving an even more expensive European car. Instead, Azarov was on foot, wearing old jeans, work boots, and the thick wool coat favored by people in this region.

"What do you want?" a man in a crisp uniform said, clutching the AK-103 strapped across his chest. "You know this area is off-limits to workers."

Apparently, there was a limit to how closely Utkin wanted to mix with the people whose history he professed to share.

"I have an appointment."

The man's expression turned from irritation to caution. He gripped his weapon a little tighter. "You're Grisha?"

Azarov nodded and was immediately surrounded by five guards culled from Russia's special forces. One ran a metal detector over him and, when satisfied that no weapons were present, motioned for Azarov to follow. They moved away from the mansion, back toward the town with two armed men falling in behind.

It wasn't particularly surprising that the meeting wouldn't be held in Utkin's home. The billionaire would suspect that Azarov had familiarized himself with the venue and would want to keep his visitor off-balance. An intelligent precaution taken by an intelligent man. In the end, though, his machinations would be of little importance.

They walked back along one of the muddy streets as derelict men scurried into alleys and unoccupied buildings in an effort to stay out of their way. The journey ended at a rusted door etched with the name of what had once been a prominent Russian oil company.

They stepped inside and Azarov was pointed to a chair—the only thing that remained in the entry hall. The walls had been stripped bare and the luxurious carpet was now stained and matted. One of the guards went through a door at the back, while the other two kept their eyes locked on Azarov. Of course, the man he was there to meet would make him wait. A reminder to Azarov of his subordinate position. It was always so.

Based on the information he'd been provided, Dmitry Utkin had little formal education. He had been nothing more than a petty criminal at the end of the Soviet era, though one with exceptional cunning and foresight. He'd moved quickly to take advantage of the opportunities presented by the fall of the Berlin Wall and had been one of Boris Yeltsin's early supporters. When Yeltsin rose to power, and he began parceling out Russia's riches to men who had been loyal to him, Dmitry Utkin was one of the first in line.

The assets, tax breaks, and government contracts he'd received were worth hundreds of millions of U.S. dollars and Utkin had transformed that initial fortune into an energy-based empire that spanned the globe. His growing power and influence inside Russia was what had brought Azarov there.

A thin man with graying hair and tinted glasses appeared in the doorway and hurried toward him. Mikhail Zhestakov was the CEO of Utkin's primary holding company—a man in his early forties with no ties to Soviet corruption or organized crime. By all reports, he was a highly competent and reasonably honest businessman. At least when viewed through the lens of Russian commerce.

"I'm so sorry to have kept you waiting," he said, extending a hand. "Dmitry is ready for you now."

Azarov stood and followed him through a dimly lit hallway with the two former special ops men following close behind. It finally opened into what had once been an opulent outer office but now smelled like the den of some unidentified animal. The entire back wall was frosted glass, with a single door of the same opaque material.

They passed through and he found himself in an expansive office that seemed to have been renovated just for this meeting. The dust and grime were gone and the overhead lights cast a fluorescent glare across the room. Furniture was still sparse, but centered along the back wall was a large desk.

Azarov initially ignored the man at it, instead taking in the details of his new environment. There were no windows and the soldiers he'd entered with went immediately for the corners of the room behind him. The third had taken a position to his eleven o'clock. Zhestakov retreated to the remaining available corner, looking increasingly nervous.

It was clear from Zhestakov's background and demeanor that he was not a threat, so Azarov deleted his existence from his mind and glanced back over his shoulder. The frosted glass wall had a horizontal crack about a meter from the floor that crossed almost its entire length. The door appeared to have been left unlocked but was too large and heavy to open quickly.

"It was my understanding that this was to be a private meeting," Azarov said, finally turning to face Utkin.

"These are my most loyal men. I trust them with my life. More than I would say for you, Private Filipov."

It was a name Azarov hadn't heard in many years and he didn't bother to hide his bemusement.

"Of course I know who you are," Utkin said. "A poverty-stricken nobody from a place no one has ever heard of. A failed athlete and a soldier whose service was so brief as to be completely inconsequential. An errand boy a long way from home. You'd do well to remember who paid for your training, boy. Remember who made it possible for you to become what you are."

His words were an overstatement, but not without a kernel of truth. While Azarov worked for Russia's president, it was impossible to separate the government from the oligarchs who acted as the country's nobility. Russia existed as a complex web of political bureaucracy, organized crime, and unrestrained capitalism. The enormous sums of money generated by men like Utkin was made possible by the favoritism of the govern-

13

ment. And that favoritism was paid for through an elaborate system of bribes and patronage controlled by President Maxim Vladimirovich Krupin.

"Why has Krupin sent one of his representatives here?" Utkin said, glancing at his security men for reassurance. "And why you, Grisha? Am I supposed to be frightened?"

It was an excellent question. Though he could be quite persuasive, Azarov wasn't a negotiator. He was a problem solver.

"You've spoken out publicly against the president and you've met with exiled men in London, sir. Understandably, this has caused the president concern."

"Exiled," Utkin repeated. "That's a pleasant characterization."

Azarov nodded noncommittally. The men in question had made the mistake of displeasing Krupin. In retaliation, the FSB had accused them of corruption and tax violations, forcing them to flee with little more than the clothes on their backs. Once they were gone, their holdings had been split up and doled out as patronage to more loyal men.

It was an arrangement that took advantage of the greed of the remaining oligarchs and had worked for decades. Those simpler times were now coming to an end, though. Russia's economy was collapsing and that was emboldening its power elite. Utkin most of all. He, more than the others, had a predator's ability to smell weakness and exploit it.

"Are you here to make me one of them, Grisha? To chase me off to the West? To take all that I've worked for?" He shook his head. "The world has changed, my friend. I have interests that range far outside Krupin's shrinking sphere of influence."

"I think you misunderstand my purpose."

Utkin ignored him, warming to his subject. "Russia is drowning in its own filth, Grisha. It's a closed system based entirely on corruption, threats, and the rape of its natural resources. No other country will respect Krupin's wishes with regard to me. I'll be a billionaire living in Monaco, not a pauper. He may believe he still has that kind of power but, if so, he's delusional."

"Might I remind you that the corruption and rape of natural resources are what generated your great wealth? You didn't buy your mineral and energy rights. They were given to you."

"But not by Krupin. By one of his long-dead predecessors." Utkin waved a hand around the office. "And now I'm being slowly bled of what I have. Mother Russia can no longer provide."

Azarov thought of the garish mansion at the edge of town. "And yet you seem to be living well."

"For how much longer, Grisha? Tell me that. There are strikes all over the country. Teachers, health care workers, and low-level bureaucrats are walking off their jobs because they haven't been paid. Oil prices have collapsed because of American production and the Saudis flooding the market. And as if that wasn't enough, economic sanctions caused by Krupin's military adventures are twisting the knife in my side. The ruble has become so volatile that my wife can't use them to buy jewels and shoes from those French pigs she loves so much. I might as well relocate my business to Nigeria."

"I understand the weather this time of year is quite beautiful."

Utkin smiled but otherwise didn't respond.

All of the oligarchs had the same complaints, but Utkin had taken his grievances one dangerous step further. He had gone to a rally and publicly placed the blame for Russia's problems at Maxim Krupin's feet. He'd then written a check for the back pay of government workers in towns his company controlled. The idea that this was an act of kindness or benevolence was laughable. The man was capable of neither. Much more likely it was a first step into the political arena—a poorly veiled threat to Azarov's master.

Utkin put his feet on a drawer pulled out from the desk. "I want you to understand my position, so that you can report it accurately, Grisha. I don't give a shit one way or another about Russia. But the fact that it's collapsing causes problems for my business. And while I acknowledge that the drop in oil prices is beyond our control, Krupin's mismanagement of the country is not. Russia's government has become nothing more than a tool to bolster the power and wealth of one man."

"A man with an eighty-three percent approval rating."

"But it used to be ninety," Utkin responded. "The sheep remain docile until they get too hungry, Grisha. If the disparities between the ruling class and the peasants gets too large, there will be a backlash. Look at our own history. The Bolsheviks butchered the aristocracy and we ended up with more than a half century of communism. Now we have this—"

"I'm here to assure you that the president is regaining control."

Utkin didn't bother to hide his skepticism. "All these strikes that are happening would have never gotten off the ground five years ago, Grisha. No one would have dared. And the murder of Krupin's leftist opponent last month shows desperation. I assume that was your handiwork?"

In fact, it wasn't. The assassination had been a simple matter. Nothing that demanded his talents.

"The world is watching, Grisha, and we're starting to look like some sub-Saharan backwater."

Azarov didn't disagree, but it wasn't his place to make judgments on Krupin's governance. Only to follow his orders.

"There have been some issues, but they'll soon be resolved, sir. The president is quite confident."

Utkin actually laughed. "That's why you were sent here? To repeat the same bland assurances? Wonderful! Please tell me how Krupin plans to protect my interests. I'm rapt with attention."

"I don't know the details," Azarov admitted.

In fact, he didn't know anything at all about Krupin's plan. Or even if there really was one.

"Ever the unquestioning servant, eh, Grisha?" The skepticism on Utkin's face gave way to a benevolent smile. "Maybe you should come work for me. It would have to be better than this."

"The president is convinced that you'll be pleased with the results of his program."

Utkin's smile faded. "And yet he sends you. Why? If he's so confident in his economic policy, why not just call me to discuss it? Why the clumsy attempt to intimidate me?"

"Again, that's not my purpose."

Not surprisingly, Utkin was unconvinced. "Krupin's quietly amassing men and materiel on the Latvian border, Grisha. Can we expect another military excursion that will do nothing but drain our resources and court a confrontation with the Americans? Is that his plan?"

Azarov wondered the same thing. Many Russians felt that the breakaway states had been stolen from them during the Soviet collapse.

Flexing this kind of military muscle—the only kind of muscle Russia still had—spoke deeply to their nationalism.

"People are starting to look clear-eyed at the condition of their lives, Grisha. Flag waving and military spectacles aren't going to keep them compliant for much longer. Is this how Russia is to end? With one man's desperation to maintain power at all costs?"

The hypocrisy of the oligarchs became tiresome quickly. Like Krupin, all Utkin cared about was his own power. In the same position, he would act no differently. It was time to put an end to this meeting and go home. Azarov liked being in Russia less and less as the years wore on. There was a darkness in his country that penetrated deeper into him each time he crossed its border.

"Can I tell the president that he can count on your support, sir?"

Utkin didn't answer and Azarov kept his eyes locked on the man, though he was really focused on his peripheral vision. The former soldier to his left had an open jacket and his arms crossed against his chest, keeping a hand close to his shoulder holster. With no windows, or even framed photographs, there were no reflections Azarov could use to assess the situation behind him. He could only assume the remaining two men were similarly alert.

"Tell Krupin that he'll get my support when he shows results. Until then, I will protect my own interests. Just like he does."

Utkin picked up the only document on the desk and began pretending to read. The meeting was over.

Azarov gave a submissive nod and turned, starting for the door. His tactical position was immediately improved. There was now only one man behind him and the glass wall, while frosted, was reflective enough to display his vague outline.

Neither the man behind nor the one waiting at his one o'clock had their weapons out. The man ahead and to his left had a silenced AR-15 hanging across his chest. An intimidating and impressive weapon, but one that would be hard to bring to bear quickly. His pistol was in a holster on his hip, held in place with a Velcro strap that would slow its retrieval.

Azarov couldn't blame them for their carelessness. This wasn't a battlefield and they had their unarmed opponent outnumbered three to one. In such situations, it was difficult not to become overconfident.

The man on the left moved across his path in order to open the door and Azarov casually kicked the back of his foot, knocking it sideway behind his other leg. He stumbled, instinctively tightening his hands around the assault rifle instead of throwing them out to break his fall toward the wall. When his head came even with the long crack in the glass, Azarov grabbed him by the belt and shoved him violently forward. The hope was that the glass would shatter and his head would penetrate, but the material wasn't sufficiently compromised. Instead of bleeding from a fatal neck wound, he landed facedown, dazed from the blow to the skull.

Azarov spun and dropped, landing back-to-back on top of the man, pinning his weapon beneath him. In the brief moment it took him to free the guard's holstered pistol, Azarov analyzed the tactical situation.

The man now on his left had a pistol out and his finger was already tensing on the trigger. Based on the barrel's position, though, the first round would go well above Azarov's head and the recoil would create a brief delay before a more accurate shot could be fired. Mikhail Zhestakov was facedown on the floor with his hands protecting the back of his head, as expected. Utkin was clawing clumsily at a drawer which undoubtedly contained a weapon that he had never used to do anything more demanding than execute a bound prisoner.

The soldier at the back of the room, though, was another matter. He was swinging his weapon smoothly in Azarov's direction. There was no fear or panic in his eyes, only calculation. In another tenth of a second he would fire and he would hit what he was aiming at.

With no time to bring the pistol up in front of him, Azarov fired it from an awkward position near his hip. The round went a bit lower than intended, hitting the man just below and to the right of his nose. Sloppy, but still sufficient to spray the contents of his head across the panicked Dmitry Utkin.

The man to Azarov's left fired and, as expected, the bullet went high. This time, Azarov was able to extend his arm fully and his shot impacted directly between the guard's eyes.

Azarov shoved the pistol into the back of the man beneath him, using it to propel himself to his feet while firing a single round. A moment later he was standing with the weapon's sights lined up on Utkin.

The aging oligarch had his hand wrapped around an old Makarov pistol but he froze just as it cleared the drawer. Unbidden, he dropped it and backed away with his hands in the air.

"You live up to your reputation, Grisha."

He was neither stupid nor a coward. He knew what was coming and would die defiant and on his feet. It was how Azarov preferred it. There was something about killing cowards that he found distasteful.

"I'm sorry our meeting will end like this."

Krupin had ordered him to shoot the man in

the stomach and then to deliver a lengthy diatribe about the futility of defiance, but Azarov considered it both pointless and disrespectful. He fired a single round into Utkin's forehead, followed by a round to the stomach in case Krupin should ever bother to look at the police reports.

He then set the pistol on the desk and went to help Zhestakov to his feet. The businessman's eyes were wide and wet, and he backed away until he bumped into the wall.

"Dmitry's empire is temporarily yours," Azarov said, straightening his coat and checking for any blood that might have spattered on him. "You'll manage its breakup and distribution to the other oligarchs and then you'll take a position of responsibility in one of their organizations. Is that acceptable?"

He nodded silently.

"The president wants you to understand that he doesn't blame you for Utkin's behavior and admires your business acumen."

Azarov didn't bother to wait for a second hesitant nod, instead turning and stepping over one of the bodies on his way to the door.

Once outside, he dialed the phone in his pocket.

"Can I assume that Dmitry was uncooperative?" Maxim Krupin's voice.

"Yes."

"And that you've taken care of it?"

"Yes."

"You handled the situation even more quickly than I expected. I thought that piece of filth would keep you there for hours whining about corruption and the fall of Russia."

"May I ask the status of the Mitch Rapp operation?" Azarov said, changing the subject. There was little value in discussing Dmitry Utkin further. The threat he posed was at an end. This was very much not the case with the American CIA agent.

"A rare error on your part, Grisha. Everything is moving forward smoothly. The reconnaissance and preparations are complete and it appears that taking the woman will be a simple matter."

"I'm pleased to have been wrong," he said without conviction. He could still feel the slight queasiness he always suffered when Rapp's name came up. Azarov had no involvement in Krupin's Pakistan operation or in his plans to keep Rapp from interfering. It was the way he preferred it. At least for now.

"Tell me," Krupin said, obviously not willing to allow his subordinate to direct the conversation. "Did Dmitry beg?"

"Yes," Azarov lied.

"The man was a pig," he said, sounding predictably pleased. "He cared nothing about Mother Russia."

"And yet he was a powerful man who the oligarchs looked to for leadership."

"Your point?"

"You didn't exile him, sir. You killed him. Are you certain that distributing his assets to the others is going to be enough to appease them? There's a difference between intimidation and fear. The latter can make men unpredictable."

"He was gunned down like the animal he was. They could expect no different outcome."

"Yes, sir."

Krupin had always been mistrustful, but the Arab Spring had amplified that to a dangerous degree. Watching dictators much more entrenched than himself being ousted and killed had caused the man to become paranoid. No slight was too trivial or player too insignificant to escape his notice. All were dealt with in the same ruthless manner.

With Utkin, though, Azarov wondered if Krupin had finally gone too far. If this time he had lit a fire that could not be extinguished.

Chapter 1

Near Franschhoek
South Africa

Mitch Rapp eased his rental car onto a quiet rural road and began winding his way through vineyards. The sun had just hit the horizon, turning the craggy mountains orange against a clear sky.

The scene couldn't have been more different from the smoggy, traffic-choked Pakistani cities he'd spent the last two months in. Swapping the stench of diesel and sweat for the idyllic setting of South Africa's wine country should have been a pleasant change. If anything, though, it had tightened the knot in his gut.

When he'd killed the fundamentalist director of Pakistan's intelligence apparatus a few weeks ago, blowback had been inevitable. But now it had grown beyond even his and Irene Kennedy's worst-case scenario.

There was still no question that Ahmed Taj's elimination had been necessary in order to keep Pakistan's nuclear arsenal out of the hands of Islamic hardliners. Unfortunately, his death had left a power vacuum that was pushing the already unstable country to the brink. Umar Shirani, the head of the army, was using the growing chaos to continue Taj's effort to oust the country's relatively moderate president.

One of the keys to his plan was to gain control of Pakistan's nuclear arsenal, confident that the world would be forced to back anyone with the means and will to incinerate a large swath of the region. Or, if not back, at least not oppose.

To that end, General Shirani had taken the country's nukes from their secure locations and was moving them around Pakistan in order to keep the civilian government from extending its authority over them. Of course, he said that his actions were to keep the weapons safe in the increasingly unstable environment, but no one actually believed him. He was forcing a showdown—making Pakistan's politicians and power elite choose sides.

Rapp and his teams had been charged with trying to track the weapons' movements and to make sure that none of Pakistan's terrorist groups got hold of one. It was a virtually impossible task. They were being asked to follow the constantly moving individual components of the world's seventh-largest nuclear arsenal while being actively opposed by its sixth-largest army. It was a little like the old cup and ball magic trick, but with a hundred balls—each one of which had the potential to explode and take out a major city.

Rapp rolled down the window and accelerated the vehicle, navigating by his memory of a map he'd glanced at months ago. He'd never actually been to the area, instead relying on a CIA team that specialized in selecting these types of locations.

And that's exactly what Irene Kennedy had tried to get him to continue to do: rely on specialists. Despite everything that was happening in Pakistan, though, he couldn't bring himself to pass this one off. So he'd put Scott Coleman in charge and boarded the CIA's Gulfstream G550 for South Africa.

A mistake? Most likely. Dereliction of duty? Maybe. But better to deal with this situation personally over the next twenty-four hours than to spend the next week trying to micromanage it from Islamabad.

The phone on the passenger seat chimed and he grimaced when he saw it was another text from Monica Estridge. The subject was the same as the last twenty unanswered messages from her. Granite.

He'd given the surprisingly relentless interior designer complete dominion over finishing the construction of the house he'd started before his wife was killed. Unfortunately, she didn't seem to understand the simple concept of "complete dominion." He had no idea how many swatches, paint colors, and wood finishes there were on the planet, but he was pretty sure she wasn't going to rest until he'd looked at every one.

The dirt road began to climb toward a mountain striped with cliff bands and Rapp made sure he kept the vehicle's speed at a level that wouldn't attract attention. When he reached the top of the first rise, he spotted the gray roof of the home he was looking for.

A ten-foot-tall wall topped with colorful shards of broken glass ringed the property and the trees had been cut back almost to a neighboring farmer's vines, leaving an open perimeter with an unobstructed view.

The scene probably wasn't appreciably different than it would have been if he'd been riding in on horseback at the turn of the twentieth century. Just beneath the surface, though, was a state-of-the-art security system that was not only connected to local police and a private security response team but to the CIA's top people in the country.

At his direction, Claudia Gould—now Dufort—and her daughter had moved in recently. Despite a long, painful history and the death of her husband at the hands of Stan Hurley, Rapp couldn't get her out of his mind. They seemed to be tangled together in a way that no amount of effort could reverse.

It was hard to reflect on his relationships with women without using the words "disaster" and "catastrophe." On particularly bad days, "cataclysm" also sprang to mind. His first love had died in the terrorist attack on Pan Am 103 when he was still young. Years later, his wife and unborn child had been murdered by Louis Gould, the late husband of the woman living in the spotless Cape Dutch house he was passing.

Since then, Rapp had tried futilely to find someone he could fit into his life. His wife, Anna, had been an idealist and in some ways that was why he'd loved her so intensely. While he was constantly mired in the dark, she saw the world with unflagging optimism and hope. Being with her helped him regain the humanity that sometimes seemed to be slipping irretrievably away.

In retrospect, though, their relationship hadn't been all sunshine and flowers. Anna had struggled constantly with what he did for a living. Intellectually, she understood that men like him were necessary, but he'd come to believe that on a deeper level she thought he might be part of the problem. Just another violent man who kept the world from becoming the utopia she thought it could be.

So, another Anna Reilly was out.

He tried going in the opposite direction and took up with a talented Italian private contractor, but the relationship was doomed from the start. On the bright side, she was beautiful, exciting, and completely unconcerned with his lifestyle.

On the other hand, he'd never been able to shake the feeling that for the right price, she'd start chasing him around the bedroom with an ice pick.

After Donatella, his relationships could be categorized as brief encounters that barely rose above the level of one-night stands. A former Secret Service agent. A hedge fund manager his brother had introduced him to. A redheaded air force pilot who flew support on a few of his ops.

But Claudia felt different for some reason. They'd first met years ago when he'd come to settle a score with her husband. He'd put a gun against her head, and to say the look in her eyes haunted him would be an overstatement. But he sure as hell hadn't forgotten it.

Claudia's background wasn't spotless like Anna's, but neither was it drenched in blood like Donatella's. She had a beautiful daughter and a soul that was just damaged enough for her to consider allowing someone like him into her life.

That sense of possibility was why he'd gotten personally involved with relocating Claudia and providing her with an immaculate new identity. Or at least an identity that he'd been assured was immaculate. Now, a reliable informant had told him, someone was looking to snatch her. Precisely who or why, no one seemed to know.

The likely bet was that one of her late husband's enemies had come crawling out from under a rock for some petty revenge. It was the kind of amateur bullshit that really pissed Rapp off and he was there to set an example that would discourage the next asshole.

It was another reason not to get Irene Kennedy's people involved. As the director of the CIA, there were lines she shouldn't cross. And his plan to identify the people stalking Claudia and then mail them back to their employer in FedEx envelopes was probably one of them.

Chapter 2

The light from the setting sun moved slowly up the side of the mountain, creating a lengthening shadow at its base. Rapp set his pace to stay just below the transition from dark to light, a location that would generate the most visual distortion for anyone looking up from ground level.

The terrain was steep enough that he had to use is hands for balance and loose enough that his boots occasionally sent a cloud of dirt and gravel cascading to the valley below. Like most plans created on paper, the climb he'd mapped out was in constant need of on-the-fly revision.

He came to a gap in the narrow ledge he was following and stopped for a moment, looking down more than a hundred feet to the tops of the trees he'd parked beneath. The mountain offered an ideal vantage point. The rural highway leading to town was just visible in the distance and he had full view of the dirt road that led to Claudia's house. A couple hundred more feet in altitude would give him a view of her fence line.

Range would be almost a mile and a half to the house. That would make it impossible for a shooter to use this position to cover an attack on her home—something he'd made sure of before he approved its purchase. Unfortunately, the curving road came within a quarter mile of the base of the cliff. A reasonable distance for a gifted sniper with the right equipment.

In truth, the property had never been ideal. Rapp would have preferred to put Claudia and her daughter in one of the heavily secured condo buildings in Cape Town's business district. The complexities of getting to her in the crowded city center were far more daunting than they were in this quiet rural area.

There were factors to consider beyond security, though. What kind of childhood would Anna have in the city? While his views on children had gone out of style over the past few decades, he'd always thought they needed room to run. What would he and his brother have done if they'd been stuck in a concrete and glass box as kids? Most likely gotten into even more trouble.

The gap in the ledge in front of him was narrow enough to jump, but the landing was strewn with rocks that would make an unacceptable amount of noise when his body weight came down. Instead, Rapp detoured up a gently overhanging cliff that led to flatter terrain. He went hand over hand, following a prominent crack system as the wind started to pick up.

He moved as quickly as he could. Despite his having selected clothing roughly the color of the rock, his outline would stand out against the wall of stone. Throwing an arm over the top, he slipped onto a ledge and went still, scanning the valley for any sign of humanity. Nothing. For now, things were going his way.

The snap of falling rock sounded above and he slid his Glock from beneath his jacket, rolling onto his back as a stream of dust and debris just missed him. He centered his sights on a flash of movement and tracked a furry torso for a few moments. Four baboons in total, including a large male that he'd rather not tangle with. Given a wide enough berth, they wouldn't be a problem and might even provide some cover for his movements.

Rapp continued upward, taking the most vertical route until he was well above what he considered the optimal position for taking out Claudia and her daughter. Having secured the high ground, he traversed south, keeping an eye on the tangle of ledges below. It took only a few minutes to find what he was looking for.

A lone shooter lay prone on a stone outcropping about twenty yards below Rapp's position. He was wearing gray-and-green fatigues, sighting through a scope attached to a Barrett M82 sniper rifle. All Rapp could see was the back of his head, most of which was covered by a baseball cap. A black wire led from his right ear to his jacket, suggesting that he was in contact with the ground team and probably with the man in charge of the operation.

Rapp studied the terrain between him and the sniper, deciding to continue south and then angle down toward him. The sun had disappeared behind the peaks to the west, but there was still enough of a glow that it was wise to keep it at his back. Combined with the foliage clinging to the sheer walls, the glare would be enough to obscure his approach. The problem was sound.

He moved slowly, lowering himself down the steep sections with his arms in order to avoid kicking off a rock, and crawling on the flatter terrain. Despite the short distance, it took him just over eighteen minutes to close to within ten feet of the shooter. A dense bush bordered his position and Rapp stopped behind it for one last recon.

The sniper's position didn't seem to have changed at all. He was statue-still, confirming his experience and discipline. Rapp slid the Glock from his jacket and inched forward. The man stayed focused on his scope, unaware that he was being hunted until the barrel of Rapp's gun pressed against his ear.

He jerked a bit and then went completely still again.

"Get up. And unless you want to take the fast route down to the valley, be careful how you do it."

Chapter 3

Ilya Gusev lit another cigarette and stubbed the old one out in an overflowing ashtray. The shades were drawn, leaving the room in darkness broken only by the glow of the computer monitor he'd paid cash for earlier that week.

He scanned an image transmitted from a camera mounted to the back of a truck, but little had changed. The same empty dirt road cast into shadow by the setting sun. Most of the other video feeds set up in a grid across the screen were still blank. They were reserved for the men carrying out the operation and wouldn't be turned on until it started in earnest.

The only other feed had a space blocked out in the bottom of the monitor. He expanded it and studied the view of the operation's entire theater being transmitted through the riflescope of a man perched high on a cliff face.

While it had been a great honor to be chosen to lead this operation, Gusev's initial nervousness was quickly turning to fear. The men he'd been forced to use—with the exception of the mercenary on the cliff—were completely unreliable. No, not unreliable. That implied someone who might or might not do his duty in a workmanlike manner. These men were insane. Uncontrollable and utterly incompetent.

His own men, while not exactly army special forces, were at least known quantities. At a minimum, they could be counted on to react to a given situation like human beings. Albeit a brutal and remorseless branch of the species.

These ISIS crazies were another matter entirely. While he understood the necessity of having a few of them involved, one or two would have been more than sufficient. Unfortunately, his pleas had fallen on deaf ears. At least he'd been able to convince his masters to give him the mercenary. If things went wrong, he would act rationally and professionally. The question was whether it would be enough.

Gusev squinted at an empty road near the center of the scope image and poured himself a glass of vodka to calm his nerves. Who was this woman? Based on the information he'd been given, Claudia Dufort was a thirty-six-year-old French national who had been provided a generous trust fund by her grandparents. Other than that he knew little. Based on his surveillance, he could only say that she was strikingly beautiful, did not hold a regular job, and had a young daughter.

She seemed to have no ties to crime or politics. No history that would generate powerful enemies. This begged the question: What was it about the woman that he *didn't* know? It seemed certain that she was not the simple wealthy single mother she presented. Who was she really? Who had she harmed?

Gusev took an unusually small sip of his vodka, cognizant that he needed to keep his wits about him. In the end, the woman's identity was irrelevant and he was undoubtedly better off not knowing. All he needed to do was succeed at the task given to him. If everything went as planned, the rewards would be limitless. Unfortunately, failure would be punished just as lavishly.

The scope image shook and the Russian focused on it again. The mercenary behind it, a young American, was one of a new generation of assassins. Not terribly experienced, but well trained and possessing the technological skills necessary to operate in a world that transformed itself almost hourly.

What had drawn Gusev's attention was less the image itself and more the sudden violent shake of it. Kent Black was nothing if not disciplined. His uncanny ability to lie completely motionless for hours on end was one of the reasons he'd been selected for this mission.

The dark feed from the body cam the American was lying on began to move as he slowly rolled over. Gusev felt a surge of adrenaline when a pair of boots came into focus. Black wasn't alone on the ledge. Someone had managed to climb to his position unnoticed and come up behind him. The camera swept upward, displaying the shadowed outline of a Glock and then a face that was lit just well enough to be recognizable.

Mitch Rapp.

Gusev stumbled backward, nearly pitching over his chair. He knew the face from years ago. It had been burned into his mind from a hazy black-and-white photo taken just after Rapp had executed seven Russians involved in selling arms to Hamas. What the fuck was the CIA man doing here? What connection could he possibly have to a young French woman living in South Africa? Gusev tried to calm himself but found it impossible. What should he do? Was it possible to call off the operation? Would the ISIS people that had been forced on him even follow that order? What if Rapp simply took Black's weapon and position? He could take out the entire team with no difficulty at all.

Fear quickly turned to panic. Gusev wondered frantically if Rapp knew of his involvement. Or the identity of his employer. Was the CIA man alone or did he have a team?

The Russian spun toward the door, his instinct for self-preservation overwhelming him. After a few jerky steps, though, he stopped. It was impossible. Where would he go? It wouldn't matter. He would be a hunted man. Better to fall into the hands of the Americans—even Rapp—than into the hands of the man who would come for him if he ran.

Gusev went for the secure phone next to the monitor and began to dial, a sense of dread descending on him. He couldn't be blamed for this, he told himself. He hadn't been involved in any of the planning. In fact, he knew very little about the operation and its goals beyond the specific set of tasks he'd been charged with. His responsibilities were a relatively simple matter. No one had even hinted at the possibility that there would be resistance that amounted to anything more serious than the child throwing a tantrum.

He was nearly finished dialing when the on-screen image shook again—this time even more violently. His thumb stopped, hovering over the last digit. The video feed had turned cloudy in a way that couldn't be explained by the encroaching darkness, and Gusev leaned in a little closer. After a few moments, the haze that appeared to be dust began to clear. What was revealed caused his breath to catch in his chest.

Mitch Rapp was lying motionless in the dirt with Black's knee in his back and a pistol pressed to his head.

The radio on Gusev's desk crackled to life and he heard the mercenary's voice come over it.

"Eagle to base."

The Russian didn't respond. He found it

impossible to process what was happening. Mitch Rapp, feared by even the most powerful men in the world, had been taken by a thirty-year-old contract killer.

"Eagle to base," Black repeated.

"This is base," Gusev responded with a shaking voice. "What is your situation?"

"An armed man came up on my position. I've subdued him."

Gusev watched as Black grabbed the CIA man by the hair and twisted his head so that it would display on the monitor. "Can you identify him?"

Gusev fell into a chair, his legs suddenly too weak to support his considerable weight. The young American didn't know who he was dealing with. That he had unwittingly done what so many men before him had died trying to accomplish.

"What happened?" Gusev asked numbly.

"Whoever he is, he's quiet as hell and can obviously climb. The cliff face behind my position is loose and I put a remote charge in it for just this kind of situation. He was standing right in front of it when I triggered it."

"Is he . . ." Gusev's mouth went dry for a moment and he wet it with a quick swig of vodka. "Is he dead?"

"Nah. Just unconscious. You want me to finish him?"

The Russian considered the question for a

moment. "Would it be possible to get him down alive?"

"This wasn't part of our deal."

"I'll provide compensation that you'll find more than generous."

"In that case, yes. If he wakes up and can walk. There's no way to carry him, though. Are we continuing with the op? Seems like we've been compromised."

"We're moving forward," Gusev said, trying to contain his excitement. Rapp dead would be an enormous prize. But alive? The man's knowledge of CIA operations was second only to that of Irene Kennedy. There was no way to over-estimate his value to Gusev's employer. What rewards would he reap for succeeding beyond anyone's wildest imagination? For capturing the man that everyone considered invincible?

"He is extraordinarily dangerous," Gusev said into the radio. "If you can get him down without taking any risks, do so. If there is any sign of a problem, kill him immediately."

"Understood."

"Dufort and her daughter should be only a few minutes out. Can you subdue him and still carry out your part of the mission?"

"Not a problem," Black said with confidence that would undoubtedly disappear if he knew who was lying at his feet. "I'm out."

Chapter 4

Claudia repeated her new last name to herself, trying to get it to sink in. She spoke quietly, keeping the volume of her voice lower than that of the breeze blowing through the vehicle's open windows.

"Dufort, Dufort, Dufort . . ."

It wasn't as though this was her first alias—she'd had plenty of occasions to use them in the years she'd handled logistics for the professional assassin she'd been married to. This felt very different, though. Those had been nothing more than a stack of IDs and credit cards to be used for a few days and then carefully destroyed. Claudia Dufort wasn't a convenient fiction to be used while Louis completed a contract. It was who she was now. Claudia Gould was gone forever.

She spoke a little louder, glancing over at her daughter in the passenger seat to make sure she didn't wake her. On the other hand, maybe she should. Anna had taken to sleeping too much in recent weeks. At seven years old, she was struggling to fully grasp the ramifications of her father's death. The permanence of it.

And then there was the new home, the new school, and the new friends. In the end, though, she was young and adaptable. In fact, Claudia had noticed that Anna's French accent was already taking on a few South African nuances.

So, sleeping too much or not, Anna would ultimately be fine. But what about her mother? Would she learn to inhabit her new life as comfortably?

It was an open question at this point. Over the past few months, Claudia had been able to immerse herself in the details of her new identity, country, and lifestyle. But now things were settling down and that left her with too much free time.

She had more money than she could spend in two lifetimes, so a job wasn't necessary. But what else would she do? She needed time to spend with Anna and had planned a series of adventures for them that included everything from classical music concerts to sandboarding the dunes of Namibia. It wouldn't be enough, though. After years of working with one of the most successful contract killers in the world, baking cookies and setting up playdates seemed too radical a change.

She needed something challenging but not all-consuming. Something exciting but that left her hands free of blood. Or maybe even something that helped clean them a bit. With the poverty that plagued Africa, perhaps going to work for one of the many NGOs in the area would be an option. Her talents would be a good fit, and her money would make her appealing to any charity she approached. Better yet, she could involve Anna. A reminder that not all little girls lived inhistoric homes surrounded by vineyards.

Claudia tapped the brake when she saw the glow of taillights through the dusty air. As she got closer, she started to make out the back of one of the lumbering cargo trucks that supplied the local winemakers. Passing was impossible on the winding dirt road. The massive armored SUV that Mitch had left in her garage was nowhere near nimble enough.

He was paranoid like everyone else involved in his business. Having said that, while she doubted any of her husband's enemies would bother to come looking, carjacking was rampant in South Africa. News reports and casual warnings from locals had been enough for her to put off trading in the thinly disguised tank for one of the Audi crossovers she'd been coveting.

Claudia closed to within five meters of the truck and then held that distance. The turn into her property wasn't far, and, there was no reason to hurry. No operations to check up on. No money to launder or bank accounts to conceal. And no one waiting other than two guard dogs that had yet to warm up to her but couldn't get enough of Anna. Another gift from Mitch.

Ahead, the rear doors of the truck suddenly

flew open and Claudia slammed her foot down on the brake pedal before instinctively throwing a protective arm in front of her daughter.

"Mom?" Anna said groggily. "What's going on?"

"It's fine," Claudia responded, letting the distance between her and the truck lengthen. "Go back to sleep, honey."

Nothing seemed to be falling out of the vehicle but even the upgraded headlights of her SUV couldn't penetrate very far into the trailer. She honked a few times but the driver didn't seem to notice. A moment later, the loading ramp rolled out and slammed into the ground.

This time Anna came fully awake.

"Mom?" she said, rubbing her eyes. "What's wrong with that truck?"

"I don't know, honey. I think the latch on the doors is broken."

The metal ramp continued to bump along the road, making enough noise to wake the dead. The night was starting to cool and the driver had his windows up. If she had to guess, he was probably also wearing headphones. It was a common practice and one of the many reasons that South African roads were some of the most dangerous in the world.

A moment later the roar of an engine behind them drowned out the rattle of metal and Claudia's eyes darted to the rearview mirror. There were no lights and she was confused until the front grille of some kind of military vehicle got close enough to be illuminated in her taillights.

Anna screamed when it rammed them and Claudia jerked the wheel left, trying to steer the SUV into the vines that lined the road. Nothing happened. She shot a glance in the direction of her side-view mirror and saw that a steel rail similar to a forklift's had embedded itself in her rear quarter panel. She hit the gas but the vehicle behind matched her speed, preventing her from breaking free.

Claudia locked up the brakes and twisted the wheel until it stopped, but they kept moving inevitably forward. The front of her SUV dipped violently when the front tires were ripped from their rims and she finally released the wheel to reach for her panicked daughter.

They hit the ramp and were forced into the truck's trailer, traveling along it until they slammed into the back. The SUV's air bags went off, shoving Claudia back into her seat and dazing her for a few seconds. By the time she managed to shake off the effect and make sure Anna was all right, footsteps were ringing against the steel floor of the trailer.

She looked back and saw a Humvee with a massive grille that included not only the forklift structure that had sandwiched the rear of her SUV but also a number of barbed spikes that had penetrated her rear hatch. The Humvee had no doors, which allowed its two Middle Eastern occupants to easily escape it. One was moving toward her while the other went for the rear of the truck to retract the ramp and close the doors.

The space was too narrow to allow her to open her door, but she wouldn't have even if she could. The armor Mitch had built into the SUV was all that was between them and the men outside. Anna tried to grab hold of her, but Claudia pulled away, reaching for her cell phone. No signal. The metal box they were trapped in was blocking reception.

The vehicle lurched and she looked up through the moonroof to see a man with a thick beard and wide grin. A moment later, he was in motion, swinging a sledgehammer down with a deafening crash that was immediately lost in Anna's terrified scream.

The reinforced glass held, but there was no way to know if it would continue to do so. Claudia unlatched her daughter's seat belt and pulled her close, trying to quiet her sobbing as the man continued to attack the glass.

After about a minute, the first crack formed. The man howled with glee but Claudia couldn't bring herself to look up. Her terror turned to a sensation of paralyzing guilt deeper than anything she'd ever felt before. She deserved this for the things she'd done in her life. But not Anna. She was innocent.

Chapter 5

Near Maseru
Lesotho

Rapp tried to wrench himself into a more comfortable position as he squinted into the light bleeding through the trunk lid. His hands were taped behind him, making it impossible to see his watch, but the fact that the sun was coming up suggested that he'd been crammed into the tiny space for a good ten hours. Karmic payback for all the people he'd stuffed into similar trunks over his career.

The road had become noticeably worse over the last hour and the vehicle dropped into yet another rut, ramming his head into what was probably a lug wrench. By his count, it was the twelfth time that had happened, and with every repeat, his anger grew.

Rapp knew pretty much everything there was to know about the shooter he'd found on that cliff face. His name was Steve Thompson, though these days he answered to Kent Black. Apparently he felt the new name gave him more gravitas. His father had been an abusive survivalist who years ago had taken his young son to a remote corner of Montana in preparation for the end of the world.

They'd lived there with no electricity or running water for a little over ten years before the old man suddenly disappeared. No body or evidence of foul play was ever found. In all likelihood, it had been the first demonstration of his son's unusual talents.

With little formal schooling and nowhere to go, Thompson had gotten his GED and joined the army. He'd eventually become a Ranger and seen a fair amount of combat in the Middle East. After eight years of that, he'd finally been drummed out for insubordination. There had been no specific incident that stood out. Just a general distaste for authority that he couldn't be bothered to hide.

It had been an interesting enough resume to land on Rapp's desk but he'd decided there were too many red flags. The issues with authority were only the tip of the iceberg. Thompson was a talented operator but a loner to the point of being a guy you wouldn't necessarily be able to count on when the shit hit the fan. And then there were the sociopathic tendencies, the potential begin-nings of a cocaine problem, and the fact that he'd likely murdered his own father. There was no question the old bastard had it coming, but it brought into question where the kid's boundaries were. Or if he had any at all.

The accomplice who had helped wedge Rapp into his present accommodation was more enigmatic. Judging by his accent, probably Iraqi. Early twenties with a thick beard and the wild eyes that Rapp had come to associate with ISIS.

An interesting pair, to say the least: the young American mercenary with well-documented sociopathic tendencies matched with an even younger member of a jihadist movement that wasn't in the habit of hiring contractors—particularly American ones.

The car skidded to a stop and Rapp rolled toward the front, slamming his head into the lug wrench again. The trunk flew open a few moments later and he turned away from the bright sunlight as the Iraqi grabbed him by the hair and dragged him out. The stream of Arabic insults was nonstop and he likely assumed that Rapp wouldn't be able to comprehend it. When the terrorist got around to Mitch's mother, though, Rapp swung a foot into the side of his leg, dropping him to his knees. A follow-up kick landed between his shoulder blades and put his face into the rear bumper.

"Stop!"

Rapp turned toward Thompson and looked down the silencer of his own gun. One of his least favorite things to do.

Blood was gushing from the Arab's nose as he leapt to his feet and prepared to charge, but Thompson shifted the weapon toward him. "I said stop! Both of you."

Rapp just turned and started walking toward the only building in sight.

"Wait!"

He ignored the man, using the time to take in his surroundings. The mountains were less rocky than those around Franschhoek and everything was green. Despite the clear sky and sun angling in from the east, the air didn't hold much heat, suggesting a significant increase in altitude. More interesting was the building itself. Windowless and constructed entirely of cinder block, its purpose was painted on it in faded red letters: Mortuary.

Thompson and the bleeding Arab fell in behind as Rapp pushed through a heavy wooden door.

The room was probably twenty-five feet square, with the woman and the girl he'd come to Africa to help sitting on a collapsing sofa at the far end. Claudia looked understandably distraught, while Anna was nearly catatonic. They were guarded by an armed Arab who looked just as crazy as the one dripping onto the floor by the entrance.

Finally, there was a coffin in the center of the room containing the emaciated corpse of a man who looked to have been about thirty when he died. Whether the condition of the body was from the illness that killed him or the fact that he'd just gotten a little dried out was hard to tell. At least he didn't smell.

Claudia stood and started toward Rapp but the man guarding her swung his rifle butt into her chest hard enough to knock her to the floor. Anna came to life, darting for her mother and landing beside her, crying loudly. Rapp felt his anger flare but there wasn't a lot he could do with his hands secured behind his back.

Claudia looked more scared than hurt and she pulled her daughter back to the sofa, keeping a watchful eye on the man screaming about crushing her skull and raping her dead body before doing the same to Anna. Fortunately, French and English were her only languages and she had no idea what was being said.

"Move," Thompson said, indicating a door to the left. With few other options, Rapp entered what appeared to be an embalming room.

"Sit."

He did as he was told and Thompson used more tape to secure him to the chair. When he was satisfied with his handiwork, he dumped Rapp's gun and other personal effects on a metal gurney next to a body in the process of being prepared for burial.

"He's secure?"

Rapp looked toward the door and examined the man who had appeared in it. The accent was unquestionably Russian and his appearance confirmed that. About six feet, weighing in at a soft two fifty. A few tattoos with Cyrillic writing were visible beneath the thick black hair on his arms.

"Yeah. He's not going anywhere."

"Then get the fuck out."

Thompson closed the door behind him as the Russian walked to the gurney and started going through items on it. He admired the Glock for a few seconds before starting to paw through Rapp's wallet.

"Mitch Kruse?"

"That's me."

The man let out a short laugh and picked up Rapp's phone, staring down at the screen for a moment. "What is this? It says granite."

That woman just wouldn't give up.

"It's a type of rock."

The Russian rushed forward and slammed a fist into the side of Rapp's face. "I speak English! What does it *mean?* Is it a code word?"

Rapp worked his jaws around. No serious damage but the guy had a punch. "It means I need kitchen counters, Ivan. Do me a favor and pick one."

He swung again but this time Rapp managed to duck his head enough to get the blow to glance off.

"You will give me the truth!" the man screamed. He paused, letting an arrogant smile spread across his face. "Mr. Rapp."

"Pretty pleased with yourself, aren't you, Ivan?"

"My name is not Ivan!"

"Sorry. What is it?"

"I am asking the questions," he shouted, this time swinging a fist into Rapp's stomach. "How did you get here so quickly?"

"I swam."

The man glanced suggestively at the door that led to Claudia and Anna. "Are you sure you want that to be your answer?"

Normally, Rapp would just clam up during an interrogation. It was the best way to hold out. But he needed to get this moron talking.

"You got me, Ivan. Gulfstream G550."

"Stop calling me that!" the man said angrily.

"Then introduce yourself."

The Russian grabbed a scalpel from next to the body and held it so it flashed in the overhead lights. "I suggest you start taking my questions seriously."

Rapp decided to mix it up and feigned a hint of fear. "Okay, okay. I have a personal relationship with the woman and got a tip someone was coming to kill her."

Of course, the intel was actually that kidnapping was the play, but the intentional error would goad this idiot.

"From who?"

"An informant in St. Petersburg. You should have covered your tracks better."

"Your informant knows nothing," the man

said, clearly anxious to prove that he was the smartest guy in the room.

"The people who hired you had dealings with her husband," Rapp offered. "This is just some piece of dumbass revenge."

"You rely too heavily on bad intelligence, Mr. Rapp. I was just to take the woman and the child to Afghanistan. To lead you on a chase around the world for the next two weeks before killing them."

This guy was way too easy. Certainly not Russian intelligence. If he were, Rapp would already be on a plane to Moscow, where he'd either get traded back to the U.S. or spend the next five years being wrung for everything he knew about America's intelligence capability.

No, this dipshit had the look of one of the many organized criminals that ran roughshod over the former Soviet Union. Not the stupidest-looking one Rapp had ever met, but then the bar wasn't all that high.

"You're lying," Rapp said, calculating the best way to keep the conversation going. It was obvious that the Russian was enjoying showing off that he knew more than the Agency. "I know how this goes. You're trying to confuse me. It's not going to work. What would be the point of taking them halfway around the world?"

The man turned back to the gurney and exchanged the scalpel for a saw. The way his eyes shifted suggested that he didn't know. Whoever was pulling his strings wasn't stupid enough to tell him any more than he needed to know.

Not that it mattered. There was only one answer that fit. This wasn't about Claudia. It was about distracting him and getting him out of Pakistan.

"My employers deemed it too risky to try to kill you."

While there was probably some truth to that, Rapp doubted it was the whole story. More likely his employers recognized that killing him went only so far toward damaging the CIA's Pakistan operation. What they were counting on was that he'd pull Scott Coleman and his team out of Islamabad to help find Claudia. And they were right. If he hadn't gotten the tip and instead showed up to find that Claudia had been snatched by a couple ISIS pricks, he would have wanted his top people in on the hunt.

"It appears that they very much overestimated you," the Russian continued.

"I get that a lot."

He used the flexible metal saw to smack Rapp across the face, leaving a serrated cut across his cheek. There seemed to have been no purpose to the blow. He did it just because he could.

More and more, Rapp was starting to suspect that this wasn't actually an interrogation. The Russian was trying to decide what to do. He could hand Rapp over to his employers and reap the rewards or he could keep Rapp and use whatever information he could beat out of him for his own benefit.

"I'm worth a lot to my government," Rapp said, trying to keep him on the hook. "They'll pay to get me back."

The man didn't respond for a long time, staring down at his own reflection in the saw. "I don't think the rewards would be equal to what I can get from my own employer."

It sounded like he was coming to a decision. Time was running out.

"Whoever you work for, they're not the U.S.A. What can they give you?" Rapp said, trying to get some clue as to who was behind this. "We'll match it."

"You're bound by the law. My employer isn't. Money, of course. But young girls? Drugs? An estate filled with stolen masterworks befitting an oligarch?"

Interesting, but not that helpful. In Russia it was hard to tell where the government stopped and organized crime started. You could probably find someone at the Moscow DMV to provide those things if the price was right.

"You seem like more a dogs-playing-poker guy to me."

The saw flashed again, this time leaving a jagged cut on his other cheek. Rapp could feel the blood trickling through his beard and then dripping into the open collar of his shirt.

"That's starting to get old, Ivan."

"It's nothing compared to what my employer will do to you. He'll keep you alive for years, extracting everything. You'll spend your days begging to be killed and your nights chained naked to a bare concrete floor. There will be nothing left of you but a frightened, broken old man."

He reached into his pocket and pulled out a satellite phone. That was it. He was going to call in a sitrep. Shame. He had to be one of the most talkative interrogators in history.

Rapp reached into the tape binding him and peeled off a shard of razor blade that was right where it was supposed to be. The Russian dialed as he started slicing.

Rapp's knee was partially locked when he finally stood. Ten years ago a few hours in a trunk wouldn't have affected him but now the wear and tear was starting to add up.

The Russian froze for a split second when he saw that his prisoner was free and then threw the saw before running for the door. The blade passed a good foot to Rapp's right and he just stood there stretching his back as the Russian jerked open the door and shouted for Thompson's help.

In the room beyond, the young contractor was

standing over the bodies of the two Arabs. Claudia had Anna on her lap, holding her tight and trying to keep her quiet.

The Russian retreated to the far wall, watching wide-eyed as Rapp retrieved his Glock and walked through the door, kneeling in front of Claudia and running a hand affectionately through Anna's hair.

"I'm sorry. I wish I could have spared you this."

Claudia shook her head, tears flowing past the streaks of dried ones on her cheeks. "Please don't, Mitch. Don't ever tell me you're sorry. We'd be dead many times over without you. I don't deserve any of the things you've done for me."

Rapp fished a set of keys from the pocket of one of the dead men. "Wait in the car. I'll be out in a little while."

He and Thompson watched her go before turning their attention back to the man pressed against the wall of the embalming room.

"But . . ." he stammered, pointing at the young contractor. "You've been paid! We had an agreement!"

His confusion was understandable. Killers of Thompson's caliber rarely betrayed their customers. At best it was bad for business. At worst it could be deadly.

"I'm not an idiot," Thompson said. "I work

in a pretty exclusive profession, Ilya. Did you think I wouldn't recognize Louis Gould's wife and daughter? And that I wouldn't know Mitch has a history with them? What do you think he was going to do after you were finished leading him around on his wild goose chase? He was going to hunt me down and put a bullet in my head."

"Gould? I . . . I didn't know!"

"Yeah, well, whoever you're working for did. And since they were setting me up, I figured I'd give Mitch a call and return the favor."

Chapter 6

The Russian crouched and let loose a right hook when Rapp got in range. It wasn't a bad effort—clearly the man had some training. Based on the speed, though, that training had been a lot of vodka and cigarettes ago.

Rapp ducked and shot an open palm up into the man's chin. He'd retreated against the cinderblock wall and, as planned, his head snapped back into it. Not with sufficient force to knock him unconscious, but hard enough to make his knees buckle.

Rapp grabbed him by the hair and dragged him to the gurney centered in the room. He shoved the corpse occupying it onto the floor and replaced it with the Russian. He struggled weakly but was too dazed to prevent Rapp from using a roll of duct tape to secure him to the bloodstained metal surface.

"Ilya, right? What's your last name?" Rapp said, grabbing his phone off the tray and starting to dial.

"I . . . I wasn't going to harm you," the man begged uselessly. "I don't know anything. I was just hired—"

Rapp slapped a piece of tape over his mouth, silencing him as the phone on the other end of the line began to ring. Irene Kennedy picked up a moment later.

"Are Claudia and Anna all right?" she said by way of greeting. As director of the CIA, the demands on her time got worse every year. She reacted by making everything more efficient, and that had prompted her to do away with meaningless pleasantries. Rapp wholeheartedly agreed. After almost a quarter century of working together, small talk was a waste of limited resources.

"They're fine. I'm holding a Russian who seemed to be running things. He's got two Middle Eastern sidekicks that I'm betting are ISIS."

"That's an odd combination."

"I thought so, too."

"Have you had a chance to question them?"

"The Arabs are dead and I'm just about to have a sit-down with the Russian. What I know at this point, though, is that none of this was about Claudia. It was about getting me out of Pakistan."

"Are you sure?"

"Ninety percent."

"There's only one reason someone would want to do that."

"Yeah. They're going to make a move against one of the nukes the army's moving around."

"How quickly can you get back to Islamabad?"

Rapp ripped the tape off the Russian's mouth. "Where are we?"

"I want to—"

He clapped a hand over the man's mouth, cutting off both his words and his ability to breathe. "It's a simple question, Ilya. You should answer it."

He removed his hand and the man spoke in a shaking voice. "Lesotho. Near Maseru."

"Did you get that, Irene? Maseru. Can you figure out the closest strip that'll take the G550 and have it brought in? And call Scott. Tell him that someone might be looking to make a move."

"I'll do it right away."

"Can you get in touch with the Pakistani government and tell them what's happened? See if they'll dial back the bullshit until we can figure out where the threat's coming from?"

"As you know, President Chutani's not our problem. He wants Pakistan's nuclear arsenal locked down even more than we do. But the army is another matter. General Shirani is willing to take whatever risks are necessary to create an environment for a successful coup."

"Keep me posted," Rapp said, cutting off the call and looking down at the man taped to the gurney.

"Please," he begged. "I don't know anything."

Rapp silently examined him—the expensive

65

slacks and shoes, the gaudy gold chain nested in a carpet of chest hair, the nose that looked like it had been broken a few times. The guy stank of Russian mafia.

"By the looks of you, I believe that you don't know much. But nothing at all? I'm not buying it."

Rapp picked up an embalming needle injector. "This looks like it would do some damage, doesn't it?"

"Please! I wasn't told you were involved and I didn't know who the woman was. I did it for the money. Nothing more."

"Okay. Then tell me who's writing the check."

"I . . ." he stammered, trying to buy enough time to come up with a plausible lie. "I don't know. I'm just a criminal. Drugs. Women. Gambling. My name is Ilya Gusev."

Rapp recognized it. Despite his appearance, Gusev wasn't just a piece of mindless muscle. He was a high-level criminal with his own outfit. Rapp had become familiar with him when the CIA had incorrectly suspected him of dealing arms in the Middle East.

"Sure," Rapp said. "I've heard of you."

"Then you know I'm telling the truth!"

"What I know is that you're not some small-time hustler who takes jobs from anyone with a few rubles to wave around. So either you're lying about not knowing who you're working for or you came up with this on your own."

"No! I've told you everything!"

"Look, Ilya. I don't give a rat's ass about you. I don't care if you walk out of here without a scratch or if my people have to scrape what's left of you off the floor. But I can tell you that if you keep lying to me, it's going to be the second one. Now let's start again. Who's writing the check for this job?"

"I don't know," he said, sounding like he was on the verge of breaking into tears.

Rapp looked back at the door, making sure it was closed and trying to assess its thickness. Normally, this would be a simple situation. He'd ask his questions in a way that they would be answered quickly and truthfully. Now, though, he found himself worrying that the sound might carry out to Claudia and Anna. And then there was the matter of blood. He couldn't walk out of here looking like he'd spent the day working in a slaughterhouse.

Rapp had promised himself that he was going to get a life outside of all this, but he'd forgotten the drawbacks—the constraints that he hadn't worked under since his wife died.

"You've caught me on a good day," Rapp said, pressing his silencer to bottom of the man's left foot. "But now my patience is wearing thin."

The Russian thrashed wildly, trying to break free of the tape, but he still didn't offer any employment details. Time for a change in strategy. Rapp moved the weapon from the leather sole of Gusev's shoe to his thigh, pressing the tip into his soft flesh. It would further dampen the sound.

"Are you partnering with ISIS, Ilya? They've knocked over a lot of banks and sold a lot of oil. I'll bet they have enough money to tempt even a high roller like you."

"No! I was going to shoot them and leave them for you to find. To give you a trail to follow to the Middle East."

"Why?"

"Maybe someone there wants to kill you?"

"*Everybody* there wants to kill me, Ilya. But why go through all this effort? A month doesn't go by that I don't show my face in the Middle East at least once. No one has to lure me. More likely, someone wanted me out of Pakistan. You just have to tell me who and why."

ISIS was coming under the control of Saddam Hussein's former generals, making their command and control structure increasingly sophisticated. Was it possible they'd gotten to the point that they were capable of embarking on something this complicated? The Baathist sons of bitches that the American politicians had prohibited him from killing would like nothing more than to get their hands on a nuke.

His phone chimed and he reached into his

pocket, hoping that it was Kennedy with an ETA on his ride and not his decorator with a selection of bathroom tiles. For once he got his wish. The G550 would be at a nearby strip in thirty minutes.

"Time's up, Ilya."

"No! I—"

Rapp squeezed the trigger and felt the Glock kick as a bullet tore through the Russian's leg. He started screaming and Rapp shoved a blood-stained rag in his mouth to muffle the sound.

Gusev managed to spit out the rag just as Rapp was finishing an acknowledgment text to Kennedy.

"You're a dead man!" the Russian screamed. "Do you hear me? A dead man! You have no idea what you're dealing with. Grisha is going to come for you and everything you love!"

Rapp set down the gun. Finally, they were getting somewhere.

"Who's Grisha?"

"You're going to find out," Gusev said between clenched teeth.

"Is that who you work for? Not ISIS? A Russian? Why don't you give me a last name? We can give him a call. Put him on speaker-phone while I bandage up that leg."

Gusev started shouting obscenities at him in Russian and Rapp grabbed hold of his wounded thigh. "Listen to me, you Russian piece of shit.

I've given you more chances than I've given anybody in ten years. But that's over now. There's a set of pliers on that tray over there and if you don't tell me what I want to know, I'm going to start pulling your teeth."

The rage in Gusev's eyes was replaced by panic when Rapp clamped a hand around his throat. He had been around too many men in Gusev's position to be fooled. Hell, *he'd* been in Gusev's position a couple times. The Russian still had some fight in him, but it was running out fast.

Gusev's eyes started to lose focus just as the door leading into the room was thrown open. Rapp spun and saw one of the Arabs Thompson had shot sagging against the jamb. There was an AK-47 in his hands and he pulled the trigger, using what little strength he had left to sweep it across the room.

Rapp dove to the floor, rolling to the table where he'd left his Glock. A barrage of bullets went over his head and a spray of pulverized cinder block hit him in the face, partially blinding him. All he could see was the Arab's outline and he aimed for the middle of it, firing three rapid shots that hit center of mass. The force of the rounds spun the man around and toppled him over a cart stacked with rusting embalming equipment.

Rapp got to his feet, wiping at his eyes as he

approached the man. This time there was no question that he was dead. Two hits in the chest and one in the stomach. A fourth wound could be seen on the right side of his head beneath blood-matted hair. Thompson's shot.

Rapp turned back toward Gusev and swore under his breath. The man was staring sightlessly at the ceiling with a gaping bullet wound in his side.

The sound of running footsteps became audible in the next room and Rapp lined up on Steve Thompson as he came skidding to a stop in the doorway.

"Whoa! Easy, Mitch!" He raised his hands, one of which held a Beretta 92FS. "What the hell happened?"

"I was going to ask you the same thing."

Thompson spotted the dead Arab and his eyes widened. "I popped that guy, man. I swear I did. Right in the head."

"You didn't check to see if he was dead?"

"It was point-blank range! His fucking hair caught fire!"

Rapp's finger tightened on the trigger but it was out of anger at the kid's stupidity, not because he thought Thompson had tried to set him up. Part of the Arab's head was noticeably concave and the trail of blood he'd left on his walk to the door was obvious. It was the downside of head shots. While they got around the problems posed by body armor, they could be unpredictable.

"Come on, Mitch. I'm sorry. I don't normally do this kind of close-up work."

"Get out."

"So we're good?"

"As long as I don't ever see you again."

"Not a problem, man. I'm a ghost. But hey, could you give me a lift to—"

Rapp adjusted his aim slightly and put a bullet in the wall about a quarter of an inch from Thompson's ear.

"Fuck!" the young assassin shouted, ducking and throwing an arm protectively in front of his face. A few seconds later he was out the front door and running up the road.

Chapter 7

Moscow
Russia

As was always the case when he arrived, the outer office was empty.

Grisha Azarov crossed it quickly, glancing at an ornate clock on the wall to confirm that he was precisely on time. The door at the back was open and he passed through, closing it quietly behind him.

The office was a stark contrast to the one he'd just visited in Siberia. Every wall was clad in the rich wood paneling favored by powerful men and gilt accents bordered the ceiling. Carefully restored antiques and priceless works of art were in abundance, tracing the whole of Russia's history.

At nearly twenty meters square, it took a not insignificant amount of time to cross the room and take a position of attention in front of a desk that had once been owned by Czar Nicolas II. According to legend, he had used it only once before the people rose up and killed him for his sins and the sins of his forebears. Azarov had always thought it ironic that Russia's president would choose a desk with such a history.

Maxim Krupin finished signing the document in front of him and set it aside, leaning back in his chair to finally acknowledge Azarov's presence. The politician was relatively young at fifty-two, stocky and solid. He had recently grown a jet-black mustache that, despite being meticulously groomed, still had the effect of making him look a little wild. Undoubtedly the change was a calculated effort to further intimidate the West and to ingratiate himself with a constituency desperate to have the world tremble once again in Russia's shadow.

By contrast, Azarov was clean-shaven, with a thin, muscular physique beneath a suit tailored to obscure it. The man who oversaw his training never allowed his client's body fat level to rise above that favored by professional athletes. In a world flooded with modern weapons, strength was desirable, but speed and agility were the difference between survival and death.

"You look well despite the recent unpleasantness, Grisha."

"It's kind of you to say, sir."

"Certainly better than when I found you."

Their rare face-to-face meetings always began with Krupin subtly reminding Azarov that everything he had was a result of their association.

While Dmitry Utkin's similar comment had been an exaggeration, Krupin's was fundamentally accurate. Azarov had been pulled from his special forces post without explanation just before his twenty-fourth birthday. Having distinguished himself on a number of difficult clandestine operations as well as on the army's intelligence tests, he had come to the attention of the country's new president.

Krupin had ridden a populist wave into office and was then in the process of consolidating his power. In order to facilitate that consolidation, he'd needed a man with a specific skill set and unwavering loyalty.

The Russian army had provided the former while Krupin bought the latter. Almost overnight, Azarov had gone from living in a barracks and making a few rubles a month to a life of mansions, private jets, and runway models. It had been more than the son of a poor farmer from the rural north could ever have dreamed of. Now, though, he recognized it as the Faustian bargain it was.

"Our friends were beginning to forget their place," Krupin continued. "Now they're reminded that they're only flesh and blood."

He was, of course, referring to Utkin and Russia's other powerful oligarchs.

"A weakness we share, Mr. President."

"Do I hear fear in your voice, Grisha? It doesn't suit you."

Krupin was a brutal man who had risen

through the ranks at great cost—a cost that was beginning to come due. The precipitous drop in oil prices had combined with Western economic sanctions to loosen the iron-fisted control he'd gained over the country. The control that kept both him and Azarov alive.

"They're dangerous men with extensive resources, sir."

"They have no patriotism, Grisha. No love for mother Russia. The Americans are trying to strangle us and all they care about are insignificant shifts in their stock prices. They have no vision for this country's return to its former glory."

Azarov wondered what exactly that former glory was. The dysfunctional aristocracy represented by the handcrafted desk in front of him? The genocidal mania of Joseph Stalin? The disastrous communist experiment?

In truth, his country was utterly dependent on the extraction of natural resources. Russia invented nothing. Made nothing. Contributed nothing. Its people had never had a chance to learn how.

In many ways, this is why Krupin had enjoyed such success in politics. He understood his people's thirst for relevance and had a gift for slaking that thirst in ways that were ultimately meaningless but satisfying in the short term.

"Before he died, Utkin demanded details of

your plan for the economy and proof that those plans would be effective, sir. I suspect the others will do the same."

Krupin's eyes narrowed and he leaned forward across his desk. "I will cut the Americans off at the knees, Grisha. Russia will be respected and feared throughout the world. We will exceed even the power we had at the height of the Soviet era. Will that be sufficient for these little men?"

"What you describe would indeed be glorious," Azarov said, trying to conjure the expected sense of enthusiasm.

It appeared that he was successful because Krupin nodded and sank back into his chair. "Unfortunately, I find myself in a position that I once again need to ask your help, Grisha. I was committed to keeping you out of the Pakistan operation but circumstances conspire to make that impossible."

"What's changed, sir?"

Krupin waved a hand in a dismissive gesture that seemed a bit strained. "We've lost touch with the men sent to deal with Mitch Rapp."

Azarov didn't allow himself to visibly react. Only two days ago, Krupin had boasted that the operation was going perfectly. That Rapp was falling headlong into the trap created for him.

"Lost touch?"

"Our best intelligence is that Rapp is on his

way back to Islamabad and could interfere with our work."

The operation targeting the CIA man had been planned entirely by Krupin and his logistics expert, Marius Postan. Azarov had been kept out of the loop, a move typical of the Russian president. One of the strategies he used to maintain power was to compartmentalize everything he did, never allowing anyone to see the entirety of his machinations. It was a level of secrecy that kept his opponents off-balance, but often had a similar effect on his allies.

Normally, Azarov would have requested to be included in the planning of an operation like this and Krupin would have eventually agreed. In this case, though, Azarov had decided to keep his distance. He had studied everything Russian intelligence had on Mitch Rapp, and it was hard to ignore the fact that even well-planned, well-executed moves against him tended to fail. Often catastrophically.

"Did Rapp have time to question any of the men involved?"

"We don't know for certain. The CIA is sending people but they appear to be a cleanup crew. Our best information is that Gusev was killed in short order along with the two ISIS men with him. The American that Gusev insisted on bringing in seems to have escaped."

So, yes, Azarov thought. Anyone would

eventually talk with Mitch Rapp doing the questioning, but Gusev could be counted on to give up what he knew more quickly than most. He was a soft, self-interested criminal faced with a man who had spent his life dealing with fanatics who welcomed—even courted—suffering and death.

Krupin seemed to read his mind. "Gusev knew less than nothing."

That seemed unlikely. He was running the tactical side of the operation and understood both its short-term goals and methods. It was admittedly not much, but that was very different from nothing.

"What action do you intend to take, sir?"

Krupin didn't answer immediately, instead staring out across the desk.

"After a great deal of thought, I've decided that Rapp has to be dealt with, Grisha. The Pakistan operation has been going well since he's been gone. Scott Coleman's men have been reasonably effective, but the other CIA teams are faltering without Rapp's leadership."

"Then you've been successful?"

He knew little of what was happening in Pakistan and he preferred to keep it that way. Unfortunately, it was becoming clear that his continued ignorance and lack of involvement weren't going to be possible.

"Successful? Yes. To some extent."

"Perhaps it would be better to accept that partial victory and suspend your operation until Rapp moves on?"

"I don't have enough material to achieve my ultimate goal. In this case, I'm afraid there are no partial victories."

"Do you have a sense of how you would like this to play out?"

"We're aware of a high-level Pakistani mole codenamed Redstone who is on the CIA's payroll. We've used back channels to feed him intelligence that the al Badr terrorist group is going to make an attempt on a nuclear warhead being moved through Faisalabad tomorrow. Redstone has been a reliable informant for the Americans and I think that they will take him at his word."

"So, we're drawing Rapp into a second trap after the first failed?"

"It was a mistake to put Gusev in charge. I should have never allowed Marius to do it. That's why I'm asking you to get involved personally, Grisha."

"But it's a bit like throwing a net over a bear, yes?" he said, despite knowing that Krupin wasn't interested in his opinions or objections. "Again, I have to wonder if it would be possible to step back for a few weeks."

Krupin shook his head. "The Pakistani warheads are being moved with minimal security because of the power struggle between its army and civilian government. This level of disorder isn't going to last. One or the other will soon gain the upper hand and the warheads will once again be out of my reach."

So it *was* Pakistan's nuclear weapons that Krupin was interested in. But why? There could be only one answer: while Russia controlled a nuclear arsenal capable of destroying the planet many times over, it was just for show. A multitrillion-dollar deterrent that couldn't be launched without creating an equally devastating response from the West.

The only reason Krupin would want access to Pakistani warheads was because they couldn't be traced to him. And the only reason that he would want nuclear weapons that couldn't be traced to him was because he planned to actually use them.

Sweat broke across Azarov's back but his expression remained opaque. He had killed many men in the service of Krupin, but this was something very different.

"You seem reticent, Grisha. Is the simple task of killing one man beyond you? Is this to be the first time you fail?"

"If so, I would be only one entry on a very long list of dead men who tried to move against Rapp."

"But you're not one of those men. You're unique."

While undoubtedly intended as flattery, what Krupin said was true. Azarov was an Olympic-level athlete with a lifetime of training behind him. Since leaving the military, he had enjoyed a constant stream of the best instructors the private sector had to offer. Human-performance coaches from renowned European universities, champion-ship marksmen, and world-class mixed martial artists, to name only a few. Further, he was taking a regular cocktail of performance-enhancing drugs designed and administered by a German doctor who had been banned from professional sports. It was something that he suspected would kill him one day. Things that burned bright burned short.

"I am almost ten years younger than Rapp and have suffered far fewer injuries over my life-time," Azarov said. "I've studied his techniques, psychology, and athletic background, while it's unlikely he's even aware that I exist."

Krupin smiled for the first time in their meeting. "It's nice to hear the confidence back in your voice, Grisha. It seems to become more muted every time I see you."

"It's not confidence, Mr. President. I have surprise on my side, as well as my youth, training, and, frankly, my drug regimen. Other factors favor him."

"What other factors?"

"Another decade of experience. A history of

surviving situations more dire than I've been involved in."

"You're far too valuable for me to risk you lightly, Grisha. And I wouldn't be using you now if it wasn't critical."

"The fact remains that he has been tested like no one currently alive and has demonstrated no discernible weaknesses. His enemies—most recently the very talented Louis Gould—are all dead."

"Very good," Krupin said. "Confidence is desirable, but arrogance is the refuge of fools. And again, I'm taking your involvement in this very seriously. I understand the risks to you and I'm designing the operation in such a way as to mitigate those risks."

Azarov nodded respectfully but couldn't bring himself to thank the man. He was nothing to Krupin. A tool, to be used and discarded the moment it became convenient to do so.

Once again, he found himself caught in the trap he'd walked into so enthusiastically as a young man. The question was, would this be the time he failed to escape?

Chapter 8

Over Zimbabwe
Africa

"Can I get you a soda, Anna?"

The young girl just shook her head and clung to her mother, staring at Rapp with a mix of fear and shock that was powerful enough to make him look away.

They'd been in the air for just over an hour, most of which he'd spent in the cockpit coordinating his teams in Pakistan. Dangerous moves were being made and the window to stop them was going to close fast. Preliminary intel was already coming in about a possible attempt on a nuke by al Badr in Faisalabad. Kennedy and Scott Coleman were trying to get details and corroborate them through their contacts on the ground.

"How about a cookie?" Rapp said, deciding to try again. "I think we have some in the galley."

Another nervous shake of the head.

The girl was terrified of him. And why wouldn't she be? Thank God Thompson had been the one to pop the Arabs. If Rapp had been forced to stand in front of her and pull the trigger on those psychopaths, she'd probably be hiding under one of the plane's seats.

"I know that what happened today was really scary," Rapp said, leaning a little closer to her. "Most people in the world are good. But there are some who aren't."

She continued to stare, but the fear seemed to diminish a bit. She was tough, like her mother. And, in truth, like her father.

"How do you know which ones are bad?" she said finally.

Rapp suppressed a smile that would be inappropriate given the gravity of the subject. At least she was talking to him. That was a serious victory after what he'd just put her through.

"The bad ones want to cheat you. Or steal from you. And a few—like the men back there— might even want to hurt you. The good ones try to help."

"What about that American man? Kent. Is *he* good?"

Rapp rubbed his beard for a few seconds but couldn't come up with an answer. He considered lying but couldn't bring himself to do it. It wasn't her fault that she'd been born into this world but it was a reality she couldn't escape.

"I honestly don't know."

"But—"

"Anna," her mother admonished. "He said he doesn't know."

The young girl looked at her feet. "Okay."

"Guess what?" Rapp said, feeling a bit guilty

85

about not having a better answer for the girl. "I think you should go introduce yourself to the pilots. And tell them I said to let you fly."

She glanced at her mother, who nodded, and then disappeared up the aisle. Whether it was because she was interested in getting her hands on the plane's controls or to get away from him, he wasn't sure. Probably a little of both.

"Sometimes children ask hard questions," Claudia said.

"Yeah."

He propped his elbows on his knees and got his first real look at her since he'd arrived in Africa. The tan she'd had when he'd last seen her in Greece had faded and her pale skin accented dark, almond-shaped eyes. She was thirty-six, but the disparity in their ages looked greater. Decades of desert sun, sandstorms, and memories of dead friends and enemies conspired to make him look older than he was.

The plane lurched and Claudia glanced back toward the cockpit. When she looked back at him, it wasn't with the expression he'd expected. In fact, he couldn't read her features at all.

"They're actually letting her fly."

"Are they?"

"People do what you tell them to, don't they?"

"Most of them."

"And the ones who don't?"

He leaned back, suddenly wanting to put some

distance betwe,
for a long time. 1

She switched to ,
more comfortable wit.
Louis."

He wasn't sure how to
him as better? Worse? h
remorseless sociopath who wo,   for
the right payday. Rapp was ver,   .ot that
person. But that wasn't necessarily   .lent from
the outside. In fact, he'd killed far more men
than her husband had. The difference was in the
subtleties of motivation.

"Thank you for saving us," she said finally.
"Again."

He shook his head. "It was my fault, Claudia.
It shouldn't have been possible to find you. I
missed something."

"No one can truly disappear. It's something I
know well from my time in . . ." Her voice faded
for a moment. "Your business."

"Still, I—"

"Some of Louis's enemies have tremendous
resources, Mitch. There's only so much that can
be done."

He didn't respond, reluctant to tell her that this
was about him, not her dead husband. And while
she was wrong about motivation, she was right
about the issue of resources. The CIA was the
world's expert at this, and the men who had been

very aware that he
idea that a Russian organized
ISIS had the sophistication to
off was incredibly far-fetched. They'd
someone inside the Agency or an organization with enough brute-force capacity to sift through every passport issued, house sold, and bank account opened worldwide.

No, this screamed Russian intelligence. But why? It was a given that they had a keen interest in who controlled Pakistan, but how would exacerbating the lack of security around that country's nuclear arsenal help their cause? It seemed like too much risk for not enough reward. Even for Maxim Krupin.

"I don't know what to do, Mitch. I deserve this. I didn't pull the trigger on Louis's contracts, but I might as well have. I participated and I benefited. I'm still benefiting. I have tens of millions of dollars in my bank account. All blood money. But Anna is innocent. She has to be protected."

Rapp let out a long breath. He wasn't sure why he'd thought he could get around this. Wishful thinking wasn't normally one of his failings.

"This wasn't about you, Claudia. Someone wanted to distract me."

"Why would they use me to do that? You've already given me a new life. You owe me nothing. Why would they think you'd care?"

Because he did. But he wasn't ready to say that. "I don't know."

"If this wasn't about Louis and the men involved are dead, does that mean you're taking us home?"

"No. I need to make sure your identity hasn't hit the street and that no one's going to try to follow up on this. The plane's going to drop me off and then take you to Washington. A very trustworthy man named Mike Nash is going to pick you up from the airport and take you to my apartment. You'll be safe there while I work this out."

"And by that you mean while you kill everyone involved."

If he'd been talking to his late wife, this would be where the fancy footwork started. But there was no point. Claudia understood how this worked.

"Yes."

"Can I help?"

"I think I can handle it, but thank you."

"I *can* help, you know. As ashamed as I am to say this, I was good at what I did."

"I know," he said honestly. "And if I wasn't one hundred percent confident in my team, I'd be taking you up on your offer."

She reached out and laid a hand on top of his. "I should be dead or in prison, Mitch. Instead, I live in the most beautiful house I've ever seen, in the most beautiful place I've ever been. Anna has a wonderful school and wonderful new friends. I want to find a way to repay you."

Rapp's phone chimed and he glanced down at it, expecting to find an update on the CIA crew being brought in to clean up the mess he'd left. Instead, it was a threat. But not from the Pakistanis or Russians. It was a warning that if he didn't make a decision in the next hour, his kitchen counters would be topped with pink Formica.

Rapp glanced up at Claudia. "Is that a serious offer?"

"Of course it is."

He turned the phone and showed her the text. "I'm finishing up building a house outside D.C. and this woman's driving me crazy. I'm going to set up a meeting between the two of you for tomorrow. After that, the only thing I ever want to hear on this subject is that the key's waiting for me under the mat."

Chapter 9

Islamabad
Pakistan

Grisha Azarov strode purposefully across the lobby of the Islamabad Marriott. It was after midnight, so it was virtually empty. A haggard-looking English couple was giving instructions to a bellboy in the corner and an attractive young woman was manning the reception desk. In his peripheral vision, he spotted a man coming through the door behind her but immediately registered him as benign. The hotel manager.

"It's nice to have you back, sir."

Azarov nodded politely, but didn't stop. He suspected that the man had stayed this late solely to provide that greeting and to make certain that the details relating to Azarov's arrival had been attended to.

As expected, the elevator was empty and he inserted the key for the top floor. As was customary, the hotel's most luxurious suite had been rented for him in the name of the Russian energy consulting firm he was the president of. The company had been bankrolled by Maxim Krupin with the help of the oligarchs who now made up a significant portion of his client list.

It was a cover that allowed him to take in enormous amounts of money with little scrutiny, travel to dangerous parts of the world without raising suspicion, and meet with wealthy, powerful men unnoticed. After more than a decade in business, the cover operation had become, for all intents and purposes, real. He had hired top talent in the areas of economics and geology, expanded his clientele to include such corporations as Exxon, BP, and Aramco, and gained enough expertise in the field to hold his own in a roomful of petroleum engineers.

Azarov exited the elevator and opened the door to his suite with the card key he'd been sent. The main room didn't feel much different than the lobby—an ornate mix of figured marble, rich wood, and expensive rugs.

The floor at the center was sunken and contained a conversation pit consisting of chairs and sofas surrounding a glass coffee table. A lone man rose from the chair farthest from the door, bowing slightly in greeting.

Marius Postan was fifty-one, balding, and wearing an expensive but ill-fitting suit that hinted at constant fluctuations in weight. He was another of Krupin's extra-governmental "advisors" and had been in the employ of the Russian president even longer than Azarov himself had. His sphere of influence was more on the technical side.

"It's my understanding that you have information for me?" Azarov said, walking to the bar. A bottle of Blanton's Gold Edition was waiting for him along with an elaborate arrangement of fresh flowers and a personal note from the manager.

"I think you'll want a clear head for our conversation," Postan said.

"On the contrary, Marius. I find our time together much more palatable with a bourbon in my hand."

While Azarov had been warned that the man would be waiting for him, he hadn't been told what they were to discuss. Not that it was difficult to guess. When Postan showed up in person, it meant that there was news too sensitive to transmit even over heavily encrypted lines.

"Can I assume that you're here to discuss the upcoming Rapp operation?"

Postan nodded and Azarov decided to exercise a bit of curiosity. "Before we start, Marius, why don't you tell me what happened in South Africa?"

The man's eyes flitted nervously around the expansive room. He had been responsible for planning the operation, under the watchful eye of Maxim Krupin. The problem was that while Krupin tended to take full credit for success, he was just as quick to distance himself from failure.

"Ilya Gusev was killed along with the two Iraqi men he'd been assigned. An independent contractor who goes by the name Kent Black has disappeared. I've not yet been able to determine what happened in any detail."

"I see," Azarov said, taking a seat on one of the sofas and spreading his arms across the back. "Would you like to know?"

Postan remained standing, staring down at him. "I don't understand."

"It's a simple question. Would you like to know what happened?"

"I don't see what—"

Azarov held up a hand, silencing the man. "Kent Black's real name is Steve Thompson. Early in his career as an independent, he worked on an operation in Nicaragua. Louis Gould was representing a competing interest. Thompson would have researched him enough to recognize his former wife and to know that Mitch Rapp has at least a peripheral relationship with her. Thompson is neither stupid nor suicidal, so I think we can assume that he contacted Rapp to make sure the move against Claudia Gould wouldn't be something that would bring about CIA retaliation."

Postan's eyes widened. "Have you spoken to Krupin of this?"

Azarov shook his head. "This is the first I've heard of Thompson's involvement."

"Then what you're saying is nothing more than speculation."

Azarov didn't answer, instead sipping his drink and appraising the man. As much as he disliked Postan, he couldn't help feeling a hint of sympathy. These kinds of operations were outside his area of expertise. Azarov himself should have been consulted but the president's damnable obsession with secrecy had prevented it. And now they found themselves in a very dangerous—and entirely self-inflicted—situation.

"Yes," Azarov said, uninterested in arguing. "Just speculation." He held out a hand. "You have something for me?"

Postan fished a flash drive from his pocket and handed it over.

"The plans for taking Rapp in Faisalabad are all on here?"

"Yes. He'll be arriving in Pakistan soon. Our operations have been going much more smoothly since he's been gone and there's a possibility that we'll have to suspend them if you don't—"

Azarov held up a hand, once again silencing the man. "If everything is on here as you say, there's no need for explanation."

Postan's nervousness suddenly turned to anger. He was wealthy, powerful, and unaccustomed to being spoken to with anything but deference. Moreover, he was a vindictive, control-obsessed man prone to flying into sudden rages. By all reports, both his staff and family were terrified of him.

"You think you're above all this, don't you, Grisha? That Krupin thinks of you as some kind of son. I assure you that he does not. Do you believe you can do for him what I can? The shell corporations, the money laundering, the constant adjustments that have to be made to keep up with technology and international law? You're just a killer, Grisha. The most common of men . . ."

Postan continued his diatribe, but Azarov had stopped listening. He rose from the sofa and walked behind the wet bar at the back of the room. Crouching as though looking for ice, he pulled a custom-built pistol from the shoulder holster beneath his left arm.

"Are you hearing me, Grisha? Are you even capable of understanding what I'm saying?"

Azarov stood and smiled politely. "I'm doing my best. Please continue."

He turned on the faucet and used it to fill the gun's integrated silencer with water. Despite the opulence of the room, the walls were a bit thin. The first shot from a suppressed weapon tended to be somewhat loud and wetting it would reduce the effect.

Azarov hadn't been paying attention to Postan's words but the sudden silence when he raised the weapon was still welcome. The man froze for a moment and then bolted for the door. Azarov tracked him over elevated sights, waiting until he was off the rug and over the easier-to-clean marble before firing.

The subsonic round struck the base of his skull and he pitched forward, landing face-first on the floor. Azarov laid the weapon on the bar and grabbed a trash bag from the can at his feet.

He put it over Postan's head and tied it tightly around his neck, partially to keep the mess to a minimum, but also to make sure he was dead. The .22 he'd used was extremely quiet, but lacked impact.

A little scrubbing with a bar towel wetted with ice finished the job. He retreated back to the sofa and had barely managed to skim though the contents of the flash drive before his phone rang.

"Yes."

"Can I assume that you've had your meeting and that it ended as I requested?" Maxim Krupin's voice.

"You can."

"And you've reviewed the information I sent?"

"Only in a very cursory way, sir."

"I, on the other hand, have gone through it in great detail."

That was undoubtedly meant to be more confidence inspiring than it actually was. Krupin was a genius at political backstabbing but had no real operational experience. He'd embellished the handful of years he'd spent with the KGB into something straight out of an American adventure film but the reality was quite different. He'd been responsible for spying on political dissidents and very occasionally ordering the assassination of a young idealist or aging political agitator. His understanding of men like Mitch Rapp was non-existent.

"I think you'll be quite satisfied with the plan, Grisha."

Azarov took a slow sip of his bourbon, savoring the flavor while he calculated how much to say. "I'm concerned about working with Pakistani Taliban while Rapp will be supported by Scott Coleman and his men."

"The Taliban have strong local knowledge and are willing to give their lives to ensure that you accomplish your goal."

"I think we can be certain that Coleman's people will be reasonably knowledgeable about their operating environment as well. And I suspect that there isn't one of them who wouldn't lay down his life for a teammate. Further, they're extraordinarily well trained, speak the same language as Rapp, and have a lengthy history of carrying out successful operations with him."

"I selected these men personally," Krupin said, the anger starting to creep into his voice. "Not only for their skill but for their commitment to the mission."

It was, of course, a complete lie. Krupin had selected these men because they couldn't be traced back to him. Their skill or lack thereof was a secondary consideration at best.

"Thank you for involving yourself personally," Azarov said, knowing that there was nothing to be gained from further discussion. "I understand the demands on your time."

"Not at all, Grisha. I have no priorities more important than your well-being. Other than perhaps your happiness. You continue to demonstrate your value. How can I express my appreciation?"

It was a question that had been asked many times during their relationship, but one that was becoming increasingly difficult to answer. Another car? He had a Bugatti Veyron sitting in storage in Canada and a Bentley Continental in a garage outside Geneva, to name only a few. Another house? He had four—three of which he hadn't visited in years. The only thing he wanted was the one thing he would never be granted. Freedom.

"That's very generous of you, sir. Please give me time to consider the offer."

"Of course."

The line went dead and Azarov set his phone down, staring at the body lying near the door.

In a way, he envied Krupin and men like him. They were blessed with insatiable appetites that had to be constantly fed. Money, power, possessions, women. It would never be enough. A billion euros would have to become two billion. The adulation and obedience of ninety percent of the population would have to grow to one hundred percent. Krupin and the oligarchs would scrape and strive until their last breath, never knowing a moment's doubt, introspection, or regret. Never considering there were aspects of life that existed outside their simple philosophy of *more.*

For a long time, Azarov had felt like he was drowning. Not the panicked, desperate death that most people would associate with that kind of end, though. More a sense of waves lapping over him and of a cold, endless darkness below. The road ahead was empty. He had nothing he wanted. Nothing worth fighting for.

Now, though, there was the strange sensation of adrenaline leaking into him. Soon, he would face Mitch Rapp, a man he had spent his adult life actively avoiding. There had never been any reason to court a confrontation, but now that it was inevitable he was starting to feel . . . what? Excitement? Fear? Those were clumsy words that had little meaning to him. But he felt something. Something to break up—or perhaps end—the existence he'd become trapped in.

Chapter 10

Faisalabad
Pakistan

Rapp didn't bother lowering the jet's stairs, instead jumping to the tarmac and jogging toward a car parked at the edge of the runway. The clear skies and cool breezes of the Western Cape were now thousands of miles away, replaced by Pakistan's familiar heat and yellow haze.

His flight plan had been for Islamabad, but they'd been diverted one hundred fifty miles south to Faisalabad without explanation. Based on the blond hair barely visible through the filthy windshield of a Honda Civic waiting for him, the news wasn't good. Scott Coleman was a former Navy SEAL and the principal in SEAL Demolition and Salvage, a private outfit that existed largely as backup for Rapp in ops that were best left off the books.

"Hot enough for you?" Coleman said as Rapp slid into the passenger seat. "The weather guys say we're going to break a hundred and eight this afternoon."

They weren't normally prone to talking about the weather, but those kinds of numbers had to be accounted for when planning operations. At best, speed, stamina, and precision would be compromised. At worst, heat stroke and dehydration could take out even an experienced desert operative.

"Did someone demote you to chauffeur and not tell me about it?" Rapp said, turning one of the car's AC vents on him as they accelerated toward the main road. He'd left Coleman in charge and had expected to be picked up by one of the CIA's local staff.

"We've got good intel that a nuke is going to be coming through town in a few hours and that al Badr is going to make a play for it."

"Not ISIS?"

"ISIS? No, why?"

"No reason," Rapp said. "But why al Badr? They're a second-string Kashmiri outfit. What are they doing in Faisalabad?"

"Hell if I know. I'm telling you, Mitch, it just keeps getting worse. Pakistan's got a thousand terrorist groups and I swear every one of them has their eye on the nukes the army's driving around. If someone doesn't get control of this chickenshit government fast, we're going to lose one."

He and Coleman had been in some hairy situations over the years, but this was about as agitated as Rapp had ever seen the man.

Not that he didn't agree. Pakistan was a fractured nation with almost two hundred million inhabitants and a stockpile of more than a hundred nuclear warheads—many of which were currently in motion. A screwup didn't mean getting your ass shot off, it meant watching a million people disappear into a mushroom cloud. Just the kind of large-scale problem Rapp had spent his career seeking out and Coleman had spent his career trying to avoid.

"Who fed us the intel?"

"Redstone."

Rapp nodded silently as Coleman turned onto a road that tracked north through the tightly packed buildings of Faisalabad. Redstone was one of their top assets in the region, a man highly placed in Pakistan's intelligence apparatus. He'd had a few misses over the years, but generally his intel was solid.

"If we get involved, are we going to run head-long into an ISI operation?" Rapp asked, referring to Inter-Services Intelligence—Pakistan's version of the CIA.

"I don't think so," Coleman responded. "According to Redstone, you killing the ISI's director has completely paralyzed them. Everybody's jockeying for position and playing both sides of the power struggle going on between General Shirani and the president. The fact that someone could wander off with one of their nukes is so low priority to them it barely makes their radar."

"How many are we tracking now?"

"Thirteen warheads that we know of are currently on the move. We located another two stationary ones while you were gone, putting the total we have a handle on at fifty-three. The analysts are guessing that another twenty-five are attached to missile systems that would make them impractical to move."

Rapp did some quick math in his head. "So that leaves somewhere in the ballpark of thirty unaccounted for."

Coleman nodded. "Including the one we're talking about now. We weren't aware of it until Redstone tipped us off."

It was a problem that had existed for years. The Pakistani army was paranoid about the Americans or Indians getting a bead on their nuclear arsenal, so they moved it around—on trucks, in train cars, in the trunks of private automobiles. Hell, there was credible intel that a tactical warhead had once been hauled three hundred miles on the back of a motorcycle.

It had always been an incredibly dangerous situation, but one that the Pakistani army kept more or less under control. The transfers were carefully coordinated and, even more important, the weapons were always partially disassembled and transported as individual parts that couldn't be used to create a nuclear explosion.

So, on any given day, you could count on the

fact that one or two nukes were making their way around the country monitored by an army division set up for just that purpose. Now that stupid—but reasonably well run—program was in chaos. Fully functional weapons were being haphazardly passed around by low-level officers and, in two confirmed cases, civilians. One warhead they were watching was currently parked in a retired captain's storage unit. A recon team had managed to get a fiber optic camera through the ventilation grate and the Agency was now in possession of an honest-to-God picture of a hot nuke sitting next to a set of golf clubs. At this point, the chances of the situation spiraling out of control was almost a hundred percent.

"This is us," Coleman said, cutting into an alley. He dialed a code into his phone and a rusted cargo door slid open in front of them. There were three motocross bikes in the bay and Rapp stepped out of the vehicle as they nosed up to them. The door began to close again and a moment later they were standing in the gloom provided by a single bulb hanging from the ceiling.

"The roads are a little narrower than Islamabad's and the traffic's about the same as Lahore. So, not knowing how fast we're going to have to move or exactly where this is going to go down, I figured bikes would be our best bet."

Joe Maslick, one of Coleman's top men, leaned his considerable bulk through a door to Rapp's right. His hand came off the weapon beneath his sweat-soaked shirt when he confirmed their identities.

"What's the situation?" Rapp said, following the man into the next room.

The building looked like it had at one time housed some kind of convenience store, and it was still lined with empty shelves and counters. The large front windows had been blacked out, with the only illumination coming from places where the paint had gotten scraped off.

"We've got cameras on buildings at all the major entrances to town. Our manpower is limited but we have people physically covering some of the others. Keep in mind that most aren't fighters. We scraped them up from wherever we could."

"Choppers?"

"One on standby."

"Anything new from Redstone?" Coleman asked.

"Yeah. He says we're looking for a produce truck."

"Do we have a description?" Rapp said.

"Better. We've got a plate number. I've texted it to all our people."

"Any intel on where al Badr is going to make its move?"

"No. But we have a few educated guesses." He motioned Rapp over to a large satellite photo spread out on the floor. The light was just good enough to make out detail.

"The fact that it's a truck helps us. A lot of the streets are too narrow for it to fit through, so we can rule them out." He used a car antenna he'd found on the floor as a pointer. "We've got guys on roofs here, here, and here. Obviously, they're spread out but because the buildings are packed in so tight, they're actually pretty mobile. The concentric circles around their positions repre-sent one minute of travel time each."

"What about Pakistani soldiers?" Rapp said.

"Police and military are stationed on most of the larger plazas and major intersections," Coleman responded. "All this political turmoil is causing a fair amount of civil unrest. The presence isn't heavy, though. Just a show of force to keep people in line."

"Do they know we're here?"

"The army and the cops? No, and that's the way we want it in this town. Both the general in charge and the chief of police are playing for their own accounts. We considered paying them off, but neither is reliable or competent enough to bother with. They're just covering their asses and waiting to see whether the army or the government comes out of this on top."

"So we can't count on them to help us?"

"Definitely not. More likely they're going to get in our way."

A walkie-talkie lying on the floor suddenly crackled to life. "Spotter eight to base. Come in, base."

Maslick snatched it up and pointed to the number 8 scrawled on the map in red. "This is base. What have you got?"

"I have eyes on the target. Heading northeast on Okara near where it changes names. Traffic is heavy. I think I can keep up on foot."

Maslick glanced at Rapp, who gave a short nod. "Do it. And let us know if he turns off that road."

Coleman was already going for the bikes, dragging a box of a gear out from behind them. Rapp followed while Maslick notified their chopper pilot that he needed to be warming up his bird.

The flak jackets were a nonstarter, as were the leather pants and jackets. It was just too hot and there was a good chance this could devolve into a running fight. Rapp slipped a tan-colored climbing harness over his khaki cargo pants and untucked his shirt to obscure it. A shoulder holster would be too visible so he ended up going with the setup he jogged with at home—a compact Glock 30 in a fanny pack.

Coleman was going with a larger weapon in a

CamelBak and was forced to wear a full helmet to cover his blond hair and fair skin. Rapp had been threatening for years to pay one of Coleman's contracts with a tanning bed and a shipping crate full of hair dye, but the former SEAL refused to take the hint.

"Comm check," Rapp said, putting on a throat mike and inserting the earpiece.

"I've got you," Coleman responded through the radio built into his helmet.

"Five by five," Maslick said a moment later.

"I'm going to try to get behind them. Scott, you come down on them from the north."

"Roger that. I'll see you in a few minutes."

Rapp threw a leg over the closest bike and kicked it to life. The door began to open and when it got about four feet off the ground, he ducked and twisted the throttle, shooting out into the alley.

Chapter 11

"The American scout has seen the truck and is following on foot."

Grisha Azarov didn't acknowledge the voice coming over his earpiece, instead continuing to pace steadily across the abandoned manufacturing plant. Twenty-three meters. He calculated how long it would take him to run that section from a standing start and then moved on to a massive industrial machine that dominated one side of the shop floor.

"I repeat. The American scout has seen the truck and is following on foot."

Azarov activated his mike as he paced off another portion of the building. "Understood. Authorize the driver to divert."

He stopped and took in the space around him—the disused machines rusting at its edges, the remains of the glass-walled office at its center, the piles of refuse left over from the plant's operations.

He didn't know what had been made there or when production stopped. He didn't know if the driver of the truck now headed inevitably his way was a Muslim fanatic, a trained operative, or an innocent transporter of fruits and vegetables. He was largely unfamiliar with the surrounding neighborhood, the flow of traffic at that time of day, and the strength of local law enforcement. He was forced to assume that these details had been sufficiently studied and to trust Krupin's spotters to keep him apprised of the status of the man he would soon engage in a fight to the death.

Azarov walked to the base of a crane that rose to the ceiling, scanning along it before lowering his gaze to a group of Middle Eastern men huddled at the back of the building. Their precise purpose had not been shared with him beyond the fact that they were not there to back him up. Based on their number and equipment, it seemed obvious that they had been charged with unloading something from the truck that would soon arrive. And, while it had never been specifically discussed, there was little question that the item in question was one of the nuclear warheads being moved haphazardly around Pakistan.

Azarov could feel his heart pounding in his chest and the blood rushing in his ears. Normally, his heart rate barely rose during operations—the result of years of physical and psychological training. This was hardly a normal operation, though. The ISIS-supplied terrorists and lack of information introduced an intolerable lack of predictability. The potential presence of a nuclear warhead opened a scope far greater than he had dealt with in the past. And, finally, there was Mitch Rapp.

The entire scenario was madness. He should have spent months personally planning this confrontation: walking the streets, laying out lines of retreat, cracking Rapp's radio encryption. He should have been drawing the legendary CIA agent into a trap that would cut him off from his backup and leave him facing an overwhelming force.

Instead, he was standing alone in an unfamiliar building armed with nothing but a pistol and single spare magazine.

Undoubtedly Maxim Krupin would say that it would be impossible to create a more elaborate plan without tipping off the Americans. That Azarov was being unnecessarily timid. Those objections rang hollow, though. In truth, Maxim Krupin was embarking on something so dark that he couldn't risk even the remotest possibility of being discovered.

And this left further troubling questions.

Of course, the Muslims would be summarily executed after they had served their purpose. But what about him? Azarov presumed that he continued to have the Russian president's confidence, but it would be foolish to cling too desperately to that belief. Marius Postan had been one of Krupin's most indispensable men and he now resided at the bottom of the Arabian Sea.

The radio came to life again, this time with a distinctly British voice. One of the insane men who had abandoned their world to fight a barbaric war that didn't concern them. "Three men on motorcycles are leaving the store on Jaranwala. One is going for Canal and another for Jhang. Best estimate is that they will intercept the truck in five minutes. The third American is heading northwest."

Azarov nodded silently. The men converging on the truck would be Mitch Rapp and Scott Coleman. They would be forced to improvise when they discovered it had changed course. The other man would be Joe Maslick, formerly of Army Delta. He was still only about ninety percent recovered from a recent shoulder injury, so the logical course would be to send him to the helicopter the CIA was holding at the edge of town.

Azarov pulled his weapon from its holster and checked it for the last time. Rapp would be there soon.

Chapter 12

Rapp accelerated the motorcycle up twenty feet of open street before being forced to veer around a van. He barely avoided having to jump onto a sidewalk packed with pedestrians, instead taking the side mirror off a Suzuki wagon when he threaded between it and a light post.

The situation was an ungodly mix of everything he'd come to associate with Pakistan: heat, car exhaust, and chaos. Even in what passed for politically stable times, the country was one of the greatest threats faced by the modern world—a hopelessly corrupt hornet's nest of factionalized terrorist groups, divisive government officials, and poorly monitored nukes.

"Turning right on Canal." Scott Coleman's voice in his ear.

"Copy that."

Rapp's long hair had become completely saturated with sweat, and it hung in front of his eyes, making visibility a struggle. An armed soldier posted on a street corner started paying too much attention and Rapp took a left into an alleyway. It was too narrow for cars, and that allowed him to increase his speed as pedestrians pressed their backs against the walls to let him by. The downside was that his handlebar-mounted GPS had lost satellite signal.

"I've turned off Jhang. Should be connecting to Okara in about a minute."

"Copy," Coleman came back.

"Mas. What's your status?"

"I'll be boarding the chopper in less than six minutes. Over your position in about ten."

"Ten minutes. Copy."

Rapp came out on a broad avenue and weaved around a motor scooter piled with bales of cotton. Coleman was about twenty blocks north, heading southwest on the same road as the truck containing the nuke. They'd converge on it from opposite directions and then they'd have to improvise. The key would be speed. Take out the tangos and get control of the vehicle. Then figure out how to deal with the backlash from the cops and military. Not exactly an airtight plan, but the best they'd been able to come up with on the fly.

"The truck has turned off Canal," their spotter said. "It's now moving southwest on the Karin Interchange. Traffic is moving too fast. I'm losing him."

"I'm going to cut left on Satayana and parallel him," Coleman said. "See if we can figure out where he's going."

"I'll be coming out south of the interchange and I'll try to get on his—"

A delivery truck parked on the sidewalk

suddenly pulled back onto the road right in front of Rapp. He swerved right, cutting across traffic and narrowly avoiding getting taken out by a passenger bus. With nowhere else to go and too much momentum to stop, he jumped onto the sidewalk and locked up the rear wheel. Pedestrians dove in every direction as he was funneled toward a set of stairs heading down into an open plaza.

There was no way to stop in time, so he took the opposite course of action, twisting the accelerator and standing on the foot pegs as he approached. Frightened and angry shouts erupted around him as he launched off the landing.

The staircase was only about fifteen steps in length and he cleared the last one by a few feet, bottoming out his shocks on the concrete slab below. There was a loud snap, followed by a loss of power and the sound of the bike's motor revving out of control. He ran through the gears but it was no use. The transmission was done.

Rapp leapt off, letting the motorcycle roll into a mailbox before flipping on its side. A crowd immediately started to gather and he could see the gray-and-tan shape of a cop running in his direction.

Rapp's first instinct was to go for the crowd. In his experience, the first few rows of people would offer token resistance, but the ones behind would just be following the herd. They would have no idea what was happening or who was involved.

As he got closer, though, it became clear that the cop was a good thirty pounds overweight, jogging awkwardly with an assault rifle clutched in front of his ample stomach. It would be a miracle if he could run a fifteen-minute mile without dropping dead, while Rapp could cover that distance in a third of the time.

Satisfied that there would be no serious pursuit, Rapp turned away from the expanding mob and began sprinting toward their target's last reported position.

"I'm on foot," he said into his throat mike. "Coming up on Okara."

"Are you all right?" Coleman asked. "What happened?"

"Yes, and don't ask. Mas? Where are you? My GPS is still on the bike. I'm running blind."

"On my way. We're pushing it as hard as we can, Mitch."

Rapp glanced behind him and confirmed that the cop was standing motionless on the sidewalk, bent at the waist and trying to catch his breath.

"I'm still on Satayana," Coleman said. "Try not to be too late for the party, huh, Mitch?"

Chapter 13

"I've reacquired the target," a voice said over Scott Coleman's earpiece. "It's entering a warehouse on the corner of Haali and Qaim using bay doors on the southwest side."

"Copy that," Coleman said, glancing down at the GPS on his bars. It was being updated remotely, and a few seconds later he had routing. "I'm about two minutes out. Can you keep eyes on?"

"That's a negative," the spotter responded. "They're closing the doors. I'll watch this entrance but I'm guessing there's another one on the other side of the building."

In fact, it was almost certain there was, Coleman knew. The likely scenario was that the driver had been paid to divert to the warehouse and that al Badr would have men there to unload the nuke. If Coleman had been running their operation, he'd have at least five cars parked inside and he'd roll them all out at the same time. One transport and four decoys.

On the other hand, it was possible that the warehouse itself was a decoy. That they were just routing through it in an effort to shake anyone who might be tailing.

"Roger that. Hold your position," Coleman said.

"I'm less than a minute now. Can we bring in more surveillance?"

"We have three people inbound, but ETAs are unknown."

It was impossible to estimate transit times if you were much more than a mile out. Traffic followed no discernible pattern, delivery vehicles regularly shut down entire roads during unloading, and accidents were more the rule than the exception.

Not that his lack of backup mattered all that much. None of these people were shooters.

Coleman cut down an alley, slowing to not much more than five miles an hour as he weaved through the annoyed pedestrians. When he came out on the other side, the warehouse was straight ahead. It looked like it took up the entire block, with huge, mostly broken windows that started about fifteen feet up and terminated near the roof.

He was coming in from the opposite direction of the spotter. A set of bay doors was visible, so at minimum, the north and south sides had egress points large enough for the truck.

"I'm on location," Coleman said, pulling the bike between two parked cars and shutting it down.

"Copy that," he heard Rapp say breathlessly. "Mas, where the fuck are you?"

"Should be coming over your position in a few seconds."

"Copy."

"Keep me apprised," Coleman said. "I'm going to take a look."

He kept his helmet on as he crossed the busy street, moving as quickly as he could without attracting attention. The headgear was hot as hell but this wasn't exactly a tourist area and his blond hair would stand out like a sore thumb. Undoubtedly, he'd take shit from Rapp over that in the post-op debriefing.

The bay doors were secured with a massive padlock that was hanging about eight feet above the sidewalk. There was no way it could be opened from inside, and based on the rust, it was questionable whether it could be opened at all. He decided to slip into the alley running between the east side of the warehouse and the windowless building next to it.

Less than six feet wide, it was piled high with garbage from a recent sanitation worker strike. The smell combined with the heat was a little nauseating, but it dissuaded people from using the alley as a shortcut.

"Mas," he heard Rapp say over the comm, "I can hear you behind me. I'm just about to cross Aminpura."

"Hang on . . . yeah. I've got you, Mitch."

"There's a soldier coming in on me from the west. He's talking on his radio. Do you see him?"

"Affirmative. You also have two cops straight

ahead. You're going to run right into them. Advise that you get off that street. The buildings on your right back up to an alley."

"Roger that."

Coleman started climbing a pile of garbage bags, struggling as some burst and others rolled beneath his boots. It took the better part of a minute, but he managed to get even with an intact upper window. The glass was surprisingly clean thanks to a recent rainstorm and he cupped his hands against it, trying to block out the glare.

"We're getting some preliminary reports on the building," he heard their spotter say over his earpiece. "It was used to manufacture industrial air conditioners until the company went bankrupt three years ago. It appears to be laid out as one open space with some of the machinery still on-site."

"I can confirm that," Coleman said. "There's also a small central office and a fair amount of debris."

He spotted movement at the back and adjusted his position to see better. Because he was in direct sunlight, the shadows seemed particularly deep. Not so much that he couldn't make out basic outlines, though. "I have eyes on the truck and at least two tangos. They seem to be unloading."

"Roger that," Rapp said. "Mas, I'm still a long way out on foot and those two cops have spotted me. Can you give me a lift?"

"No problem."

Coleman's eyes were starting to adjust to the light level in the warehouse and he managed to pick out two more tangos, for a total of at least four. They were pulling crates out of the truck, but none of the boxes were large enough to contain the package he was looking for. Most likely, the warhead was buried deep behind the legit cargo.

"Orders?" Coleman said into the mike installed in his helmet.

"You're there, not me," Rapp responded. "It's your call."

There seemed to be some excitement flaring in the warehouse and he watched as three of the men rushed toward the back of the truck. A moment later, they reappeared carrying something that looked a little like a simple pine coffin. Decision made.

"I'm going in."

"Roger that. Watch your ass and I'll be there as soon as I can."

Coleman half scrambled, half rolled down the trash heap and ran to a small door in the side of the warehouse. It was secured with a padlock smaller than the one on the front bays, but every bit as rusted. He retrieved his silenced Sig Sauer P226 and fired a single round into the lock. As expected, it gave way.

The flash of light was going to be a problem as

he entered so he yanked the door open only far enough to slip through sideways, immediately closing it and dropping to the floor. The men at the back of the building were too lost in their effort to open the crate to notice.

Coleman propped his elbow on the floor and aimed carefully at a man hammering a crowbar beneath the lid. He took a breath and held it before gently squeezing the trigger. The quiet snap of the gun was followed by the man's head jerking back. And then all hell broke loose.

Chapter 14

Moscow
Russia

President Maxim Krupin strode down the hall-way flanked by two men in traditional Russian military uniforms. The thick red carpet seemed to disappear into the distance, absorbing the sound of their footsteps. For the first time, the silence and grandeur failed to fill him with a sense of his own importance.

When the ornate doors at the end of the passage finally came into view, he slowed. The anger had been building in him since the moment this meeting was scheduled. The fact that it was necessary—that he lacked the power to prevent it—infuriated him. In the end, though, this was the way of the world. No dictator's grip was absolute. History was littered with the corpses of men who forgot that simple fact.

Two additional guards snapped to attention next to a pair of marble pillars and then moved to open the doors. Krupin passed through without acknowledging them.

The conference room he'd chosen was the least grand available. It was long and narrow, with a utilitarian table that extended too close to unadorned green walls. The men seated around it were somewhat more impressive—a sea of tailored suits, extravagant jewelry, and elegant haircuts. Twelve in all, they were members of Russia's new ruling class. Each had a net worth in excess of ten billion U.S. dollars, with holdings throughout the country and the world. Oil, gas, real estate, and arms were the primary sources of income, but their portfolios diversified more every year. Commercial fishing, media, construction, and agriculture played an ever-growing part. It was a complex web that was becoming difficult for him to control. And as the importance of his role diminished, so grew their arrogance.

"Gentlemen, thank you for coming," Krupin said as they all stood.

He singled out a few of the most influential men for a brief nod and then took a place at the head of the table.

"Please sit."

All did as he asked, but none returned his greeting or spoke. They were fully aware of what had happened to Dmitry Utkin and now knew that they weren't as untouchable as they had once imagined. Good. Let them speak in whispers about it among themselves. Let them lie awake at night wondering if Grisha was just outside their door. If it was their turn to face him.

Without exception, the men in the room owed

everything they had to the government. If it weren't for the gifts, payments, tax breaks, and nepotism lavished on them after the fall of the Soviet Union, they would be scraping out an existence far from the halls of power. As time passed, though, that history became easier to deny. They began to forget what had made them what they were and to believe they should have a say in how the country was run.

The arrogance of that position was laughable, but to ignore it would be unwise. While they didn't have the FSB or Grisha Azarov at their disposal, they were still dangerous. Each commanded enormous resources and great political power both within Russia and outside it. Further, most had significant ties to organized crime along with the mercenaries, assassins, and traitors who made up those syndicates. As distasteful as it was for Krupin to admit, a war between him and the oligarchs would destroy everything he had built while producing no clear winner.

"Academics have many names for government structures," Krupin started. "Monarchy, democracy, communism, socialism. But there's really only one. The world has always been ruled by a small group of men with the cunning, strength, and drive to take the reins of power. You are those men. The rest—the people outside these walls—are sheep."

Krupin's gaze moved around the table as he spoke, making eye contact with everyone seated at it. "Even the Americans who believe their democracy to be so unique are no different from us. Their politicians are members of family dynasties and owned by wealthy patrons. Information is controlled by a media flogging false narratives for profit. They call us corrupt, but we're all members of the same hypocrisy. It can be no other way."

He paused and, predictably, all eyes flickered toward Tarben Chkalov. He was in his mid-eighties and nowhere near the wealthiest of them, but there was little question that he commanded the most respect. His holdings were the most diverse internationally and he'd moved most aggressively to distance himself from Russia's system of patronage. It was this careful maneuvering that had made him the de facto leader of the oligarchs and the second-most-powerful man in Russia next to Krupin himself.

As was his custom, Chkalov stood and silently acknowledged everyone at the table before he spoke. "We all agree with much of what you say, Mr. President. And we are fully aware of our debt to the Russian government for its past favors and to you personally for your political skill. You've given the people enemies—the Americans, the breakaway states, the homo-sexuals. You've given them a sense of outrage and persecution. You've inflamed their nationalism. All these things have been extraordinarily effective at keeping attention diverted from our activities as well as your own."

Chkalov fell silent, looking down and concentrating on the empty table before him. Anyone else might have seen the pause as an indication that his mind was weakening, but Krupin knew better. The useless old woman was simply choosing his next words carefully.

"While what you say is true about the corruption of the West, there is still a great chasm between their system and ours. . . ."

Another lengthy pause, this one longer than Krupin had ever personally experienced. Maybe the insufferable old bastard *was* finally losing his mind.

"May I speak plainly, Mr. President?"

Krupin tensed, but not in a way that would be visible to the others. He'd occasionally been asked this question early in his presidency, but quickly demonstrated how he dealt with anyone too frank in their opposition. Chkalov, though, was in a very different category than the bureaucrats and minor elected officials that infested the Kremlin. There was only one answer Krupin could give.

"Of course, Tarben. We've been friends for many years and I value your opinion."

"The situation in Russia is getting bad enough

that the people are beginning to see through the fog you've created. I sense that you're aware of this and I believe that the growing danger has made you act rashly."

Another infuriating lull.

"Ukraine offered a brief populist boost to you personally but the Western sanctions are slowly bleeding us. And your ban on the importation of Western food products was the result of anger, not calculation. Putting images of the government burning millions of rubles worth of perfectly good food in a country where people are going hungry has had disastrous results."

Krupin's anger grew with every word. He managed to keep his face impassive, but the skin on his cheeks started to burn.

"I believe that the low energy prices punishing Russia's economy will persist. The Americans are producing increasing amounts of oil and gas, and the Saudis are committed to keeping prices low in order to hamper the development of renewables and to bankrupt American producers —both battles they are losing. Technology moves inevitably forward and no one in this room or in similar rooms around the world can stop that progress."

Krupin found it impossible to remain silent any longer. "Are you finished?"

It was a question that was always answered in the affirmative by the fearful men and women who worked for him. But Chkalov wasn't one of those people.

"I'm afraid not, Mr. President. I apologize if this sounds disrespectful but hard talk is preferable to the alternative."

"Then by all means go on," Krupin snapped. "But do it quickly. I have other matters to attend to."

The old man nodded respectfully. "Russia is becoming irrelevant, sir. The Americans are good villains for your television programs, but the truth is they don't hate us. They're indifferent to us. Of course, we can get their attention by occasionally flexing our military muscle, but we all know this is ultimately meaningless. The question is, why should we continue to support you? It used to be that our laws were more flexible than those in America. Now, though, there's no real danger of prosecution for men like us as long as we contribute to the right congressmen. Why shouldn't I spend my money buying influence in a country with a future instead of Russia, which has only a past?"

"Everything you have is because of the Russian government!" Krupin said, his voice echoing throughout the room. "And you continue to possess it only because I allow you to."

"What you say is true of my Russian assets, Mr. President. But they're worth less every day. I wonder if soon I won't be hoping for you to

130

nationalize them or distribute them to the other men in this room."

Krupin swallowed his anger. There was no profit in escalating this confrontation. He had to acknowledge the limits of his power. For now.

"You're too much of a pessimist, Tarben. All these things you speak of are easily fixed."

A man near the far end of the table leaned forward and spoke uninvited. "And if we ask how, will you send Grisha for us, too?"

Pyotr Druganin was the youngest and most reckless of the men in the room. He'd bet heavily on energy and his empire was teetering on the verge of collapse. While the danger Chkalov posed flowed from his status and the respect he commanded, this man's flowed from his desperation.

"Your government is bankrupt, Mr. President. Too cash strapped to even make payments to the corrupt local officials that keep your house of cards from collapsing. They're pursuing their own interests now, squeezing my businesses, creating red tape that I pay you to cut through. And I'm not so easily blinded by glorious reports of your military exploits."

Chkalov motioned for him to be silent but he refused. "You're too polite, Tarben. Too diplomatic. We talk about our demands amongst ourselves like a bunch of frightened children. Now here we are. What better time to present them?"

"I don't think—" Chkalov started, but Krupin spoke over him.

"Demands? I'm intrigued. Please go on."

He expected the other men around the table to become uncomfortable but they displayed surprising resolve. Perhaps this had been the plan all along. Let Chkalov play the respectful general while the pup took on the suicide mission.

"Western sanctions must be removed," Druganin said.

"And how do you suggest I achieve that?"

"Frankly, we don't care. But most likely it will involve ceding some of your military gains."

Krupin actually laughed at that. "You're not serious."

"I am, Mr. President. And that's not all. The lifting of sanctions alone won't be enough to stop Russia's slide. We need significant free market reforms and a crackdown on corruption. You'll also have to begin to decentralize your power. Russia is the largest country in the world and this isn't the seventeenth century. It can't be run for the benefit of only one man."

Krupin stared at Druganin, but the man refused to look away.

"You can't send Grisha for us all, Mr. President. We have the means to fight back. And we will use—"

"Enough!" Chkalov said, sensing that his young comrade was stepping over the line. He focused his hooded eyes on Krupin. "We're all aware that you ordered the death of Dmitry Utkin for his opposition. And we find this understandable. His—"

"Are you giving me your approval, Tarben? Do you believe that because I agreed to meet with you that I now serve at your pleasure?"

Chkalov refused to be drawn into a fight. "Dmitry was incautious and his actions were counterproductive. I spoke with him about this n a number of occasions. We aren't happy about what has happened, but we acknowledge that it was inevitable."

"I care very little about what you do or do not acknowledge, Tarben."

Again, the old man seemed not to hear. "Make no mistake, Mr. President. If this was the first shot in a war against us, it's a war we are capable of fighting."

The threat was completely unveiled and Krupin's jaw clenched as he looked at the stoic faces around him. He seriously considered calling in his guards and having these men executed on the spot. The government would reabsorb their companies and throw their families into the streets.

But it was impossible. They wouldn't have come here without taking precautions. Krupin was certain they had men inside the Kremlin— perhaps even among his most trusted advisors.

He couldn't afford to underestimate them. A

drop of poison, a disgruntled guard, a hidden explosive. It was almost certain that plans for his assassination were laid and that these traitors were already squabbling about who would replace him.

Silence descended on the room as Krupin considered his next move. For now, there was only one course. The oligarchs had to be put at ease. Then, when his power was fully restored, they could be dealt with.

"Can I assume that all of you are familiar with the Ghawar oil field in Saudi Arabia?"

Unsurprisingly, all nodded. It was the largest in the world and, along with the others around it, responsible for the vast majority of Saudi Arabia's output.

"As Tarben mentioned, the Saudis are increasingly committed to keeping oil prices artificially low. It harms them very little as it still provides plenty of income for the royal family. It is, however, extremely damaging to countries that aren't governed by backward tribal monarchies. Venezuela and Iran, for instance. And, of course, Russia."

"We're aware of all this," Druganin interrupted.

Krupin nodded impassively. This man would die first. Grisha would carve the flesh from his bones while his family watched.

"If I may continue. I intend to end all

meaningful production in Ghawar and the surrounding fields permanently. That will significantly reduce worldwide supplies as well as removing Saudi Arabia as the world's swing producer. In all likelihood, it will also collapse the monarchy and cause the country to descend into a civil war. The other small oil-producing states like the UAE and Kuwait will be threatened by the chaos on their borders, particularly from a strengthened ISIS, and this will significantly reduce their output as well. My economists expect oil prices to increase to as much as two hundred fifty dollars per barrel, which would translate to a tripling of gasoline prices. The U.S. will be forced to use its military to secure critical production areas at great expense to them—something that will further drag on an economy damaged by the sudden rise in energy prices. Russia's budget deficit will turn into surplus almost overnight, which I will use for economic stimulus and the expansion of our military in order to reassert Russia's influence in the region."

Krupin rose from his seat and looked down at the men. While he had hoped that it wouldn't be necessary to reveal this much of his plan, he enjoyed their stunned expressions and mute stares. "Can I assume that this will be satis-factory?"

Chapter 15

Faisalabad
Pakistan

The soldier was angling in from the right, running across an empty lot piled with garbage. His weapon was still holstered but he was young and respectably fast. Avoiding a confrontation was going to be impossible if Rapp wanted to get into position for the chopper closing from behind.

They continued on their collision course, with Rapp at a full sprint, dodging through the alarmed pedestrians sharing the sidewalk. Predictably, the soldier slowed when he got within ten yards, shouting for Rapp to stop and reaching awkwardly for the pistol on his hip.

The problem with military men in this part of the world was that they expected people to do what they were told. A good bet ninety percent of the time, but today he was going to get an education in the other ten.

Despite the stifling heat and his aching lungs, Rapp managed a brief burst of additional speed, aiming directly at the young soldier. The gun snagged before clearing its holster and Rapp stuck an arm out, clotheslining the man. He landed hard, the back of his head hitting the concrete with a dull crack.

The maneuver had multiple benefits. First, the kid was done with his chase but still breathing. And second, the pedestrians crowding the area started to panic. Instead of his having to dodge them, now they were getting out of his way.

No plan was perfect, though. The two cops coming at him from the north saw the soldier go down and pulled their weapons. Neither looked like he could hit the broad side of a barn, but that actually made the situation worse. If they decided to open up, the most likely outcome would be that they'd take out a bunch of innocent bystanders.

The buildings that Maslick had told him about appeared on his right and Rapp abruptly slowed to a walk, stepping through a set of doors as he wiped at the sweat pouring down his face.

He had no idea what the people working in the building did and there were no clues in the modest lobby. A receptionist sitting at a desk to his left looked at him with a friendly but inquisitive expression. There was a single open door at the back and he could see the cubicles lined up beyond it.

"Hi, I have an appointment to see Mr. Gajani," Rapp said, trying to control his breathing. It was the most common Pakistani name he could think of on the spur of the moment and he got lucky. The woman still looked a little perplexed but there was apparently someone working there by that name and the idea that an American might visit him was within the realm of possibility. She reached for the phone but Rapp waved a hand and gave her as friendly a smile as he could muster. "Don't bother. I'll just go on back."

He picked up his pace as he passed through the door. The receptionist didn't protest, instead just nodding submissively. In terms of her cultural situation, she was the exact opposite of the soldier he'd left lying on the sidewalk. In male-dominated Pakistan, he would expect deference while she would expect to be dismissed.

His luck held as he weaved through the cubes. A few people glanced up at the sweat-drenched man in their midst but most remained focused on what they were doing. By the time the sound of the front doors being thrown open reached him, he was already approaching the back of the building.

Demanding shouts reverberated through the building, but a moment later they were drowned out by the dull thud of chopper blades. The people around him began to stand and wander out of their cubicles when the vibration started to shake the structure.

"Stop!"

Rapp ignored the shout, continuing to walk casually toward a door in the back wall. More yelling and the sound of running feet didn't prompt him to look back. The combination of the cops and the fact that the chopper was close enough to start knocking pictures off the walls was creating a panic that would be enough to cover him for the next few seconds.

Yanking the door open created a blast of air that felt like a convection oven. He used a hand on the jamb to pull himself forward into the hurricane of rotor wash. There was a red climbing rope whipping around the narrow alley and Rapp went for it, catching the carabiner dangling from the end and attaching it to the harness beneath his shirt. A quick wave and the helicopter started to rise, lifting him off the ground.

Rapp reached for his fanny pack and retrieved his weapon, pumping a couple rounds into the wall next to the door when one of the cops poked his head through. He disappeared back inside and stuck a hand out, firing blindly around the jamb. The rounds ricocheted through the alley but by then Rapp was well clear. The chopper continued to rise until he was out of practical range of anyone on the ground and then dipped its nose and started in the direction of the warehouse Coleman had infiltrated.

A voice crackled to life in his earpiece but he

couldn't understand what was being said over the roar of the air around him. He grabbed the rope to steady himself and looked up, spotting Joe Maslick hanging out of the helicopter's open door. He pointed and Rapp followed his finger to a large building to the north. It took up the entire block and had a ring of windows around the top. Despite the sun glare, intermittent flashes of gunfire were visible through them.

With no idea of Coleman's position, the floor plan, or the strength of the opposing force, entering through one of the broken skylights was a no-go. Instead, Rapp motioned toward the roof of an adjacent building.

"Scott!" Rapp said, activating his mike. "I'm going for the high ground on the northeast side of the building. I should be in position in two."

There was no response as the aircraft started to descend. Rapp hit hard, rolling across a melting asphalt roof and coming to his knees near the low concrete wall that encircled it. The rope dropped on top of him and he looked up, pointing at the HK416 assault rifle in Maslick's hand. The former Delta operator nodded and let it drop. The rotor wash put it into a flat spin as it fell but Rapp managed to catch it. He moved right, lining up on a broken window in the side of the warehouse.

As planned, he was high enough to see about seventy percent of the building's floor. The relative darkness inside didn't make for great visibility, but it was enough.

The chopper started to rise, taking the noise and the wind with it. The oppressive heat, though, remained.

"Scott, I'm in position. I can't see the first fifteen feet of the north side of the floor because of the wall and I'm blind to the last thirty feet at the back because of the light. I have full view of the center section all the way to the east and west walls. That's your cover area. Do you copy?"

Rapp could see muzzle flashes coming from the back but they weren't enough to pick out individual targets. About all he could do was make an educated guess that Coleman was dealing with three to four men with automatic weapons.

"Scott, do you copy?"

"Fifteen feet from the north and thirty from the south," Coleman repeated back.

Rapp let out a relieved breath and swept the rifle's scope right, searching for targets. "Mas. Get your ass in position over that building and make sure nothing comes out."

"Copy that, Mitch. I'm on it."

Chapter 16

Coleman eased right, taking cover behind a rusting metal-forming machine before sprinting across the open five yards to a pile of rotting pallets. He stayed near the wall and in the shadows, which obscured him from the men spraying bullets in his direction but also made it impossible for Rapp to track him.

The automatic gunfire emanating from the back of the building started arcing to the right in search of him and he darted across another gap, rolling through the debris before coming up onto a single knee. He lined up on the flashes but couldn't find a target reliable enough to risk giving away his position. Instead, he crawled away from the wall, hoping to enter Rapp's field of view without being forced to cross into the sunlight beaming through the windows.

The gunfire went silent, which should have been a positive development, but the abruptness of it set alarm bells off for the former SEAL. It had been too loud for his opponents to hear a cease-fire order that uniformly. And that left only one possibility he could think of: they had someone coming in on him that they didn't want to hit.

He dove left just as the dull snap of a silenced pistol sounded. The round smashed into his motorcycle helmet with a deafening crash, jerking his head to the side. There was no time to worry about whether he was injured—or maybe even dead and just not realizing it yet—so instead he rolled with the force of the impact and came back to his feet. Miraculously, his body and mind were still working in concert and he began sprinting toward a stand-alone office just beyond the line that separated sunlight from shadow. Out of the corner of his eye, he saw an armed man walking calmly toward him. Not Middle Eastern and not like any terrorist he'd ever run into. No, this shooter wasn't just Caucasian; he was wearing a really nice suit.

Just before reaching the door, Coleman altered his trajectory and dove through a window. On the back wall, a puff of dust sprang up where the gunman's round penetrated. Judging by the position of the impact, his aim was once again dead-on. Had Coleman not changed course, the bullet would have hit him right between the shoulder blades.

The former SEAL found himself rolling through a carpet of broken glass with virtually no control. By the time he slammed into what was left of an old desk, his torso, hands, and arms were a spiderweb of oozing cuts.

He pressed his back against the wood and

aimed through the doorway, spotting the man coming at him in a sideways run to minimize his profile. Coleman suffered a rare moment of confusion at the speed of his opponent's approach. Rapp was the fastest guy he'd ever seen in person and this son of a bitch was noticeably faster.

It was impossible to line up a reliable shot, so he calculated that his best option was to conserve his ammo. Against a lesser opponent, he might have gone for a few near misses in an attempt

to score a psychological blow. This asshole wouldn't be so easily intimidated.

Coleman slid away from the desk through the loose glass just as the man opened up again. Three rounds hit right where he'd been a split second before, grouping in a circle just over an inch in diameter. It was an incredible display of marksmanship. Even with time to aim, it would have been impressive. But from a full run? Bullshit. No one could do that.

Coleman yanked his foot away from the open door but was just a fraction too slow. The shooter had anticipated his move and a bullet tore through the middle of his right calf, spraying blood across the floor.

Certain that the next few rounds were going to come through the flimsy plywood wall next to him, Colman pushed himself into a standing position on his wounded leg and fired four times in quick succession.

The move was obviously unexpected and the shooter didn't have time to recalibrate his aim. Instead, he grabbed a metal pillar and swung around it, changing direction ninety degrees without any loss of speed. Less than a second later, he had disappeared behind an enormous machine set up in front of an old crane.

Coleman expected the men at the back of the building to open up again, but they'd lost interest. The sudden silence seemed absolute.

"Do you have eyes on me, Mitch?" Coleman said, in hopes that his radio was still operational. "The office. One tango to the east. The others are still working on the crate. Do you copy?"

No response.

He grabbed a chunk of two-by-four off the desk and threw it through the window in front of him. The glass shattered, leaving him a clearer view as he sighted over his Sig. There was no movement near the machine the shooter had disappeared behind. The only evidence that he'd ever existed was the widely spaced footprints in the dust.

"Mitch. Do you copy?"

Again, nothing.

He could feel a slight shaking in his hands and knew it wasn't just the sprint to his current position or the leg injury. It was fear. There was something about this opponent that was different from those he'd faced in the past.

Combat was the one activity no human ever did half-assed. Situations like this were full-gas until you either won or died. But Coleman had a gnawing suspicion that this guy wasn't really trying.

He reached up with his free hand and ripped off his motorcycle helmet, further improving his vision. The side was caved in and he could see what was left of his radio dangling from it. That explained the silence from Rapp.

Without the helmet to contain it, blood began flowing down his neck and shoulder. The calf was a hell of a lot worse, he knew, but he didn't dare look.

Time was working against him. The heat had been a problem already, but blood loss would magnify its effect. Coleman was already incapable of running, and in a few minutes his mind would start to dull.

For the first time in his career, he could see no path that didn't end with him dead.

Chapter 17

Rapp swept his rifle left, sighting through the scope and finally settling on the image of Scott Coleman. His helmet was off and he was bleeding badly from the side of his head. The seriousness of the injury was impossible to determine, though. Head wounds tended to bleed profusely and when mixed with sweat could look a lot worse than they were.

He also seemed to be favoring his right leg, suggesting that he'd either been hit or injured when he'd gone through the window. What concerned Rapp most, though, was that he looked scared. It was an emotion that Coleman had never openly displayed in their years working together.

The former SEAL was pinned down in a wrecked office near the center of the building. The bottom four feet of the enclosure was constructed from plywood, with windows above, running a full three hundred sixty degrees. The ceiling was low—probably no more than seven feet, with a few damaged acoustic tiles hanging lower.

Whoever Coleman was fighting had managed to stay out of Rapp's line of sight. Based on the former SEAL's movements, Rapp's best guess was it was one man, that he was fast as hell, and that he'd taken cover along the east wall.

A shot rang out from the street below and Rapp glanced around the edge of his scope to make sure it wasn't anything he needed to worry about.

The sound of gunfire in the warehouse had sent the people on the crowded road into disarray. A few cops and soldiers had arrived on the scene and one had fired into the air in an effort to get the evacuation of the area under control. Predictably, it had the opposite effect.

When Rapp returned to his optics, he eased the rifle a little farther left, focusing on the same massive industrial machine that Coleman was locked onto. One edge of it was obscured and he assumed that the shooter had slipped behind it there. If he reappeared on the south side, Rapp would be able to line up on him. If he tried to come out on the north side, Coleman would have a clear shot.

"Mitch, I've got two tangos leaving through the back of the building," Maslick said over his earpiece. "Both are on foot and not carrying anything other than a small backpack."

"Copy that," Rapp said, scanning the mast of a crane that rose up behind the machine. "Hold your position. Don't follow."

"Affirmative."

Maslick's chopper was hovering just off the south side of the building and wasn't getting too much negative attention yet. The Pakistanis would assume that the Russian-built Mil Mi-17 was being operated by the military, but the illusion wouldn't last. When they couldn't raise it on the radio, the local commanders would figure out that it wasn't one of theirs. Hopefully, the backstabbing dysfunction the local armed forces were known for would delay that epiphany a few more minutes.

Rapp kept exploring the crane mast through his scope, finally coming to its junction with a steel track that ran the length of the ceiling from north to south. He felt a dull surge of adrenaline when he saw that it passed directly over the office at a height of about twenty feet.

"Scott!" Rapp said into his throat mike. It was possible that Coleman had been forced to remove the helmet to improve his field of view and that the radio was still functional. If that was the case, he might still be able to hear a transmission.

"Scott! Do you copy?"

No reaction.

Coleman was one of the best soldiers he'd ever worked with but he had a tendency toward two-dimensional thinking. In a way, it was the result of his training. Even in spec ops, the U.S. military was a little too focused on there being a right way and a wrong way for a battle to develop.

Rapp's mentor, Stan Hurley, had been a hell of a lot looser. He'd stressed creativity and improvisation over learned knowledge. One of his many mantras fit this situation perfectly: *If everyone else is thinking right and left, you fucking well better be thinking up and down.*

Hurley's premonition became a reality a moment later when Rapp saw a flash of dark gray near the top of the machine. His finger tensed on the trigger but he had no shot.

"Look up," he muttered, but Coleman's gaze remained fixed straight ahead.

The figure moved quickly along the grid-work that made up the crane's mast, staying behind the heavy steel and as deep in the shadows as possible. Whoever this prick was, he was talented. Beyond climbing the vertical surface faster than most people could run up a set of stairs, he maintained a weaving path that kept him obscured from as many angles as possible.

It took only a few seconds for him to reach the horizontal track and slip behind it. Rapp kept his scope locked on, but that section of rail was solid. He could see occasional flashes of sleeve and pant leg at the bottom but nothing that he could score any damage hitting.

The man's plan of attack was obvious at this point. He'd simply get above the office and drop. It was around twenty feet to the ground, but hitting and breaking through the ceiling would absorb some of the impact. As strategies went, this one was incredibly risky. He could hit the edge of the desk, the roof could hold, or he could get hung up on his way through. Despite those unknowns, it was the best option and likely the one Rapp himself would have chosen. The element of surprise was everything against an opponent as formidable as Scott Coleman.

Rapp resisted the overwhelming urge to go over the side of the building and run for the warehouse. His gut was screaming at him to get into this fight but his head told him that it was impossible. By the time he pushed his way across the street and into that building, it would all be over.

Rapp reluctantly adjusted his scope to focus on the area above the office. This tango wasn't going to give him a shot while he was climbing but there was no way he could avoid exposing himself forever. He'd have to make the drop, and in that split second, he'd be vulnerable.

Rapp controlled his breathing, willing his heart to beat slower and relaxing his shoulders. He'd have only one chance at this.

Movement at the edge of his scope surprised him and he tried to adjust his aim as the man swung from beneath the crane well to the left of the office below. He let go and came in at an angle instead of dropping straight down. Again,

Rapp's finger tensed on the rifle's trigger, but the unexpected move reduced his chance of a hit to near zero. In all likelihood all he would do is give his presence away to both the tango and the soldiers gathering on the street.

The figure arced through the air, firing a rapid series of shots into the roof below. He came down hard and the addition of sideways momentum made the impact even more dangerous. Despite the complexity of the landing, he handled it with what could almost be called grace, disappearing through the roof in a dense cloud of dust and debris that made it impossible for Rapp to pick out a target.

The haze was immediately lit up by the flash of shots being fired but there was no way to know who was doing the shooting or if they were hitting anything.

"Come on, Scott," Rapp muttered, feeling the rage building over his inability to help his friend. "Get him up. Get him up where I can see him."

Scott Coleman's initial instinct was to drop at the sound of the shots, but then he registered that they were coming from above. Instead he threw an arm protectively over his head and crouched, firing upward in a wide pattern.

He felt an impact to his right shoulder and a moment later the entire ceiling collapsed, raining shards of rotted two by fours and shattered plywood down on him. The unmistakable thud of a body hitting the ground sounded behind him but he didn't bother to spin. His gun arm was now useless and he had to assume that his adversary was already lining up a shot.

Instead, he dove over the desk, feeling another bullet impact in his right side just before he slammed headfirst into the floor. It felt like a graze and he ignored it, kicking back against the desk and sending it sliding toward his attacker.

He switched his gun to his left hand and aimed beneath the desk at a flash of movement. Blood loss and the awkward firing position combined to make the shot go wide.

And then his opponent was on him.

A hand clamped around Coleman's left wrist and immediately gained control of it. The former SEAL's wounds hadn't left him with much strength to fight with, but it wasn't just that. His wrist felt like it was in a vise.

The dust was clearing and they were face-to-face, on their knees. Coleman would have liked to die on his feet, but there was nothing he could do. The man was too strong. Too fast. The butt of his gun was arcing inevitably toward Colman's head. There would be a flare of pain, a loss of focus, and then it would be over. The dark eyes locked on him were the last thing he would ever see.

But then the man hesitated. A split second of confusion flashed across his features, as though he wasn't sure what he was looking at. As though he'd been expecting someone else. It was all Coleman needed. He used his injured arm to grab a chunk of wood and slam it into his opponent's gun hand.

The blow dislodged the weapon, but the man was in motion again. He grabbed a knife from his waistband and Coleman tried to dodge right, but his body would no longer obey. The blade penetrated his side and he felt the dull ache of the steel sliding into him. When it stopped on bone, the man released the hilt and grabbed Coleman's right elbow, yanking it upward in an effort to flip him on his back.

Knowing that if he went down, he was never getting back up, Coleman threw his weight forward, ignoring the sensation of his already injured shoulder being torn from its socket. He used his good arm to wrap the man in a bear hug and, with one last desperate burst of strength, lifted him.

Chapter 18

Rapp kept his scope trained on the warehouse's empty window frame, focusing on the small office at its center. Every few seconds a body part would come into view above the plywood wall, but it always disappeared too quickly to discern who it belonged to. The only thing that was crystal clear was that Scott Coleman was overmatched. His attacker was moving with incredible speed and power, while the injured SEAL was on the ragged edge, barely able to defend himself.

A knife appeared and then plunged down, causing Rapp's breath to catch. He gripped the rifle a little tighter, but didn't attempt a shot. While there was no doubt he could hit one of them, which one was no better than a coin toss.

"Get off your ass," Rapp said quietly. "Get him up."

The decision to go for the high ground had initially been a no-brainer. In the anticipated scenario of Coleman coming up against a number of moderately well trained jihadists, the danger was that they would split up and go for position. A sniper with a wide field of view was the ideal tool to deal with that situation. This, though, was something very different. It should have been him down there. Not Coleman.

A shot rang out from below and a chunk of concrete shattered about two feet to Rapp's right. The cops had finally noticed the lone gunman on the rooftop. He ignored them, keeping his rifle trained on the battle taking place inside the warehouse.

"Come on, Scott," he repeated under his breath. "Get him up."

As though his friend had heard, the tops of two heads suddenly rose from behind the wall. It occurred to Rapp that he'd been wrong about Coleman's conspicuously blond hair. At that moment, it was the most beautiful thing in the world.

He immediately adjusted his aim to the darker of the two heads but was a fraction too slow. Coleman's attacker shifted his weight and swung the SEAL left, using him as a shield against anyone looking down on them.

The scene seemed to slow down and every detail came into razor-sharp focus. Coleman's right arm was useless, hanging at a grotesque angle in its socket. Beyond that and the knife sticking from his side, it was impossible to assess the number or seriousness of his wounds. There was just too much blood.

His attacker, by contrast, appeared to be uninjured from the fall and in complete control. He had Coleman by the shirt and was lifting him up while simultaneously ducking down, further reducing Rapp's line of sight to him.

His actions made it likely that he'd been tipped off that there was a sniper on the roof north of him. In the same situation, Rapp would twist a little farther and drop onto his back, pulling Coleman down on top of him. Done correctly, it would drive the knife the rest of the way in and provide cover from a shooter controlling the high ground.

Clearly the man had come to exactly the same conclusion. He continued to turn, beginning to disappear behind the plywood wall with Coleman in tow. Rapp knew that if he lost sight of them without acting, his friend was a dead man.

He adjusted his aim slightly and squeezed the trigger. Maslick's meticulously dialed-in rifle bucked against his shoulder and the crack of one of the most critical shots he'd ever fired assaulted his eardrums.

As planned, the round missed both men, instead shattering what was left of the office window they were standing in front of. Shards slammed into the back of Coleman's head and stuck there. The ones that didn't, though, sprayed into the face of his opponent.

The man shoved Coleman back, slamming him into the window frame and dropping out of sight. Rapp watched his friend slowly slide down and fired a pattern around him. The tango would be trying to get behind the desk and kick through what was left of the flimsy rear wall. From there he'd have enough cover to reach the rear exit.

"Mas, you've got a man heading for the back door. Bloody face, nice suit. Kill the mother-fucker."

"There are a lot of civilians back here and I gave you my rifle," came the response. "I have the door gun. How big a mess do you want me to make?"

Rapp swore under his breath. There was no way they could open up on a crowded street with a weapon like that. In one of the most anti-American countries in the world, it would be seen as an act of war.

"Belay my last order," Rapp said through clenched teeth. "Let him go."

"You want our people to try to follow him?"

Hell yes, he did. More than anything. He wanted them to track him to his safe house and then he wanted to kick down the door and look into his eyes before splattering his brains all over the wall. But one of his people was already down. That was enough.

"Negative. No one gets anywhere near this guy. Is that understood?"

"Copy that. We're letting him walk."

Another shot came from below, this time hissing past his right ear. Rapp turned and fired five rounds in rapid succession, each one coming within inches of one of the five armed men in the street. They all scrambled for cover as Rapp turned and ran crouched toward a sturdy-looking ventilation pipe.

He tied the end of the rope still running through his harness around the base and then played out some slack. With the guns below still silent, he ran toward the edge of the roof, launching himself over the low wall bordering it and into the air. The rope caught him with a spine-wrenching jerk about fifteen feet down. He released his brake hand and dropped the rest of the way, hitting the concrete rolling, and coming to his knees behind a parked car.

"I'm on the ground and heading for the warehouse," he said into his throat mike.

"Copy that," Maslick came back. "I see you. The front's locked and you've got a lot of company out there. Scott got in through the alley on the southeast side."

"Copy."

Rapp came up over the hood of the car and fired a few more well-placed rounds, punching holes in the vehicles, walls, and street signs the Pakistanis were using for cover. Nothing close enough to cause injuries, but plenty close to get everyone thinking about just how important their job was to them.

Despite the hundreds of garbage bags rotting in the heat, the entrance wasn't hard to find. The lock had already been shattered by Coleman's

Sig, so Rapp pushed the door open and slipped though.

Predictably, the shooting started almost immediately. Automatic fire stitched a line of holes in the wall above, forcing him to stay low in the shadows. He moved right and dropped to the floor, landing exactly where Coleman had, based on the marks in the dust.

The HK rifle rounds impacted a hell of a lot harder than his Glock, so he didn't bother going for his normal head shot. The first tango took a round to the chest, flipping backward over the crate he was standing in front of and disappearing behind it. The second was hit in the ribs and dropped like a bag of rocks when both lungs and his heart were punctured.

Rapp sprinted for the demolished office at the heart of the building. Coleman was lying on his back in the debris from the collapsed roof and shattered windows. His eyes were open but he didn't so much as twitch when Rapp dropped the rifle next to him.

"Mitch," Maslick said over his earpiece, "give me a sitrep."

"I took out two tangos. They look like the last ones. Scott's down. Stand by."

"Down? Is he all right?"

"I said to fucking stand by."

He pulled his Glock 30 from the fanny pack strapped around his waist and moved away from the office, crossing the shop floor while watching for movement. Once at the back, he stepped over the body of one of the men he'd shot and looked inside the open crate lying on the floor.

"I have the warhead, Mas. Drop me a cable and a box of ammo for your HK."

"Copy that."

Outside, the roar of the chopper intensified. Rapp threw open one of the bays and squinted against the dust being kicked up by the rotors. The civilians Maslick had been concerned about seemed to have fled, and Rapp went for the line descending from a reel in the helicopter's open door. Weighted down with the metal ammunition box, it was easy to get hold of and he pulled it inside.

When he reached the crate, he found there was nowhere to connect the hook, only smooth steel and a garish depiction of the Pakistani flag. With no other option, he just wrapped the cable around the tail fins.

"All right," he said into his throat mike. "Reel it in!"

The line went taut and he winced as the weapon started bouncing across the concrete floor. The CIA's experts had told him these things were hard to set off and now he was going to find out if they were right. It hung up on the bay door for a moment and then went through, taking some of the frame with it.

"We've got it!" Maslick said. "And you've got a group of Pakistani cops and soldiers coming at you from the north. They've blown the lock on the front doors and are getting into position to open them."

"Copy that. Now get that thing out of here."

"What about you and Scott?"

"Go!" Rapp said, scooping up the ammo box and running back to Coleman. It turned out that he was still breathing, but in a shallow, labored way that Rapp had seen too many times before.

The sound of grinding metal rose up from the front of the building but he didn't bother to look at what was causing it. Instead, he lifted Coleman into a fireman's carry and grabbed the rifle and spare ammunition with his free hand.

The main door was nearly fully open but none of the Pakistanis were visible as he ran across the shop floor and took cover behind the same machine Coleman's attacker had. He laid his friend on the concrete and pulled the magazine from Maslick's rifle, quickly slapping in a fresh one as he watched the shadows of the men moving around in front.

They didn't seem all that anxious to enter, and he used the time to dial Irene Kennedy on his satellite phone, patching it through his earpiece.

"Mitch!" she said upon picking up. "I'm getting reports of a firefight in downtown Faisalabad."

"That's me. Most of the terrorists are dead and Maslick's in the air with the nuke."

"Where are you?"

"Pinned down in a warehouse. You need to get on to the government and tell them to pull their men back. So far I've been shooting wide but if they move in on me I'm going to start dropping them."

"I'll do it right away. Where's Scott? Is he with Joe?"

A small metal canister came sailing through the open door and bounced a few times before starting to spew tear gas.

"He's with me. He couldn't make it to the chopper."

"Why? Is he injured?"

"Sooner would be better than later on that call, Irene."

He disconnected the line and used Maslick's rifle to shoot out some of the still-intact windows near the ceiling—more to put the fear of God into the men considering charging him than out of concern about the gas. The building was too large and well ventilated for it to have much effect.

A weak hand gripped Rapp's leg and he looked down to see Scott Coleman's eyes fix on him. The injured man managed to speak but when he did, a thick mix of blood and spit drooled from his mouth.

"I'm done, man. Get out of here."

Rapp shook off memories of Stan Hurley, who had looked up at him in a similar condition a few weeks ago. The difference was that he'd been an old man dying on his own terms. Coleman wasn't.

Rapp knew that any hint of concern or sympathy would just weaken his friend further. He was a soldier. One of the best in the world. And that's the way he deserved to be treated.

Rapp pulled the pistol from his waistband and slapped it into Coleman's limp hand. "Quit whining and make yourself useful."

Chapter 19

Joe Maslick was lying on the metal floor of the chopper with his head hanging out the open door. He'd been raised by dirt-poor parents in a trailer park tucked into the mountains of South Carolina. When he graduated from high school, he'd never been out of the state. Never eaten Chinese food. Never seen the ocean, except on his family's static-ridden TV.

Thinking back on that made him wonder how the hell he'd ended up in Pakistan, staring down at an atomic bomb. That cashier's job at the local gas station was looking better and better.

"This thing's swinging really bad," he said into the mike attached to his headset.

"You want to come up here and fly, asshole?" was the predictable response.

The man at the controls was Fred Mason, a retired navy pilot who now flew search-and-rescue missions out of California. Coleman brought him in when second-best wasn't an option.

"It'd just be good if it didn't go into the tail rotor, you know?"

"I didn't remember you being the nervous type, Mas."

They climbed out of range of the cops and soldiers below, but Maslick could still make out detail around the warehouse. The front entrance was open and there were at least ten cops and soldiers lined up next to it. Smoke was curling from the bay doors but none of the men appeared to have masks on. The general impression was that no one was in charge. That should play in Rapp's and Coleman's favor.

The nuke settled down and he started to use the winch to reel it up. When it got close, the copilot came back to help him wrestle it inside. Even with the two of them, it was a herculean task. In addition to the weight, there wasn't anywhere to get a good grip. They got it partway in the door a couple of times but it always hung up and fell back onto the cable.

The pilot heard all the swearing and glanced back for a moment. "Watch your asses, boys!"

The left side of the chopper suddenly dipped, slamming Maslick into the back of the door gun and rolling the nuke up onto the skid. Then the floor dipped right, tossing him into the other wall. When the aircraft leveled out again, the weapon was inside and rolling lazily toward a cargo net hanging from a set of eyebolts.

"Asshole!" Maslick said, rubbing the back of his head as the copilot trapped the nuke in the net and began securing it.

An urgent beeping indicating an incoming

satellite call echoed through Maslick's headphones and he cut out the two pilots before picking up. "Go ahead."

"Give me a sitrep," Irene Kennedy said in a worried tone.

"We have the nuke on board and we're heading home, ma'am."

There was a pause that suggested she wasn't as happy about that as she should have been. "I've lost contact with Mitch."

"I wouldn't worry about that, ma'am. We just left him and the situation didn't look like anything he wouldn't be able to handle."

Another long pause. "Scott's injured and I can't get through to General Shirani or the local police commander to get them to issue a standdown order. I need you to go back for them."

Maslick wasn't sure how to respond. Rapp had made it clear that he was to get their cargo to safety. And, while Kennedy was technically in charge, he was only mildly afraid of her. Rapp, on the other hand . . .

"That's a negative, ma'am. I have my orders."

"You take orders from me and those orders have changed!"

He was a little startled by the force of her response. In all the years he'd known her, he'd never heard Irene Kennedy raise her voice.

Maslick suffered a rare moment of hesitation. If she was right—and she almost always was—

then his team was in trouble. Rapp would never leave Coleman and the Pakistanis would eventually get organized enough to surround that building. The thought of abandoning them was a thousand times worse than the thought of dying with them. On the other hand, he had no idea what Rapp would do if his orders weren't followed to the letter. It never really happened.

Finally he pressed a button and linked in the pilots again. "Turn us around, Fred. We're going back."

"What? Could you repeat that?"

"You heard me."

"You realize you're literally sitting on a nuclear bomb, right?"

Maslick looked down. He actually *was* sitting on it. "Do it, Fred."

The chopper banked hard and Maslick used his free hand to switch to the frequency monitored by Rapp. "We are inbound to your position. Do you copy?"

The response was barely intelligible due to interference. "That's a negative. Continue on your previous heading."

Maslick couldn't shake the feeling that he was a dead man. The only question was whether it was a lucky shot from a Pakistani or a perfectly placed one from Rapp. "Be advised that we are operating under revised orders and will be over your position in approximately three minutes."

Rapp swung his rifle around the machine he'd taken cover behind and scanned through the dissipating smoke. No one had appeared in the open door. Maybe they'd finally realized they didn't have masks and were waiting for reinforcements. If they were smart—and that was a big if—they'd put men on the surrounding buildings and position teams behind barricades to cover the exits. At that point, they could lob in some more gas or, better yet, just wait him out. With no water and temps pushing a hundred ten, he wouldn't last much longer than twenty-four hours. And Coleman probably wouldn't make it another twenty-four minutes.

"We're in our descent," came Maslick's voice over his earpiece.

Rapp's jaw clenched and he looked down at Coleman. The pistol had slipped from his fingers and he wasn't moving. His head wound probably looked worse than it was, but the knife sticking out of his side was likely exactly as bad as it looked. Then there was the blood flowing from his shoulder and leg.

"Scott."

No reaction to his voice at all. It was possible that he was dead but it didn't matter at this point anyway. They were going out together or not at all.

He switched Maslick's rifle to full auto and

emptied the magazine into a steel pillar near the door. The metal made an impressive racket and would be enough to delay anyone who might have built up the courage to launch an offensive. He tossed the rifle and pulled Coleman onto his shoulder again. Scooping up the pistol that had fallen from his hand, Rapp started for the back of the building at a full run. He was about halfway there when the deafening whine of a chain gun started up outside. Hopefully, it was Maslick shooting and not an incoming Pakistani aircraft.

He came out into the bright sunlight just as Maslick let loose another burst. He was firing into the air over the top of the surrounding buildings, but it was enough. If there had been any soldiers in the alley before his arrival, they'd taken the hint and run like hell.

Despite Coleman's dead weight, Rapp managed to grab the rope dangling from the chopper and attached it to his harness. He slid Coleman off his shoulder and wrapped his arms around the injured man. Maslick was leaning out the open door and when he saw that Rapp was ready, he motioned for the pilot to start climbing.

They were only about ten feet off the ground when someone started shooting from an alley to the north. Rapp's pistol was in his waistband and there was no way to get to it. Coleman was slippery with blood and his weight was being multiplied by the chopper's climb. It was all Rapp could do to not drop him.

"Mas! Get that son of a—"

But the former Delta operator was already ahead of him. The door gun opened up again and the alley entrance disappeared in a cloud of shattered concrete.

They finally cleared the tops of the buildings and started streaking east. Above, Maslick was rigging the winch to pull them up and Rapp tightened his grip on Coleman despite the fact that the muscles in his forearms felt like they were on fire. The SEAL slipped and Rapp barely managed to loop a leg around him in time to keep him from dropping four hundred feet to the street below.

By the time they made it to the chopper door, Rapp had been forced to grab Coleman's shirt in his teeth to make up for the fatigue in his arms. The metallic taste of blood was yet another reminder of his friend's condition.

"I've got him!"

Maslick's powerful arms appeared and dragged Coleman's limp body upward. When he was safe, Rapp grabbed the skids and pulled himself inside, rolling across the floor as the aircraft's nose tilted forward and Fred Mason pushed the chopper to its limit.

Chapter 20

CIA Airfield
Central Pakistan

Rapp leaned over the chopper pilot's shoulder and pointed at a C-17 Globemaster transport plane below. It was parked at the end of a line of buildings containing the Reaper drones the CIA used against terrorist cells operating in the region. "Put us down there!"

The skids touched down about twenty yards from the Globemaster's open rear cargo door. The sun had dipped below the horizon and the lights inside the plane silhouetted a group of soldiers pushing a gurney in their direction. Inside the plane, Rapp could see rows of bunks and walls lined with state-of-the-art medical equipment. For all intents and purposes, the plane was a flying hospital—manned by multiple medical teams and equipped to handle everything from basic triage to severe burns.

With so many unknowns relating to the Pakistan operation, Kennedy had kept the Globemaster close in case things went south. Rapp didn't like to plan for failure, but Kennedy was obsessed with covering every angle. In this case—as in so many before—she'd made the right call. Coleman could be stabilized on their way to the U.S. military hospital in Germany.

Rapp jumped out of the open door as Joe Maslick and the copilot began sliding the stretcher containing Scott Coleman toward him.

They'd managed to stop the visible bleeding, but there was no question that he had internal injuries beyond their ability to deal with. The former SEAL's skin had gone pale, creating a stark contrast to the blood spattered all over it. He'd still been alive when they'd checked ten minutes ago, but it was impossible to tell just by looking at him if that was still the case.

He didn't move at all as Rapp took one end of the stretcher and started sliding it out of the aircraft. Shouts became audible from behind and a moment later he was enveloped by one of the C-17's medical teams. A moment later they had Coleman on a two-wheeled gurney and were rushing him back to the plane. A nurse in desert camo was straddling him, pulling off his bandages and checking for a carotid pulse. Another was running alongside, cutting through Coleman's pants leg with a pair of scissors.

One of the corpsmen lagged and Rapp grabbed him by the back of the collar, jerking him to a stop.

"We need one more gurney."

"Sir?" the kid said, eyes widening. "We were told one injured man."

He had the look of a new recruit. Smart and well trained, but not yet certain of his role in this shit storm.

"Just get me the gurney," Rapp said.

"We have another team. I'll—"

"Stop talking and listen to me. Don't get another team. Don't ask for help or tell anyone what you're doing. Just get me the fucking gurney. Is that clear?"

The man was understandably scared and confused, but nodded.

"You have one minute."

When he started to run, Rapp pushed himself back into the chopper and pointed to the nuke. "Let's get it out of here."

It took some wrestling, but they managed to drag the warhead to the doors just as the corpsman reappeared. He took a hesitant step backward when he saw his new patient and then another when they rolled it into a position where the radiation hazard symbol was visible.

"Sir? We're authorized to pick up three men. One injured. No one told me anything about . . ." His voice faded for a moment. "About anything else."

"I'm telling you about it now," Rapp said, pushing the gurney to the edge of the chopper's door. Maslick and the copilot put their shoulders to the warhead and gave it one last shove. The gurney's tires bulged when the weapon landed, but everything held together. Rapp threw a blanket over it before pointing at Maslick and then to the Globemaster. The former Delta operator jumped out and helped the corpsman push the warhead toward the open cargo hold.

Rapp slapped an open palm loudly against the side of the chopper and leaned inside. "Get out of here, Fred. And like always, forget any of this ever happened."

"That'll be a pleasure," the pilot said, flipping a few switches above him. "Tell Scott we're pulling for him."

Rapp jogged toward the plane as the dust kicked up and the helicopter started rising into a darkening sky. The C-17's four jet engines were already spooling and the cargo bay door was on its way up. Rapp grabbed its edge and flipped himself onto it, rolling to his feet inside.

He ignored Maslick and the corpsman trying to strap the nuke into a bunk and walked forward. There was a dividing wall near the front and he skirted around it before stopping at its edge. Coleman had five people working on him. IVs and oxygen were in place and his clothes were gone. Bloody rags that had been used to clean him up enough to search for hidden wounds were piled on the floor.

Rapp wasn't sure how long he watched. How long he listened to the voices go from commanding to desperate and back again. The details of what they were doing, the meaning of what they were saying, was lost on him.

A scalpel flashed in the overhead lights and Rapp saw it slide between Coleman's ribs. He just lay there like a piece of meat.

"Mitch?"

Rapp ignored the voice behind him and continued to watch the medical team work on his friend.

"Mitch? Dr. Kennedy is on the phone for you."

Rapp turned slowly toward Maslick, who was sheepishly holding out a satphone.

Instead of taking it, he grabbed the man by the throat and drove him back into the fuselage. "I told you to get that nuke out of there! Were my orders not clear or are you just too stupid to understand them?"

"I'm sorry," Maslick managed to get out past the pressure on his windpipe. "Dr. Kennedy overrode you. She sent us back."

Rapp could hear her tinny voice shouting unintelligibly from the phone lying at his feet. The plane started to taxi and he finally released Maslick, shoving him toward the back of the plane. The former soldier retreated unsteadily as Rapp scooped up the handset.

"Mitch!" Kennedy said. "Are you there? Mitch!"

"I'm here."

"Joe went back on my express orders. He tried to talk me out of it."

"Not smart, Irene. The cops were moving in and we had no idea what their capabilities were. They could have taken down Fred's bird."

"There was no other option. I contacted President Chutani but he said there was nothing he could do to pull them back. General Shirani wouldn't even take my call."

"Then you should have left us."

"I guarantee you that Shirani was going to force a fight. Video of you gunning down a bunch of soldiers before getting taken out by an RPG is just what he needs to stoke Pakistan's anti-American elements. It might have been enough to turn the tide against the civilian government."

She was probably right, Rapp knew. Her grasp of the intricate power struggles from Washington to Beijing to Islamabad was second to none. The nuke was safe, he was alive, and Coleman was in the hands of the best combat trauma people in the world. It didn't help, though. His anger just kept building.

"So this was about Pakistan, not about me and Scott."

"Of course," she said, not bothering even to try to be convincing. "I consider both of you completely expendable."

The plane's wheels touched down and the engines roared as the massive aircraft came to a stop.

Rapp didn't move from his position on a cot bolted to the fuselage. He watched silently as Coleman, utterly still and surrounded by his medical team, was wheeled out the back.

It wasn't their planned stop in Europe. The docs had told him that Coleman wasn't going to survive long enough to get there. This U.S. air base in Afghanistan was the closest thing that had the surgical capabilities they needed.

He continued to sit, staring at the wall in front of him, until an air force colonel came stalking up the open loading bay.

"Who's in charge here?"

When Rapp didn't react, Maslick subtly pointed.

"Who the hell are you?" the man said, putting his hands on his hips and positioning himself in front of Rapp. "I got a call saying that a plane was coming in with a medical emergency. Nothing about on whose authority, where it was from, who was on—"

He suddenly fell silent and it was obvious why. The blanket had slipped off the nuke strapped into a bunk to his left.

"What the hell did you bring onto my base?"

"Nothing you need to worry about," Rapp said finally. "You just need to make sure my man gets the best care available and call me in a fast transport to the U.S."

With an expression of disgust, the officer examined Rapp's filthy clothing, long hair, and thick beard. "CIA," he spat. "Fuck you. You don't walk onto my base and start giving orders."

"Look, Colonel. I'm bone tired and we both know I'm going to get what I want. Why not just skip straight to that part?"

"You have confidence, I'll give you that. Exactly why is it you think you're going to get what you want?"

"Because I have a nuke."

The man's eyes shot toward the warhead again. "But where did you get it and where are you going with it? Because you're not getting me involved in some bullshit CIA operation without authorization."

It worried Rapp that he was actually thinking about killing the man. And not in some vague, theoretical way. He had his eye on a large wrench stowed against the fuselage and was picturing beating the officer's skull in with it.

"Okay, Colonel," he said, reluctantly abandoning the idea. "Then let's get you authorization."

He smirked. "What? From Irene Kennedy? I don't work for her."

The anger flashed across Rapp's face and Maslick inched closer, putting himself in position for an intercept. The Delta man tensed when Rapp reached behind him, but then relaxed when nothing more deadly than a phone appeared.

"Would the president be good enough?"

"My ass," the man said. "You Agency pricks are all the same. You swagger around and bullshit about how the White House hangs on your every word. I've been around way too long to fall for that."

Rapp switched his phone to speaker and dialed a number that went to a private switch-board at 1600 Pennsylvania Avenue.

"White House. How can I help you?"

"Could you put me through to the Oval Office, please?"

"Connecting you now."

The still-unnamed air force colonel started to look a little uncertain.

"Oval Office."

"Gloria, it's Mitch. Is he available?"

"He's meeting with the vice president right now. Do you want me to poke my head in?"

Rapp looked inquisitively at the man in front of him, who shook his head violently.

"No, it's not that important."

"Should he call you when he's out?"

Again, Rapp looked up and again he got a vigorous shake of the head.

"No, I'll just catch up with him when I get back. Thanks."

By the time he disconnected the call, the anonymous colonel was already headed for the exit.

"Fast transport," Rapp called after him.

"I'll find the closest one and get it in the air,"

he responded without looking back. A moment later he had disappeared down the tarmac.

"Helpful guy," Maslick said.

Rapp stood. "Lock this plane down. No one gets on or off until we're ready to transfer that nuke. I'll be back in twenty."

Rapp hated the smell of hospitals. It was a stale antiseptic stench that he'd come to associate with failure and loss. He walked up to a large reception desk and looked over it at a woman in a crisp air force uniform. "Excuse me, ma'am. One of my men just came in here."

Her eyebrows rose a bit. "Are you the guy running our CO ragged?"

News had a way of moving quickly on military bases. "Yeah."

"Congratulations. No one knew he could move that fast," she said, sliding a clipboard toward him. "Your man didn't have any tags or a name. Could you give us his information?"

"Sure," Rapp said. "How is he?"

"They've taken him into surgery."

"With respect, ma'am, that's not what I asked."

"I know."

Rapp nodded his understanding and picked up the clipboard. "Is there somewhere I can fill this out? Somewhere private?"

"We've got a little chapel down the hall on the

right. Nothing fancy but I don't think anyone's in there."

He followed her directions, pushing through a set of double doors before dropping the clipboard in a trash can and dialing Irene Kennedy.

He thought about the deaths of his wife and unborn child. About his brother, whom he hadn't seen in more than a year. About his old friend Stan Hurley bleeding out in his arms only a few weeks ago.

And now Scott.

The line began to ring and Kennedy picked up almost immediately. "How is he?"

"Not good. He's in surgery."

"And the warhead?"

"Joe's watching it. I've ordered up a transport."

"You're still planning on bringing it here?"

"We've been wanting to get a look at Pakistani nuclear technology for a long time. This might be our only chance."

She didn't respond.

"You disagree?"

"No, but I'm getting a lot of pushback from the Pakistanis. They know we have it and they want it back."

"Call Chutani."

"He's one of the ones pushing back."

"Bullshit. He'd be dead if it weren't for me and that nuke would be in the back of a van with a bunch of terrorists."

"Still, he's the president of Pakistan and he's trying to hold on to power. Shirani can use this against him."

"Then stall. It's not like we need it for a month. I'll deliver it to Craig and tell him his tech guys have twenty-four hours to learn everything he can."

"This isn't like snatching some mid-level ISI operative or hacking into one of their computers, Mitch. This is a nuclear weapon. What do I tell them?"

"That it's a holiday weekend. That my plane ran out of gas. Or maybe that if they don't want us to take them, they shouldn't drive them around in fucking fruit trucks."

"I've briefed President Alexander and he's given his authorization, but he asked some questions that I had a hard time answering. We know they have nukes. We know they work. How much are the details worth to us?"

Rapp let out a long breath. "There's something not right here, Irene. Something we don't understand."

"What makes you say that?"

"A Russian mobster working with ISIS, for one. Why?"

"To get you out of the way so they could get their hands on a nuke. With Saddam Hussein's former generals starting to take charge, ISIS tactics are getting more sophisticated. They have money and it's not hard to believe that they'd use it to hire outside contractors."

"But our information was that the people looking to snatch this nuke weren't ISIS. They were al Badr. The two groups aren't really connected."

"Agreed."

"And then there's what happened to Scott."

"What did happen? Was he ambushed?"

"Not in the way you're thinking. It was one guy."

"One man? Are you sure?"

Rapp dropped onto a bench. "I'm sure. And this guy went through Scott like he wasn't there."

"That doesn't seem possible."

"I'd say the same thing if I hadn't seen it with my own eyes."

"Did you get a good look at him?"

"Marginal."

"And?"

"White guy around my size. Dark hair. Mid-thirties. Medium complexion."

"You didn't recognize him?"

"Nope."

She fell silent for a moment, considering what she was being told. The number of people who could hope to even survive a confrontation with Scott Coleman was incredibly small. But to do it easily? If there was someone like that out there, how could Mitch Rapp have never run across him?

"Look, Irene. A guy like this doesn't work for

the Mob and he doesn't take contracts from a bunch of half-assed terrorists. In fact, he doesn't contract himself out at all or I'd have heard of him."

"But you think he's important."

"My gut says that if we can find him, we'll have the key to this thing."

"The key? Or a target for revenge?"

Rapp ignored her question. "I figure there's a seventy-five percent chance that he came up through a solid spec ops program. So, probably European. And since the Russians seem to have their fingerprints all over this thing, I'd start there."

"What about the other twenty-five percent?"

"He could have been trained by the ops side of one of the intelligence agencies like I was."

"That's not a lot to go on, Mitch. Elite white soldiers in their thirties casts a pretty wide net."

"One more thing to add to his profile, Irene. This guy's an athlete. Maybe he stopped competing when he was young, but at some point, people noticed him."

"So, gifted white male teens playing some sport in some country. Not that helpful."

"Yeah, but again, we know that the Russians are involved. So I'd start with the former Soviet athletics program. Records still exist and people who worked in it are still alive. Maybe we'll get lucky."

Chapter 21

Above Southwestern Virginia U.S.A.

"We're on our final approach," Rapp said into his headset. "Could you give us runway lights?"

No response. They were coming in between two heavily wooded mountains, the outlines of which were barely visible in glow of the moon. The colonel whose name Rapp still didn't know had managed to scrounge up one of the Air Force's Gulfstream IIIs but, ironically, pilots had been in short supply. That left Rapp and his rusty flying skills in the right seat.

"I repeat. We are on our—"

"I can't find the fucking switch," a familiar voice interrupted. "Hang on. I think it's behind this bush. Yeah, I've got it."

Two rows of lights appeared to the north, outlining a runway that had been used probably no more than ten times since the Cold War. The pilot banked toward it and steepened their descent.

"Some genius," Rapp said into the mike hanging in front of his mouth.

"What, I'm an electrician, now?"

"We'll be on the ground in two. Try not to

touch anything else until then. I'd rather not put this thing into the trees."

"No problemo, man."

Rapp glanced back into the cabin. The luxurious seats he was used to in the CIA's G550 were conspicuously absent, replaced with a few frame-and-canvas benches bolted to the rear bulkhead. Joe Maslick had piled some blankets and cushions next to the warhead and was sound asleep with his head propped against the nose-cone.

"Mas! Get your ass up. We're landing."

The former Delta operator jerked awake.

"Is that thing secure? We don't need it chasing us around in here when we touch down."

"We're good," he grumbled. "But there are better things to wake up next to."

Rapp faced forward again and watched the approaching lights. Surprisingly, Maslick's comment made him think of Claudia Gould. He tried to shake it off by telling himself that any relationship between them was doomed, but her image wasn't so easily dismissed.

His relationships had always been a study in extremes. Maybe Claudia was the right balance. But was it worth the inevitable pain? The responsibility? The constraints? And more than that, was it fair? Anna was dead. Hurley was dead. Scott was likely dying. The people closest to him didn't do well and Claudia was responsible for more than just herself. She had a young daughter who needed her.

The wheels hit the ground and a set of headlights flashed to their eleven o'clock. Rapp pointed them out to the pilot before trading his headset for a phone and heading back into the cabin. Irene Kennedy's private line rang a good five times before she picked up. When that happened it usually meant she was in the midst of the three hours a night she managed to sleep.

"Have you landed?"

"Just touched down," he said, helping Maslick unstrap the warhead. "What's the update on Scott?"

Rapp expected the long silence that always preceded reports of the death of a friend, but the news turned out to be slightly more upbeat.

"The calf was all soft-tissue damage and the shot that hit him in the shoulder shattered his collarbone but isn't anything a metal plate can't fix. The dislocation was worse than the bullet wound. The head injury was more serious than we initially thought. Beyond the concussion, he has some hairline skull fractures."

"And the knife?"

"He just got out of a four-hour surgery and they think they've repaired the damage . . ." Her voice trailed off.

"But?"

"But the blood loss and heat stroke were

extremely serious. The doctors have induced a coma and the expectation is that he'll never regain consciousness. If he does, they don't know if he'll have brain damage."

Rapp grabbed the nuke's nosecone and began dragging it toward the door. "Where is he now?"

"On his way to Bethesda in the C-17 you evacuated him in. I'm sure you already know this, but I want to say it anyway. We're bringing in the world's top people. Everything that can be done will be done."

"His mother's still alive," Rapp said. "That's the only family he has. Did you tell her?"

"I haven't. She's in the early stages of dementia and I think it would be better if we didn't contact her until we know more. Certainly not until he's in an American hospital bed."

"Or an American grave."

"I don't think there's any point in considering that possibility right now."

"What about the guy who's responsible?"

"We have some shaky cell phone footage. He had facial wounds that obscured his features somewhat but our people were able to clean it up and get some solid stills. We have them out to intelligence agencies worldwide but so far no hits."

Rapp jumped out of the plane and moved away. The night had turned cool but the humidity still hung in the air. He crossed the runway as the lights blinked off and walked into the damp brush at its edge. There was no wind. The only sound was an engine starting up a few hundred yards to the west.

"Tell your people to find him, Irene. Not tomorrow. Not next week. Now."

"I understand what you're feeling, Mitch. Believe me, I do. But we're doing the best we can." She paused for a moment. "In the meantime, I need you back in Pakistan. After what happened, the Pakistani army is tightening its procedures for moving the country's arsenal, but there's the danger that this wasn't the only warhead targeted. In fact, the army pulling back could make the problem worse."

"Terrorist groups trying to make a move before the window closes," Rapp said.

"Exactly."

"I'll fly back as soon as I can."

"Thank you. With both you and Scott gone, our operation there is starting to unravel. And on top of that, we need to return their device. The political pressure is getting heavy and we're seeing action by the army that we don't like. This could be the first sign of a coup by General Shirani."

Rapp let out a long breath. Pakistan run by Shirani would be a disaster. The current president was a scumbag but at least he was a secular, Westward-leaning scumbag. Shirani was a wannabe fundamentalist dictator with an insatiable thirst for power and a deep hatred for the United States.

"We'll work fast," he said as an old pickup rolled to a stop next to the jet. "I'll contact you if we find anything interesting."

Rapp disconnected the call and walked back onto the tarmac in order to greet the man stepping out of the truck. Craig Bailer was a full three inches taller than Rapp, with thick, tattoo-covered arms extending from a T-shirt extolling the virtues of Pabst Blue Ribbon. His gaunt face was shadowed by three days of stubble and a baseball cap equally enthusiastic about PBR.

"How's it going, Mitch? Been a while."

Despite his outward appearance, Bailer held three PhDs—one in nuclear physics and two in fields Rapp couldn't pronounce. Kennedy had snapped him up after he'd unexpectedly walked away from Lockheed Martin but he'd hated Langley, hated his job, and hated being cooped up in an office. Toward the end of his tenure at headquarters, Bailer had spent most of his time working in the motor pool. In fact, it was he who had tricked out Rapp's Dodge with full armor, run-flats, nitrous, and bulletproof glass, among other things. The people in personnel were fairly certain he was the best-educated and best-paid auto mechanic in history.

When he inevitably quit, Kennedy had gone

into crisis mode. It had been Rapp's idea to move him into an abandoned Cold War missile facility in a remote corner of Virginia. If Bailer wouldn't go to the mountain, they'd just move the mountain to him.

Despite the huge financial outlay, though, Bailer spent less time at the facility than he did in the local drunk tank. The Agency only brought him in when there was a job no one else could handle. And that's just the way the gregarious redneck liked it. He had a legitimate machine shop about twenty miles away where he fabricated custom parts for spy satellites and hot rods.

"Good to see you," Rapp said, extending a hand. "Sorry about the short notice."

Behind them, Joe Maslick had the warhead balanced in the plane's open hatch. "Where's the transport?"

"Right here," Bailer said, slapping the side of his truck. He jumped in and backed up to the plane before getting out again to rearrange a cooler and some shovels to make room.

"Roll it on in," Bailer said.

"That's a three-foot drop."

"It's not a bottle of nitro, Mas. Do you have any idea how many intricate reactions it takes to set one of these things off?"

"No."

Bailer grinned. "Me neither. But I figure it's got to be more than two."

Rapp gave a subtle nod and Maslick rolled the weapon out the door. It hit the bed of the truck with an earsplitting clang, nearly bottoming out the shocks.

"Hop in the back, Mas. There's not enough room for all three of us in the cab."

Maslick jumped in, his two-hundred-twenty-pound frame pushing the chassis the rest of the way down. "Anything in that cooler?"

"Would I leave you hanging?" Bailer said, sliding behind the wheel.

Rapp opened the passenger door and picked up a stick of dynamite lying in the seat. Bailer grabbed it and tossed it into the back. "I was doing a little fishing last weekend. So how's the Charger?"

"Stereo sounds like shit," Rapp said as they accelerated up the tarmac.

"Yeah, I had to take out the main speakers to make room for the Kevlar. They've got some thinner stuff now and I've got a great sound guy I work with. You should bring it by."

Maslick banged on the top of the cab with a beer can and Bailer held a hand through his open window to take it. "You want one, Mitch?"

"No."

He popped it open and took a healthy slug as the vehicle bounced across a grassy field. With the shocks already at their limit, the nuke was making quite a racket bouncing off the sides of the truck's bed, but Rapp didn't worry about it. If Craig Bailer said it wasn't a problem, it wasn't a problem.

They finally skidded to a stop in an unremarkable part of the field and Bailer pointed to the visor above the passenger seat. "Could you hit that garage door opener, Mitch?"

He did and a moment later they were descending on a massive elevator platform once used to move intercontinental ballistic missiles.

"So are you looking for anything special, man? Or do you just want to know if the Pakistanis can detonate the thing without blowing their dicks off?"

"Irene wants a rundown of the technology and power," Rapp said.

"What about you?"

"Someone tried to steal it. I want to know who."

"No problem. I'll bring in some of the forensics guys I work with. Anything else?"

"No," Rapp said, watching the gray concrete walls slip slowly by.

"You all right, man?"

"Yeah."

"You sure? Because it's a beautiful night and we have a cooler full of beer and a stolen A-bomb. It don't get any better than that."

Chapter 22

North of Islamabad
Pakistan

Grisha Azarov pulled his hat down his forehead and tilted his face into the upturned collar on his jacket. The sun was gone but the heat was still hovering at thirty-eight degrees Celsius, making his choice of clothing both uncomfortable and likely to attract attention. Fortunately, the private airstrip was all but abandoned at this time of night.

He jogged up the steps of his company's Bombardier Challenger 650, heading for the back as the pilot closed the door. The interior had been redesigned to his specifications, reducing the number of seats and adding a sofa long enough to sleep on without causing stiffness. He entered the expanded bathroom and closed the door, leaning over the sink and staring into the mirror.

His face was dotted with bandages that a few hours ago had matched his skin tone but were now dark with blood. He began peeling them off, pulling glass from the wounds he hadn't had time to clean during his escape. None were serious enough to need stitches, though the half-moon slice on the bridge of his nose was deeper than he'd realized. That one had been too close. Less than a centimeter from his right eye.

He couldn't help but be reminded of the severe acne he'd suffered as a teenager, the damage from which had been repaired during the plastic surgeries he'd undergone before going to work for Maxim Krupin.

The phone lying on the counter next to him came to life with a number that belonged to the president's secure cell. Azarov considered ignoring the call, but giving into that temptation would be unwise in the extreme. Instead, he inserted a Bluetooth headset and picked up.

"Good evening, sir."

"What the hell happened, Grisha? My people in Pakistan report that Mitch Rapp is still alive and that he has the weapon."

"I can't confirm those reports with certainty, sir. But they seem credible."

Krupin let out a lengthy string of expletives in Russian. "I should have seen through your false bravado and known you'd fail me."

It was an entirely predictable revision of their last meeting. Azarov had done nothing to hide his concerns regarding a confrontation with Rapp and had gone so far as to recommend against it. Krupin, though, would never admit to an error and was already shifting the blame. It was always odd to watch these deflections because of the strange honesty to them. Azarov had come to believe that they were less a deliberate reaction to failure than an unconscious one. Krupin saw himself as infallible and lapses in his own judgment tended to cause unbearable cognitive dissonance. Typically, that dissonance was resolved at the expense of one of his underlings.

"My bravado or lack thereof was of no importance," Azarov said, cleaning his wounds with alcohol. "I never saw Mitch Rapp, though it seems likely that he fired the shot that injured me. He sent his man Scott Coleman into the warehouse and I dealt with the situation."

Krupin ignored him. "The Pakistanis are demanding the weapon back, but the Americans are delaying. We have to assume they're examining it."

"That seems reasonable."

"I'm not interested in your opinions on this or any other matter, Grisha! I'm interested in your actions. The Americans won't just be looking at the Pakistani technology, they'll be looking for clues as to who was behind the attempt to steal it. And unless the Pakistanis can exert sufficient pressure to get it back immediately, it's almost certain that the our alterations will be discovered."

Azarov had a growing understanding of Krupin's activities in Pakistan, but he was still in the dark as to the man's ultimate goal. What alterations was he referring to?

When he spoke again, Krupin seemed to have recovered the icy façade that he liked to wear. "For the first time in our relationship, you've disappointed me, Grisha."

Azarov pulled the pistol from the holster beneath his left arm and placed it on the counter. It seemed unlikely that Krupin would act rashly where his young enforcer was involved. In the current unpredictable environment, it would be more advantageous to send Azarov to his death in a way that furthered his plans than to summarily execute him. Having said that, it would be a mistake to count on his indispensability as Marius Postan had.

"At this point, I can only offer my apologies, sir. My hope is that despite this setback, your Pakistani operations were successful and that now you have what you want."

"I do. But with Rapp alive and in possession of the Faisalabad warhead, it's possible that Irene Kennedy will get a glimpse into my plans."

"She's a political appointee," Azarov said. "Certainly she's controllable."

"Not as much as one would expect. We've contacted people sympathetic to us in their Congress and found many of them to be afraid of her. Even more so, of Mitch Rapp. That's one of many reasons he needed to be dealt with. The problem is that your incompetence has tipped him off. He'll become cautious and retreat."

Azarov actually laughed out loud at that. "Mr. President, in all likelihood, I've killed his primary lieutenant and closest friends. I can tell you with great certainty that a confrontation between myself and Mr. Rapp is now inevitable."

Maxim Krupin cut off the speakerphone and looked across his desk at Tarben Chkalov. The powerful oligarch said nothing, instead staring at the speaker with aging eyes.

Krupin found it difficult to hide his anger at having the old bag of bones there. At being forced to consult with this man in affairs of state—the affairs of a country that he had sacrificed everything to control.

But even great autocrats such as France's Louis XIV had been forced to cater to nobles and religious leaders. While Russia's people could be drugged with the illusion of power, its oligarchs demanded more tangible rewards. Like stray dogs, they occasionally had to be thrown scraps from his table.

"Irene Kennedy will discover your tampering," Chkalov said. "She's many things, but stupid is not one of them."

Krupin had anticipated the criticism and managed a respectful nod. "The men involved were from a Pakistani terrorist group. I don't see how this—"

"But Ilya Gusev in South Africa was not. Nor

is Grisha. Certainly there were witnesses in Faisalabad. And in the modern society we live in, someone always has a phone with a camera. Even if Grisha can't be specifically identified, it will be obvious to anyone with eyes that he isn't Middle Eastern. And are we even certain that Scott Coleman is dead? Rapp went to a great deal of trouble to get him out."

"The Americans have a sentimental bias against leaving their fallen behind."

"Perhaps. But if he *has* survived, I suspect that Grisha's face is indelibly burned into his mind."

"What are you suggesting, Tarben?"

Chkalov forced an unconvincingly subservient smile. "I wouldn't presume to suggest anything, Mr. President. I was merely pointing out that your attempt to divert blame to ISIS and other similar groups may be at risk."

"The Americans are terrified of the Muslims and blinded to all other risks by that fear. They'll believe that their mainland is under a nuclear threat and will pull back to defend themselves. By the time they realize the truth, it'll be too late."

"They would say 'circling the wagons,' " the old man said. He was fond of flaunting his mastery of English. "I agree with regard to the American politicians. They both fear the Muslim threat and need it to keep their electorate motivated. Kennedy and Rapp, though, are different. They're not afraid and they don't have to worry about elections. Further, they're as knowledgeable as anyone alive about the groups you are trying to use to blind them. More knowledgeable than even you, perhaps."

"You overestimate them, Tarben. Kennedy is hemmed in by the increasing dysfunction of the American government and Rapp is nothing more than an assassin. Gifted in that realm admittedly, but hardly sophisticated enough to understand the forces at work here."

Chkalov just nodded.

Chapter 23

Southwestern Virginia
U.S.A.

The dull ring of a knock on the steel door echoed off the walls. Rapp sat up on his cot, looking through the semidarkness at the rusting pipes and crumbling ceiling. During the height of the Cold War, this is where the ICBM missile crews bunked. Now the room was little more than a relic of a largely forgotten conflict.

The only illumination was coming from a single battery-powered light on the floor. There was no functioning power in the room, and the lack of electric heat gave it the feel of a meat locker. Despite that, Maslick was snoring loudly in the top bunk, the fog of his breath rising rhythmically into the still air. For now, his role in this was over. He'd focus on recovery until he was needed again.

The knock came again, this time followed by the sound of the door scraping open.

"Mitch?" Craig Bailer's voice. But more subdued than normal. "Are you awake?"

"Yeah," Rapp said, sliding off the edge of his bunk. "What time is it?"

"Four in the morning," Bailer said, motioning

Rapp down a corridor fashioned from a concrete pipe twenty feet in diameter.

"Have you found anything?"

"After we made sure it was safe, we gave the forensics guys priority. They wanted prints, DNA, fibers, and God knows what else before my people contaminated it any more than it already has been. When they were done, we started with X-rays, MRI, and metallurgy."

It was hard not to notice that Bailer was avoiding his question. "And?"

"Well, it's definitely safe," he said in an enigmatic tone. "We're most of the way through the teardown—getting pictures and working on a virtual 3-D model."

They came out of the pipe and arrived at a set of titanium blast doors that were part of the fifty million dollars in modifications the CIA had made. He pressed his palm against a pad set into the wall and the doors slid open to reveal a world of bright fluorescent light, stainless steel, and glass. No fewer than twenty people were milling around what had once been one of Pakistan's most advanced nuclear weapons. Now it was nothing more than endless rows of individual parts laid out on a stark white floor.

"I hope you know how to put that thing back together," Rapp said as the doors slid closed behind them.

"No worries. I took pictures with my cell phone."

Rapp had always found watching Bailer in his element to be a bit surreal. Despite looking like a truck driver, it was abundantly clear that he was the smartest guy in the room. Gray-haired men in lab coats approached him with clipboards to sign, deferential nods were aimed in his direction, and numerous people vied for his attention to get approvals, ask questions, and have their work checked over. Rapp didn't bother to pay attention to any of it. Computer screens full of complex diagrams and math equations were well outside his operating theater. Which was exactly the reason they went to such lengths to keep Bailer happy.

"What aren't you telling me, Craig? The thing's not going to blow up, right?"

"Definitely not."

Bailer motioned him onto a platform that ran across the back wall. The people working on the computer terminals there suddenly found reasons they needed to be somewhere else, increasing Rapp's apprehension. They knew who he was and didn't want to be around when he got the news.

"How bad is it?" Rapp said as Bailer brought up a false-color image of the nuke on a monitor.

"Pretty bad, Mitch. We stitched this together out of the scans we made. "Metal shows blue, plastics and carbon fiber are black. Radioactivity comes up red."

"What do you mean? There is no red."

"Exactly."

Rapp considered what he was seeing for a moment. Was it possible that Umar Shirani was smarter that they gave him credit for? That he was circulating decoys along with live nukes to keep the endless list of Pakistani terrorist groups off-balance?

"So this is a fake?"

"No. This is a working bomb. But the canister that should contain its nuclear fuel is empty."

"Empty," Rapp repeated quietly. "So the Pakistani army removed the fissile material before they moved them? They're shipping it separately?"

Bailer's face transformed into something that was between a frown and a wince. "That was my initial thought, too. But it doesn't add up."

"Explain."

"The empty canister is a really good fake, but it isn't made from the same steel as the other parts."

"So? It makes sense that they wouldn't have been manufactured at the same time as the device. That useless prick Shirani could have had them produced later as an additional security precaution."

"Two problems with that theory. One, my gut says that the canister wasn't made in Pakistan."

"And two?"

"That's the bigger problem: how the original canister was removed. Whoever did it knew what they were doing and had the right tools, but I can tell you they were in a hurry. There are some pretty deep gouges, a disconnected wire, and a cracked switch."

Rapp thought about the warehouse where the terrorists had pulled the nuke from the truck and opened the crate. "What are we talking about, Craig? How much time?"

"With a little training, you could change out the original canister with a fake in as little as four minutes."

"How big and heavy is it?"

"Call it a fifty-pound hatbox."

"Shit," Rapp said.

"My thought exactly."

Rapp turned and walked a few paces, staring out over the activity below as he dialed his phone.

"Hello," Irene Kennedy said. By the sound of her voice, she hadn't been asleep.

"We have a problem."

"Yes?"

"The canister holding the fissile material has been replaced with a fake."

"So the Pakistani army decoupled it?"

"Craig says no. My guess is that the people in that warehouse got out with it. We were watching for them to move the entire unit and we didn't have the manpower to track them all."

There was a long silence over the phone. "It doesn't make sense to me, Mitch. I can understand them taking it but replacing it with a decoy? Why would they go through the trouble? And how would they have built it? Was it a convincing fake?"

"Yeah, but Craig's betting that it wasn't made in Pakistan."

"That's even less believable, then. I'd be skeptical if this was al Qaeda or ISIS. But al Badr is—"

"The minor leagues," Rapp said, finishing her thought.

"Exactly. The fact that they were even going after a nuke was surprising. Now you're telling me they figured out how to not only remove the fissile material container but manufacture a convincing replacement? That strains credulity to the breaking point."

"Al Badr or not, someone's got the critical piece for building a nuke, and I'm guessing it's not one of our friends."

"Agreed. Have Craig reassemble the weapon so we can get it back to Pakistan. The situation's heating up and we can't afford to keep it any longer."

"Shirani's going to blame us," Rapp pointed out. "He'll say we took the fuel and use the accusation to pump up the religious fanatics. It could be enough for him to take over."

"No question. But I'm not sure what we can do about it at this point. We need to focus on making sure no more fissile material is removed from the Pakistani arsenal."

"Mas and I can jump a plane back to Pakistan, but this makes our job a hell of a lot harder. We've been looking for people moving against entire nukes. They're big, heavy, and visible. If all they need is a wrench and a few minutes alone, we've got an entirely different game. Now it's just a matter of slipping some low-level army officer a few grand or sneaking into the back of a train or truck while it's on the move."

She didn't respond.

"Irene?"

"I need you to come to Maryland before you leave, Mitch."

He tensed. "Why?"

"The surgeons in Afghanistan missed some perforations in Scott's small intestine. Our people have repaired them but Scott has a serious infection."

"Bottom line?"

"They're doing everything they can, Mitch—"

"Bottom line, Irene!" Rapp said, the volume of his voice rising. Some of the scientists working below turned and shot him a nervous glance.

"They think he'll be gone before sunrise."

Rapp disconnected the call and turned back to Craig Bailer.

"Everything okay, Mitch?"

"You're done. Get that thing put back together."

"Can I shave a little off that canister? No more than a few thousandths of an inch. With some time to analyze it, I might be able to tell you where it came from."

"As long as you can do it in the next few hours."

"Not a problem."

"Craig, I need a favor."

"Sure. What?"

"My plane's gone and I need to get to Bethesda. Fast."

Bailer nodded thoughtfully. "Yeah. I think I can help you out."

Chapter 24

Near Dominical
Costa Rica

Grisha Azarov eased his pickup along the badly rutted dirt road, keeping his speed under thirty kilometers per hour. Not that he couldn't go faster. He'd paid almost two hundred thousand U.S. dollars to have the vehicle custom built. It looked like a thousand others roaming Central America, but beneath the stock Toyota body was a 600-horsepower off-road racing machine. Based on his tests, he could maintain almost two hundred kilometers an hour on roads that most people crawled along at the pace of a horse-drawn cart.

He was relieved to be out of Pakistan, away from the CIA men operating there, and outside Maxim Krupin's intelligence network. It was a beautiful day in Costa Rica. Humid, but unseason-ably cool. Skies were clear and the sound of the jungle around him calmed his mind. In many ways, this was home. Or at least the closest thing to a home he would likely ever have.

Azarov turned onto an even rougher road and began climbing, scanning the dense trees on either side but keeping his window open and his left arm hanging out. The glass wasn't bulletproof and even if it had been, anyone Krupin sent to punish him for his failure would use a weapon sufficient to defeat any armoring.

Azarov had given his situation a great deal of thought on the flight to Panama and the long overland drive that followed. He was reasonably confident that Krupin wouldn't attempt to have him killed in the near term. Not certain enough that he didn't have a loaded pistol resting in his lap, though.

At thirty-five, he was probably at the peak of his abilities and on the verge of his inevitable decline. He assumed that Krupin recognized this and would be looking for a replacement. Perhaps he'd even found one and was now in the lengthy training and grooming process that Azarov himself had endured. Would this new recruit one day be sent for him? Would that be the boy's test to prove his worth?

Perhaps. But for now, he suspected the benefits of his continued existence outweighed the drawbacks. Still, he had never known Krupin to completely ignore a failure by one of his people. The Russian president felt it set a bad example.

Azarov came to the top of a rise and reached for his cell phone, knowing that he would have a signal until he started dropping down the other side. He dialed and tossed the phone on the dash.

"Hola, Grisha."

"Hola, Juan. Are you well?"

"My back went out again last week," the man responded in Spanish.

Azarov smiled. Juan Fernandez had been running a fruit stand outside the small town of Dominical since he was a child. He knew everyone in the area and was the clearinghouse for local gossip. If anyone suspicious was hanging around the area or asking questions, Juan would know.

For the very reasonable price of three million colones per year, they had an ongoing agreement that Azarov would call him when he was approaching the area. If Juan's answer to the inquiry about his health was *bueno*, then there was a problem. Conversely, if it was an honest recitation of the Costa Rican's many real and imagined infirmities, he had noticed nothing unusual.

"Sorry to hear it. Have you gone to see the doctor?"

"Doctors," he spat. "What do they know? They tell me I'm healthy. But I'm eighty years old. I ask you: How can I be healthy at my age?"

"Clean living," Azarov suggested. "Does Olga need me to pick anything up?"

"No, she was in town shopping just yesterday. But I hear a rumor that there's a problem with your refrigerator."

Azarov was feeling better and better about his situation. If only Russian intelligence had people as thorough as Juan Fernandez.

"Thank you, my friend. I'll see you tomorrow. We'll have a drink."

He disconnected the call and dialed Olga, the woman he lived with. She didn't pick up, but that wasn't unusual. She wasn't terribly reliable and had been angry at him when he last left. If Olga had any gift beyond her startling beauty, it was her ability to hold a grudge.

He accelerated to fifty kilometers per hour and passed by a partially hidden right turn. After a few hundred meters, he saw another, but decided at the last moment to pass it by, too. Finally, he drifted onto the third.

The locals had thought he was crazy when he'd had five separate roads built to his mountaintop home. The land itself had cost less than half a million U.S. dollars. Another million had built the house. The kilometers-long driveways, though, had cost more than the land and buildings com-bined.

They were yet another insurance policy. Anyone hired to come after him would be hesitant to try to take him at his house—the home field advantage was difficult to overcome. Much better to do it during his approach. The five different routes created a situation where one would need a fairly large team to cover every possibility. Just the kind of team that Juan Fernandez would be likely to notice.

The quality of road was bad enough to make it impassable for cars available from standard rental agencies. Again, this was accomplished with significant forethought. As obvious as Russian assassins would be in this quiet surf haven, ones piloting unusual four-wheel drives might as well simply announce their presence personally to Juan.

He pressed the accelerator a bit harder, increasing his speed to over a hundred kilometers an hour. The sound of the engine became deafening—something the people who built the truck had refused to correct, insisting that they worked tirelessly to give it just the right growl. When he approached a small bridge, he slammed on the oversize brakes and diverted right, plummeting down the bank and hitting the stream below hard enough to send water arcing over the roof.

The massive shock absorbers barely cycled through half their travel and the snorkel kept the motor running smoothly during the crossing. When he came to the top of the opposite bank, the truck lofted a good meter in the air. He hated bridges. Too exposed. But Olga insisted on them and he had to admit they could be quite useful during the rainy season.

Azarov accelerated further, reaching a speed

that would make it difficult for even a topnotch sniper to track him from the jungle. Difficult, but not impossible. He wondered sometimes if it would have been safer to live in a city. He owned high-rise flats in both New York and London, cities with countless security cameras, twenty-four-hour crowds, and sophisticated police forces. But he hadn't set foot in either for years. He needed this place. The remoteness. The silence. The distance from the reality he'd become trapped in.

When the house came into view, he began to slow. It was a massive stucco-and-glass structure, open in a way that, if he skidded to a stop, the dust would drift through the living area. In light of that, he continued to ease back on the throttle. What he didn't need was for his reunion with Olga to begin with her screaming at him for an hour in Russian.

Her car was parked in the driveway but she didn't come out to greet him. Normally, he would have slipped his weapon in his waistband instead of keeping it in hand, but the depth of the silence bothered him. Even the insects that sang in the surrounding jungle seemed unusually subdued.

"Olga?"

No answer. It was possible that she was up at the gym, but unlikely. She tended to maintain her spectacular figure through youth and starvation more than exercise.

Azarov had designed the house to allow him to efficiently clear the rooms while making it impractical for anyone to get behind him. He worked his way through it quickly, finding nothing unusual until he reached the master bedroom.

Olga was sitting on the bed wearing a yellow bikini he remembered her paying over a thousand euros for in Paris. She was held upright by her arms, spread wide and secured to the headboard with wire. Her chin was resting on her chest, causing her blond hair to hang down enough to hide her face, but not enough to hide the long gash across her throat.

Blood from the wound had dried across her breasts but was still wet where it had soaked into the mattress. He slid his gun into the back of his pants and stood motionless in the doorway, staring down at her.

Olga Smolin had been a gift for a particularly difficult job he'd completed in Ukraine. A runway model from Tomsk, she'd been beautiful, reasonably good in bed, and a passably competent administrator of his household affairs. On a more basic level, she had been a deeply unhappy young woman. She didn't like the remoteness of Costa Rica, but even in the world's great cities, she seemed to feel nothing was good enough. It made taking pleasure in the simple things impossible for her.

Or maybe she just felt trapped. Like he did.

Azarov freed her and covered her body with a bloodstained sheet. Though she wasn't a woman he would have chosen, he would miss her. But that was the point, wasn't it? Krupin once again demonstrated his skill. Azarov had been punished in a way that was extremely visceral but not sufficient to start a war between them.

He heard the crunch of gravel out front but didn't reach for his gun. His punishment had been meted out. There was nothing more to fear.

"Hello?" he heard a familiar voice call. "Is anyone here?"

Azarov came out of the hallway just as a young woman with a cooler in her hands took a hesitant step into his living room. She was an American surf instructor who provided home management services for some of the wealthier foreign owners.

"How are you, Cara?"

She jumped at the sound of his voice, but managed to keep from dropping the cooler. "Oh, hi, Grisha. I'm fine, thanks. What about you? What happened to your face?"

"A car accident. The window shattered."

"Oh, man. I guess you should consider yourself lucky that nothing hit you in the eye, huh?"

"Very lucky."

Cara Hansen was in many ways the complete opposite of the woman Azarov had spent the last two years living with. She was just as beautiful, but in a natural, perpetually disheveled way that contrasted with Olga's icy perfection. She always had a smile on her face, and seemed to think neither of the past nor the future. While Olga had everything and appreciated nothing, Cara had very little and loved all of it.

Azarov had known her in a peripheral way for years, but paid no attention to her. He'd never looked into her background or had a conversation with her that didn't involve some problem with his house or meaningless small talk about waves or the weather. He couldn't. If Krupin knew how he felt about this twenty-nine-year-old Californian expat, it would have been her, and not Olga, bleeding into his mattress.

Azarov pointed to the cooler. "To what do I owe the pleasure of your visit?"

"Oh. Yeah. Sorry. They told me you needed a bunch of ice. Party or broken fridge?"

"The latter."

"I could take a look at it."

"That's not necessary."

"It's no problem," she said, pushing past him into the kitchen. She put the cooler on the island and opened the refrigerator, crouching down to get a closer look.

He watched with calculated indifference as she poked her head inside.

"Seems fine. The light's on and it feels cold."

"It comes and goes."

"Well, I wouldn't eat any of this stuff, then," she said, standing and turning toward him.

He made sure not to look at the way her shirt clung to her or the tantalizing strip of skin between the bottom of it and the top of her shorts.

"That's good advice, Cara. Thank you."

"Where's Olga?"

"Russia."

"Cool trip. When's she coming back?"

"Probably never."

"Oh," she said, suddenly looking a bit uneasy. "I'm sorry."

"Me too."

She thumbed toward the door. "You want the rest of the ice I brought? I feel like they told me way too much."

"Sure. Just in case."

He followed her out and she brushed a hand along his truck. "This thing must be faster than it looks. I could see you kicking up dust all the way from town."

"Really? Interesting. It's something I've never given thought to."

Cara cocked her head inquisitively, but then just grabbed another cooler from the back of her

Suzuki. He pulled out the last one and followed her back to the house.

She put the cooler down on the floor next to the dishwasher but didn't make a move to leave.

"Thank you," he said, not sure why she was just standing there. Did she know something? That Olga hadn't left? Had she noticed someone lurking around the house? He assumed that Krupin had sent a lone female to kill Olga. Juan couldn't be blamed for overlooking the presence of an unaccompanied eastern European woman on the local beaches.

"Hey, you know, since you're . . . I mean, since your food's probably bad, I'm getting together with some friends tonight at Patrón's. You should come down and get a bite to eat. Maybe have a drink. You seem like you could use a few."

"Thank you for the invitation, Cara, but I've been traveling for the last thirty hours and I think I'm just going to go to bed."

"Yeah, I understand. Maybe some other time."

"Maybe."

She finally turned to leave and he watched her go, waiting until the sound of her car faded before he carried one of the coolers to the bathroom and emptied it into the tub. Krupin thought of everything.

Another ten minutes work and Olga was on ice. She'd keep until he figured out how to dispose of the body and mattress without running the risk of piquing anyone's interest.

After cleaning the bedroom, he wanted nothing more than to lie in his hammock and drain a good bottle of bourbon. Instead, he stripped off his bloody clothes and put on a pair of running shorts. There were only two hours of daylight left, so he grabbed a headlamp from the shelf next to his running shoes.

Mitch Rapp was coming. Not today and probably not tomorrow. But soon.

Chapter 25

Highway 81
Virginia

There were two more hours until sunrise and the dead-straight road was empty of taillights. Rapp was pushing Craig Bailer's modified Corvette hard, but it seemed to be handling the stress with ease. The stereo had been replaced with controls for a fire suppression system mounted to the roll cage, so the only thing audible was the roar ofthe V8 and the slight whistle of aftermarket turbochargers. Joe Maslick's bulky frame was crammed into a passenger seat that Bailer had jury-rigged specifically for this trip. Typically, he hadn't said a word since they'd left.

The radar detector sounded, prompting Rapp to glance down at the vehicle's speedometer. One hundred sixty miles per hour. In the rearview mirror he saw a police cruiser's lights go on, already distant enough to be just a pinpoint. A moment later, they went dark again. He'd called in a number of favors and cleared the path to Walter Reed, where Scott Coleman was on life support. The Vette's plate number had been given to Maryland and Virginia police, with instructions that under no circumstances was it to be pulled over.

Rapp tried to concentrate on the missing fissile material and how it tied back to Pakistan, but found it impossible. Scott Coleman had been at his side for almost his entire career. The former SEAL was patriotic, unwaveringly loyal, and courageous. But he was more than that. He was a man who somehow had never allowed himself to be sucked into the darkness that constantly swirled around him.

The death of Rapp's mentor Stan Hurley was still a fresh wound but in many ways a different one. Hurley had been, first and foremost, a killer. A man filled with rage at the injustices of the world and consumed with visiting misery on the people who caused them. He'd died the way he wanted to—the way he had to: full of bullet holes, with his enemy bleeding from a fatal wound that he'd inflicted. For some reason, it wasn't the future Rapp had seen for Coleman. More than any of them, he deserved something better.

He considered calling Kennedy for an update but immediately abandoned the idea. If Coleman was dead, Rapp wasn't ready to hear the news. The thought of spending the next two hours crawling along at seventy miles an hour was for some reason unacceptable. At least now there was urgency. A goal to push for. Even if it turned out to be an illusion.

He felt a tap on his shoulder and glanced over to see Maslick pointing to the fuel gauge. Even at normal speeds, Bailer's Vette wasn't exactly economical. Being driven like this, it was going through gas like there was a hole in the tank.

"Five more miles on the right!" Maslick shouted over the roar of the engine. "The GPS is showing a station less than a quarter mile off the highway. We should be able to get in and out in under four minutes."

The end of the whitewashed hallway had been cordoned off and was empty except for a lone man in a dark suit. One of Irene Kennedy's security detail.

"Is he still alive?" Rapp said, skirting the barriers that had been set up.

"Last I heard, Mitch."

Rapp wasn't sure how to feel about that. Whether he wanted to see his friend struggling to cling to the last few moments of life or if he'd just rather see him gone. He told himself that it didn't matter. Everyone ended up the same way eventually.

Kennedy appeared from a door to his right, wearing a meticulously pressed gray suit jacket and skirt, but looking tired. Her dark hair was pulled back, making the sadness on her face even more stark.

"I'm glad you made it."

"Where is he?"

She led Rapp down the corridor to a transparent wall that looked in on one of the hospital's inten-sive care units. With the bandages on his head and a respirator covering much of his face, Coleman was almost unrecognizable. A small patch of blond hair and an exposed arm full of needles were the only things left to identify one of America's greatest and most loyal warriors.

Maslick stared through the glass for a few seconds and then just walked away, his broad shoulders sagging in a way that actually made the man look small. He'd lost his best friend, Mick Reavers, in a firefight only a few months ago. The price of America's war on terrorism had begun to weigh heavily on him.

Rapp saw motion in his peripheral vision and glanced right to see a figure approaching with two cups of coffee. For one of the few times in his life, he wasn't able to hide his surprise.

Claudia Gould put down the cups and rushed forward, throwing her arms around him. "I'm so sorry about your friend, Mitch."

He just stood there, unsure how to react. Kennedy watched carefully from a few feet away. There was no question that she was the one who had called Claudia. The two women had a long and complicated relationship that had only gotten stronger after Hurley had killed

Claudia's hus-band. But why bring her here now?

"I know how close you and Scott are," she said, pulling away but keeping her gaze on him.

"Thanks," he said, taking a hesitant step back.

"When we met again, I thought I would be telling you all about your house and the horrible amount of your money I'm spending. It seems stupid now."

The strange thing was that he wanted to hear about the house. He wanted to go with her to see it and to listen to the endless details of how she'd chosen things he had no interest in at all.

"How's Anna?"

"She misses her new home and her new friends, but Irene's son has been spending time with her and she's quite taken with him."

"I'll get the two of you back to the Cape, Claudia. I promise."

"I know."

The silence that followed dragged out until Kennedy reached for Rapp's arm and gave it a gentle tug. "Could you excuse us for a few minutes, Claudia? I need to talk to Mitch."

"Yes. Of course," she said, suddenly looking a bit uncomfortable. "Should I . . . Should I stay here?"

"I'd appreciate that. Please let us know if there's any change."

Her discomfort was understandable. It seemed

almost certain that at some point she'd created a dossier on Coleman. History, habits, address, family ties—all designed to give her husband an edge if he ever came up against the man. Now she found her world turned upside down. The people she had once spent time calculating out how to kill were now her protectors.

Rapp followed Kennedy down an empty hallway. "Any new information?"

"On Scott's condition? No. He's on intravenous antibiotics but the doctors don't think they'll work. They keep telling me he won't make it another hour, but he keeps proving them wrong."

They entered a break room and she took a seat in a plastic chair at its center. Rapp pushed the door closed, not speaking again until the latch clicked.

"What's Claudia doing here?"

"I thought you could use a friendly face."

"Are you trying to handle me, Irene?"

"We just lost Stan. And now this. I'm not trying to handle you, Mitch. I'm trying to help you keep perspective."

"Have you talked to his mother yet?"

Kennedy shook her head. "Her dementia is worse than Scott let on. That's the other reason Claudia's here. He has no family other than his mother, and his close friends are all in Pakistan working for you. I can provide him with security but I can't stay here for much longer. Claudia can."

"What have you got on the guy who did this?" Rapp said, changing the subject.

"We're still working on it."

"I don't want to hear that you're working on it, Irene. I want to hear that you know who he is and where I can find him. If the people you have on this don't start providing me with some actionable intel, I'm going to come to Langley and crack some skulls."

"I understand, Mitch. I do. But we have more pressing issues than revenge right now."

"What issues?"

"We've ID'ed two of the men Scott killed. They weren't al Badr. That was likely just a piece of misinformation to throw us off track. They were ISIS."

"So you can identify two random Arab ass-holes but not one of the top professional killers on the planet?"

"It wasn't hard. And one of them was British. Both of them had Facebook pages identifying themselves as members of ISIS and putting their area of operation as Iraq. I think we can be confident that the man who attacked Scott is less active on social media."

Rapp walked to a soda machine in the corner. The change slot had been taped up so he slammed a hand into one of the buttons and was rewarded with a cold Coke. He would have preferred some-thing stronger but had sworn off alcohol until he pulled his life together. Something that, at this rate, might take a while.

"Look, Mitch. We have to consider a few things."

"What things?" he said, opening the can.

"First, the possibility that the fissile material in that weapon wasn't the primary target. That it was just an ancillary benefit."

"What was the target then?"

"You. Think about it. We get information from one of our most trusted informants leading us to an abandoned manufacturing plant where a highly trained assassin is waiting. The reasonable assumption would have been that you—not Scott—would be the one to enter the building. And that assumption would have been right if your motorcycle hadn't broken down."

"Yeah. The same thing occurred to me."

"Whoever's behind this wasn't able to distract you in South Africa so they decided to get rid f you. That seems obvious. And unfortunately, the why of it also seems obvious."

"Because their move against that warhead wasn't a onetime thing. They want me out of the way so they can get more."

She nodded. "Either warheads or fissile material. And if it's the latter, they may already have it. How much of Pakistan's arsenal might already be compromised? How many of their warheads now have empty fuel canisters? ISIS could be creating dirty bombs for deployment in U.S. cities. Worse, they could be developing their own nuclear weapons."

"ISIS? Look, I know they're getting more sophisticated now that Saddam's old generals are taking command positions, but building a nuke? That seems far-fetched."

"Yesterday, I would have agreed. But, according to Craig, whoever manufactured that decoy canister is extremely knowledgeable and well equipped. It doesn't take much anymore, Mitch. You know that. It won't be long before nuclear weapons technology is a century old. In an age of computer-aided design, CNC machines, and 3-D printers, how hard is it really to put a weapon together? It's the fuel that's difficult. Weapons-grade fissile material takes an enormous amount of infrastructure to create."

"And then there's the Russian involvement," Rapp said.

She nodded. "Beyond Ilya Gusev in Africa, we've got the pictures of the man who attacked Scott. Based on his features, I'd say there's greater than a fifty percent chance that he's of eastern European descent."

"But what's in it for the Russians? Why would they get involved in something like this?"

"Those are two pieces of the puzzle that I haven't been able to put together. What I can tell you, though, is that Maxim Krupin is one of the most dangerous men in the world. From the outside he seems to have iron-fisted control of Russia, but it's not true. His supporters are loyal only to the point that he's making them money, and he has countless enemies who will attack the moment they see an opportunity."

"And the cracks are starting to show."

She nodded. "We're predicting that the Russian economy will shrink another four percent this year and that government revenue could be down as much as thirty percent. Krupin's power—and the country itself—just isn't sustainable in the current environment. It's an example of the dark side of low oil prices. On the surface it seems that weakening regimes like Russia and Venezuela would be a good thing. But weakness can turn to chaos in the blink of an eye. You wouldn't believe how much time I spend trying to get politicians to focus on Russia. It's a country with sixteen hundred nuclear warheads controlled by a single man. And, having met Krupin on a number of occasions, I can tell you that there is nothing he won't do to maintain his position. Including turning the planet into a burned-out cinder."

"I feel like we're getting too far ahead of ourselves, Irene. What we need to do now is assess the damage and make sure no more is done. Our first order of business should be finding out how many of Pakistani's nukes have been compromised. And that means you're going to have to get me in front of President Chutani and the general."

"That's easier said than done, Mitch. Our relationship with Pakistani army command isn't exactly warm and those two are on the brink of taking opposite sides in a civil war."

"Contact General Shirani and tell him I'm on my way back with the nuke. Tell him that if he's not there when I land, I'm going to hand it over to Chutani in front of a bunch of television cameras. And I'm going to use those cameras to tell the Pakistani people how their president forced the Great Satan to return their weapon while the army sat around with its thumb up its ass."

Kennedy considered that for a moment. "It might just work. Shirani's trying to portray himself as a strong leader who can strike fear into the hearts of Pakistan's enemies. Your narrative could cut his legs out from under him."

Rapp downed the rest of his Coke. "Joe and I are going to head back to Virginia and get that nuke in the air. Let's talk later about how and where to deliver it."

"Not so fast, Mitch. I'm meeting with President Alexander in an hour and he wants you there."

Rapp shook his head and started for the hallway. "Meetings are your job, Irene. Tell him I'll see him when I get back."

Chapter 26

Near Dominical
Costa Rica

Grisha Azarov leapt over a rotting log and immediately ducked beneath a branch arcing down from his right. It would have been easier to drop and roll, but that maneuver would cost him time. In his experience, almost three quarters of a second.

He entered a clearing and increased his speed, taking the steepest line up a dirt slope, staying low to minimize his profile. While he doubted there was anyone hiding in the dense foliage on either side of him, it had happened before.

His thighs felt like they were on fire but his lungs and heart were handling the workload with an ease that surprised even him. A carefully administered drug regimen increased his blood's ability to carry oxygen to his muscles, but today that had been supplemented with an inhaled substance that he knew nothing about. He'd expected the perfor-mance improvement to be subtle as it had been in the past when his pharmaceutical cocktail was adjusted. It was anything but.

Azarov maintained his momentum through to

the top of the hill and found himself on the top of a butte that jutted from the jungle. To his right, he could see the ocean in the distance and at his ten o'clock was a stucco-and-glass building that encompassed a little more than two hundred square meters. Next to it, a man in his late sixties was standing behind a table with a laptop computer on it.

Azarov pulled two custom pistols from their shoulder holsters as the man dodged right and grabbed a long steel pole. He swung it toward Azarov just as the Russian came to a stop and took aim at a paper target five meters away. On the end of the pole was a life-size silhouette constructed
of aluminum to make hits clearly audible.

The man used it to try to interfere with Azarov's aim as he fired both weapons at the target. When he was empty, he dropped one of the pistols and reloaded the other while moving left. When the magazine clicked home, he went into a two-handed stance and emptied the weapon into a target set up thirty meters to the east.

The older man dropped the pole and retreated to his laptop, squinting at the screen through the glare of the Costa Rican sun. "How did you feel?"

Linus Heis's clipped German accent was no different than it had been the first time they'd met—when Azarov was a seven-year-old biathlete with dreams of making the Soviet Olympic team. It had been Heis who had found the slight heart murmur that disqualified Azarov and changed the course of his life. In subsequent years, the murmur had proved to be completely irrelevant and the scientist was still defensive about what may have been the only mistake he'd ever made in the field of human performance.

"I felt good. My heart rate seemed lower than normal at the top of the climb."

"Fourteen percent lower," Heis agreed. The approving expression was unusual for the stoic German. "And that translated into steadier hands. Your accuracy was one hundred percent."

"What about my speed?"

The man's barely perceptible smile disap-|peared. "You beat your personal best by two percent."

"Two percent? Impressive."

Heis shook his head. "It should have been three point six. Did something go wrong? Did you stumble on the way up?"

Azarov considered lying. There was nothing that infuriated Heis more than when one of his arcane calculations failed to predict reality. The purpose of this exercise wasn't to make the old man happy, though.

"No. Nothing."

"You should have been faster," he repeated.

"I'm sure you'll find the problem and correct it, Linus. You always do."

The German folded his arms in front of his narrow chest. "I'm not so sure. Your shooting is excellent but your running is suboptimal. It occurs to me that firing a weapon is easy while running is hard. I wonder if the problem isn't physical. If it's mental."

"I've taken more psychological tests than I can count, Linus. And I've been involved in more operations than I can count. There's never been even a hint of weakness. You know this."

"Things change, Grisha. People change. You're not as young as you once were. We all slip eventually. But I admit that my concern may be premature. It's three degrees warmer than when you set your prior personal best, and despite living in this godforsaken jungle furnace, you've never dealt well with heat. Or perhaps you're just not fully focused. It would be understand-able after what happened to Olga."

Azarov resisted the urge to glance right. She was buried at the edge of the clearing, next to a man he'd inadvertently killed in a training session six years ago. It was a pleasant spot, with a view of the ocean and particularly vibrant flowering trees. Not that either of the two had cared much about the wonders of nature, but he felt obligated to do what he could to honor their memories.

"Is that it?" Heis probed. "Is it Olga?"

"Yes," he responded, but it wasn't true. It wasn't Olga and it wasn't the heat. It was everything else.

Anxious to change the subject, Azarov pointed to a pistol lying next to Heis's computer. "What's that?"

The man glared at him for a few seconds more but then decided to drop the subject of his pupil's mental state for the time being. "A new weapon for you to try. Nadia is quite proud of it."

Azarov picked up the gun and turned it over in his hands.

"It's a full two centimeters shorter than what you're using now. That should increase the speed of your draw significantly. Your current weapon takes too long to clear its holster. Also, the integrated silencer is three millimeters smaller in diameter."

"Does it still perform?"

"Better, in fact. She's reduced sound output by one decibel."

Azarov aimed at the five-meter target. "May I fire it?"

"Of course."

Heis was right. The report was noticeably duller. Balance was better. Accuracy and recoil were unchanged.

"It's quite light."

"Almost a twenty percent reduction in loaded weight," Heis agreed.

"Drawbacks?"

"It can use standard nine-millimeter rounds, but to get the full benefits, it needs custom ammunition."

"Durability?"

"If you use the recommended ammunition, she estimates that you'll be able to fire two thousand rounds before you start to see a degradation in performance. With commercially available rounds, service life will be cut in half."

"How much?"

"Seventeen thousand euros. Rounds are another eight euros each."

Azarov stared down at the weapon. Mitch Rapp still used a Glock 19 with an AAC Ti-RANT 9S suppressor. A reasonably accurate and reliable weapon. A bit loud and long, but it had the benefit of being extremely common.

"I'll take three. And a thousand rounds."

"I'll pass that on. Now let's get into the gym. I have you scheduled for a brief strength work-out before your swim."

As they walked, Heis lectured him on the need to push harder, to go deeper. The drug regimen created a situation where his mind no longer understood the full capabilities of his body. He needed to learn to break through the limitations his subconscious was imposing on him.

Azarov was barely listening. His mind was consumed by Mitch Rapp. How would he perform on Heis's tests? Could he and his technologically unremarkable Glock have achieved one hundred percent accuracy? In all likelihood, yes. But how quickly could he have completed the run? In his youth, he had been exceptionally fast. The X-rays Azarov had been provided, though, showed a new reality. Years of damage that had left him with thickening scar tissue and thinning cartilage. Would he be able—

"Grisha! Are you listening to me?"

Azarov smiled and bowed his head respectfully. "Every word, Linus. Every word."

Chapter 27

Near Bhakkar
Pakistan

This time Rapp was in the left seat of the CIA's Gulfstream G550. The negotiations to get this meeting set up had been short but contentious. The President of the United States had threatened to use his political clout to cut off every dime of foreign aid to Pakistan. Irene Kennedy, for her part, had made a number of more subtle threats that included General Shirani's home address and a new class of stealth drone.

No negotiation was completely one-sided, though, and the U.S. had been forced to compromise on a few points. Unfortunately, the first thing to be sacrificed was Rapp's team. Shirani had made it clear that he would walk if Rapp didn't come alone. They'd managed to get him to allow a pilot, but Rapp had decided to forgo someone competent at the controls in favor of Joe Maslick, who was parked nervously in the copilot's seat.

Beyond Rapp's questionable ability to safely fly the G550, the airstrip below them was hardly the quiet, abandoned field that they would have liked. Instead of descending into a few blowing plastic bags and a herd of goats, they were about to land on a strip crawling with soldiers.

"Looks like about two hundred men total," Maslick said, peering through the windscreen with a pair of binoculars. "Call it a hundred west of the strip and a hundred east. Tanks, artillery, and fixed machine gun placements just for starters. Looks like they're using the runway as some kind of half-assed demilitarized zone."

"Can you tell who's who?"

"Based on the uniforms you've got Shirani's guys west. Chutani's presidential guard is east, backed up to the only four buildings still standing. Our intel was right. They look like they haven't been used in twenty years but they're still solid enough to provide some cover if everyone starts shooting."

"What about SAMs?"

"Nothing visible, but you know they've got handheld stuff down there somewhere. If the shit hits the fan, we're probably better off running away from the plane, not toward it."

Rapp eased forward on the yoke and started their descent while Maslick continued to examine the opposition. They were only a couple hundred feet above the ground when Maslick looked around the side of his binoculars.

"Mitch. You're too high."

Rapp ignored him.

"Mitch. Seriously, man. You're too fucking high. We're going to overshoot the runway."

"You want to fly this thing?"

"Oh, shiiiiit!" Maslick shouted in response, putting his feet up on the instrument panel to brace himself.

The landing gear slammed into the runway two-thirds of the way down. Rapp applied the brakes and reversed the engines, but they were still going a good twenty knots when they jumped the end of the tarmac and headed off into the sunbaked mud beyond. The plane bounced wildly over the rough terrain while Rapp fought to keep the tips of the wings from hitting the ground and sending them cart-wheeling across the desert. They finally came to a stop in a cloud of dust thick enough to blot out the sun.

"I told you we were too high!" Maslick said. "Why didn't you just come around for another approach?"

"Where are we?" Rapp asked, calmly shutting down the engines.

"What? What the hell are you talking about?"

"Simple question, Mas. Where are we?"

The former Delta operator thought about it for a moment, an expression of understanding slowly spreading across his features. "Not parked right in the middle of two hundred guys with itchy trigger fingers?"

Rapp thumbed toward the back. "Start unstrapping that thing and let's get this over with."

When Rapp jumped down to the desert floor, the dust haze had cleared just enough to see a black SUV speeding toward them with a single armored vehicle right on its tail. Both skidded to a stop fifteen feet away and one man got out of each. The first was a captain from the Black Storks, a spec ops group controlled by General Shirani. The other was a member of President Chutani's elite guard. Undoubtedly, every detail of this operation, including who would meet the plane, had been carefully negotiated by the two men vying for control of Pakistan.

"Do you have the warhead you stole from us?" the soldier demanded, while Chutani's man struck a more respectful pose.

"Right here," Maslick said, rolling it to the plane's door. "Enjoy!"

He gave it a hard kick and it dropped the four feet to the ground with an ominous clang that made both men jerk back in fear.

"Load it up," Rapp said, slipping into the passenger seat of the SUV. The air-conditioning was running and he pointed the vents at himself while the two men looked at each other in confusion. Finally, they were forced to work together to drag the warhead to the army transport. Rapp flipped the radio on and searched for a decent station while they wrestled it into the back.

It was a solid ten minutes before Chutani's sweat-drenched man finally climbed into the driver's seat. He started the engine and led out as Maslick watched from the open door of the G550.

"We weren't informed that you were going to land like that," the man said nervously.

"Wind," Rapp lied.

He'd saved Saad Chutani's life and taken out the man's main rival at the ISI, but Rapp still didn't trust him. Like all Pakistani politicians, he was happy to ally himself with America when it benefited him. The moment it no longer did, though, he'd turn on his Western benefactor faster than the idiots in Washington could ever imagine.

"Is everything ready?" Rapp said.

"Yes. It's just as we discussed."

They rolled down the middle of the two forces, finally pulling up to a low stone building with a roof that looked like it was on the verge of collapse. Rapp stepped out of the vehicle, making sure not to make any moves sudden enough to startle one of the hundred or so soldiers aiming guns at him.

Two men came out of the building's only door and an army major indicated for Rapp to put his arms up. He complied, allowing himself to be thoroughly frisked. When the soldier was satis-fied, one of Chutani's men went through the motions of repeating the process. The president didn't want to give anyone the impression that he was too cozy with America's CIA, an organization with approval ratings in Pakistan just below those of Satan.

They went inside, where the process was to be repeated by two more men. The first was recognizable as one of Shirani's most trusted advisors, a squared-away soldier with an impressive physique despite being north of sixty years old. He did an even more thorough job, sliding his fingers along the inside of Rapp's waistband and insisting that he remove his shoes so that they, too, could be inspected.

Chutani's man was cut from very different cloth. He was in his early twenties and thin in a way that suggested mild malnutrition. His skin was blackened and marred by a lifetime under the Pakistani sun, but freshly cut hair and an impeccable uniform made him look respectable enough to pass as a young officer.

In fact, Raza Khan was an extremely gifted pickpocket that Chutani's people had pulled from prison less than fifteen hours ago. He'd been given the choice of performing a small service in return for his freedom, or having his sentence changed from five years to death. Apparently, he hadn't found the decision difficult.

Khan began to frisk Rapp, starting at the top and moving down as Shirani's man looked on attentively. The young criminal lived up to his reputation and more. If Rapp hadn't been expecting it, he wasn't sure even he would have noticed the tiny Glock 39 slip beneath his shirt and into the waistband Shirani's man had searched only moments before.

"Are we done?" Rapp said as Khan stepped away.

The pickpocket gave a short nod and opened a door at the back, motioning him through.

The room was windowless and completely empty except for the two men standing silently at opposite ends. President Saad Chutani was a tall, imposing figure with sharp eyes and a suit that was miraculously free of the dust that covered so much of his country. General Umar Shirani was shorter and had a gut held back by the straining fabric of his uniform. He wore the grand mustache favored by Pakistan's military elite, and a prominent scar ran down one cheek—a souvenir from Pakistan's 1971 war with India.

Neither of the men moved, clearly not willing to get any closer to one another than was necessary.

Shirani was the first to speak. "You've returned my country's property?"

"Yes," Rapp responded. "For what it's worth."

The soldier's eyes narrowed as he tried to understand the meaning of Rapp's words. "Is that another threat? Because if you don't believe we can get—"

"General," Chutani cautioned, "before we jump to conclusions, maybe we should let Mr. Rapp explain."

"I'd be happy to. That bomb's a dud. There's no fuel."

"What are you talking about?" Shirani said. "You—"

"The canister that was supposed to contain the warhead's fissile material is a fake," Rapp said, cutting him off.

"This is your doing!" Shirani shouted, pointing an accusatory finger. "You stole our weapon and sabotaged it! Now you're trying to blame the army. You want to discredit me. To discredit my leadership."

"Who do you think you're talking to, General? Don't accuse me of things we both know I didn't do."

"My people saw no terrorists in Faisalabad. Just your people and your helicopter. You wonder why we move our arsenal on a regular schedule? Because of this. Because of the outlaw CIA, killing our people and trying to destroy our ability to defend ourselves." The aging soldier turned to Chutani. "You made a grave mistake allying yourself with this man. The people of

Pakistan don't want our country to be run from Washington. We are a proud—"

Rapp rushed him, ramming a forearm into Shirani's throat and driving him into the wall. The general had been a formidable warrior once but had spent his last twenty years sitting on his ass, a luxurious lifestyle that reduced him to slapping ineffectually in Rapp's general direction.

Rapp used his free hand to take hold of the soldier's hair and drag him to the floor. A moment later he had the Glock pressed against Shirani's forehead.

"You . . ." the general stammered. "My forces are just outside. You can't kill me."

"Are you willing to bet your life on that?"

"You'll die minutes after me. You won't do it. Americans are cowards."

Rapp grabbed the general's sleeve and ripped it from his uniform. The man resisted but couldn't prevent Rapp from stuffing the starched fabric in his mouth.

"Mitch," Chutani cautioned from behind. He sounded scared. "Perhaps you should—"

"Shut up," Rapp said without looking back. "You signed on for this."

Fucking politicians. They were all the same. Tough as nails when they were barking orders from a distance. But if there was any danger of blood splashing on their five-thousand-dollar suits, they shrank away.

"How many?" Rapp said, pulling the sleeve from the man's mouth.

"What? I don't know what you're—"

The sleeve went back in and Rapp reached for the man's ring finger, snapping it at the middle joint. The sound of shattering bone was surprisingly loud in the concrete cube of a room. Shirani screamed through his gag, but Rapp didn't immediately remove it. Better to let the pain work on him for a while.

Kennedy was increasingly convinced that fissile material had been taken from more than just the warhead Craig Bailer had examined. And Rapp found it hard to swallow that Shirani would be completely in the dark about terrorist groups tinkering with his nukes. The man was a scum-bag and a thug but not a complete idiot. If he'd gotten even an inkling that his arsenal might be compromised, he'd order a comprehensive assess-ment.

"How many of your warheads are missing their fissile material?" Rapp repeated, pulling the sleeve out again.

"I don't—"

He replaced the gag and this time targeted Shirani's index finger. He needed to get this moving. The Pakistani had more fingers than Rapp did time.

"Mitch . . ." Chutani said. "He may not know. We—"

"I said, shut up!"

Rapp pulled the gag out again and the man coughed violently, apparently on the verge of vomiting. He'd undoubtedly done much worse to people who had opposed him over the years. Based on the look in his eyes, though, he didn't much like being on the receiving end.

"You can make this stop, General. How many?"

"Six!" he managed to get out. "There are six including the one you have."

"Who's responsible?"

"We don't know. I didn't bring in the ISI, so we're doing the investigation internally. Not Taliban. We know that. My people suspect ISIS. We don't have much penetration into their network."

"Where are they? Where are the nukes that have been compromised?"

"We've moved them to a nearby missile facility in order to examine them."

Rapp pressed the barrel of the gun harder against Shirani's forehead.

"No! I told you what you wanted to know. If you kill me, you and Chutani will never get past my men alive."

"You should have never agreed to let Chutani's people take the east side of the runway, General. I've got five drones circling overhead and they're going to rain hell down on your forces while the president's men take cover behind the buildings. Then it'll just be a matter of cleaning up the mess."

The story was only partially true. The drones were there, but Rapp had no idea if the wrecked buildings would hold up to the firestorm they were capable of unleashing.

"There is an alternative," Rapp said.

"What?"

"You take me to those nukes and resign."

"I won't."

"Don't be stupid, General. You have what? A hundred and twenty million dollars squirreled away in accounts all over the world? Take your family and your mistresses to London. Buy a mansion and live the good life. Or die here. Now. In this shithole."

Shirani looked at the president. "Are you sure about this? Are you sure that your position is strong enough to survive the retaliation of the army?"

Chutani shook his head. "I'm not sure, Umar. But you've lost control of our nuclear arsenal and put weapons-grade plutonium in the hands of fanatics. One way or another, this must end. Our country and our arsenal must come under responsible civilian control. If we both die here in an effort to achieve that, so be it."

Chapter 28

President Chutani had returned to Islamabad, leaving Rapp with a contingent of his top men. The string of armored vehicles containing them stretched out in front of and behind the one he was sharing with General Shirani. The road was well maintained but the sand from the empty plain had blown across it in places, occasionally bogging down the convoy.

Now, though, their destination was finally in view. A half mile away, Rapp saw a massive building shimmering in the heat. It was unremarkable in every way—a squat rectangle built from local materials and ringed by a generic chain-link fence. According to Irene Kennedy, the American intelligence community had no knowledge of the facility's clandestine purpose and identified it as a legitimate textile manu-facturing plant.

The motorcade eased to a stop and Rapp watched through the windshield as Shirani's chief of staff leaned out of the lead car to bark orders at a guard in civilian clothing. A moment later, the convoy was progressing into the courtyard.

Shirani was sweating profusely next to him,

causing stains to spread down the sides of his uniform. Rapp had straightened the soldier's broken fingers, but he was still in a fair amount of pain.

Or was it more than that? The motorcade consisted of thirty of Saad Chutani's elite guard, but Shirani would have at least that many loyal army regulars inside. Was he thinking about abandoning his promise to quietly resign in favor of taking his chances in an all-out fire-fight?

They pulled up in front of a peeling door and stepped out into the heat. Along the line of vehicles, Chutani's men did the same, keeping their weapons out of sight. Rapp followed Shirani into a tiny office that stank of the chemicals used on the factory floor. The man standing behind the only desk was wearing the collared shirt and bland tie of a factory manager, but neither was effective in disguising his military background. He gave a crisp salute and pressed a button beneath the desk, unlocking a door at the back.

The shop floor probably would have looked pretty authentic if it weren't for the warheads lying in various states of disassembly. Further, Rapp's eye immediately picked out a series of seams in the concrete floor that undoubtedly hid operational nukes. If he had to guess, probably installed on Shaheen 1A ballistic missiles.

The engineers working on the warheads stopped and turned, a few attempting awkward salutes. A man whose uniform designated him an army major hurried toward them, stopping short a few feet away and firing off a somewhat crisper salute than the academics under his command.

"Welcome to Bhakkar, sir."

"Where do we stand with the investigation into the missing fissile material, Major?"

"We have confirmation that these are the only five," he said, glancing at Rapp but not daring to ask questions. "The remainder of the arsenal has been examined, with the exception of the one in the Americans' possession."

Shirani nodded. "It's in a vehicle outside. Send a detail to retrieve it."

"Right away, sir. What else can I do for you? We weren't given your agenda. Are you here to see the American prisoner?"

Rapp's eyebrows rose slightly, while the general's expression darkened. He hadn't mentioned anything about a prisoner and apparently hadn't expected his subordinate to bring up the subject. It was one of the problems that accompanied a reputation for volatility and brutality. Having everyone falling over themselves to anticipate your next demand could backfire.

"Of course we're here to see the prisoner, you idiot!" Shirani said, trying to cover. "Now, where is he?"

The major hurried toward the back of the building with Rapp and the general following. They stopped in front of a steel door and Rapp stood quietly as the increasingly anxious soldier tried to get the latch unstuck.

"We're in the process of interrogating him," he said, finally freeing the rusted handle. "But so far he's said very little. We know he's American from his accent and he's identified himself as a member of ISIS."

"That will be all, Major."

"Yes, sir. Let me know if I or any of my men can be of assistance."

Rapp watched him go before turning his gaze on Shirani.

"I forgot to mention him," the general blurted, anxious to avert further wrath from the CIA man. "Under the circumstances, I think—"

"Shut up," Rapp said. "All I want to hear from you is where you captured this man."

"An ISIS group tried to hijack a truck containing one of our warheads on the road between Naal and Khuzdar. We had an army unit training nearby and they managed to capture this man as he was trying to escape."

"The others got away?"

"Two were killed, but otherwise, yes."

Out of the corner of his eye, Rapp saw Joe Maslick come around the corner and head their way.

"Get back to your engineers and tell them we're going to be expecting a full report on their findings. And this time I suggest you don't leave anything out."

"It was a mistake!" Shirani insisted.

"Get out of my sight."

Maslick skirted the wall as the general hurried past him.

"Give me a sitrep," Rapp said when his man was within earshot.

"We're solid. Everyone working in this place is regular army but their security procedures are shit. They've got four armed guys patrolling the fence line but everyone else is working under their cover as factory workers. Their weapons are all secured in an armory under the building. I've spread Chutani's men around the facility and on the perimeter. Sidearms only but that'll be plenty to take the place. If it has to go down, it'll probably take less than two minutes and we could conceivably get out of it with no casualties."

"Good," Rapp said and then pointed through the partially open door. "Now there's someone I think we need to meet."

They went inside and Maslick shut the door behind them before taking a position behind a lone man shackled to a chair.

"Looks like you've had better days," Rapp said.

The man raised his head, revealing a

pulverized face partially hidden by a beard similar to the one Rapp wore.

"You're . . . You're American?" he said, saliva and blood rolling from his swollen lips as he spoke.

"Yeah."

"Are you from the embassy?"

"Not exactly."

"You're here to take me home?"

"I don't know. Who are you?"

He didn't answer, but Rapp had a pretty good idea. The accent was middle-America but he had black hair and a dark complexion. A second-generation immigrant from somewhere in the Middle East.

Rapp would never understand how foreign parents—largely grateful for everything America had given them—could raise children like the man sitting in front of him. How someone brought up in a good neighborhood by moderate Muslims turned to radicalism. What was it about living in a free, prosperous, safe society that chapped their asses so bad?

"Look, you sound like you want to go home, but I don't know where that is. American accents are easy to fake. I'm not sure you're really my problem."

He stared at Rapp through blackened eyes for a good thirty seconds, but finally spoke. "I'm from Durango. In Colorado."

"You got a name?"

"Eric Jesem. You can look it up. Now take me home."

"Home? You joined ISIS. This is your home."

"I'm an American citizen!" he shouted, but the effort caused him to cough uncontrollably. His evident agony suggested he had a few broken ribs to go with the bruises on his face. "I . . . I have rights!"

"What about the rights of the women and children you and your friends have raped and killed?"

"They live in the new caliphate. Under God's law."

"But you don't," Rapp said. "Is that what you're telling me? They live under God's law but you get yours from Thomas Jefferson?"

"Take me back to the States! I know my rights. I get my day in court."

"Why don't we try it this way. You tell me everything you know and if it's useful, we'll get you to an American hospital."

"Bullshit. I don't have to talk to you. I don't have to incriminate myself. It's in our fucking Christian constitution."

"Look around you, Eric. Where do you think you are? Does this look like a Colorado police station?"

"I serve the one true God."

Rapp switched to Arabic. "You butcher your way through civilian populations."

Jesem just stared blankly at him.

"Are you kidding me?" Rapp said, switching back to English. "You're sitting there lecturing me about Islam and your parents didn't even teach you to speak its language?"

"You have to take me home! I'm an American citizen."

"Sure. I'll just run you back to Denver so you can get some great medical care and do a little skiing before you get back to your genocide."

"No," he said, starting to sound a little less certain of his position.

"No what? You don't ski?"

"I just . . ." Tears started to flow, mixing with the dried blood on his cheeks. "I just want to go home."

"Don't you dare start crying about missing America. I will fucking yank your dick off and feed it to you."

Jesem managed to stifle his sobs just as the satphone in Rapp's pocket started to vibrate. The number on the screen was immediately recognizable. Irene Kennedy.

"Go ahead," he said, picking up.

"I just got a call from Umar Shirani. It seems your plan worked."

"He's even more of a coward than I gave him credit for."

"He says there are five more canisters missing

259

and that his people are going to send a full report within the hour."

"Give it to Craig. He's in the process of analyzing samples from the warhead I brought him."

"Mitch, I don't have to tell you that this situation has just gone from dire to potentially catastrophic. Even if the people who took the fissile material don't have a way to detonate it, they have enough to build a dirty bomb that could make Washington or New York uninhabitable."

"Who are you talking to?" Jesem said. "I want a lawyer. Tell them I want a lawyer!"

"What was that?" Kennedy asked.

"The television," Rapp said, leaning against the wall and examining Jesem. His beard and hair were almost identical to Rapp's, but the similarities didn't end there. They had the same coloring and build. And, though it was hard to judge exactly with him seated, they even seemed to be about the same height. He was undoubtedly younger than Rapp, but with all the damage done by Shirani's men, someone would have to be looking pretty closely to notice.

"We're out of time," Kennedy continued. "Anyone with the ability to coordinate an operation this sophisticated has a plan that's equally sophisticated. That fissile material could already be coupled with bombs small enough to smuggle across the U.S. border."

"Agreed. Any movement on finding the man who took out Scott?"

"Yes, but it's not an easy task. There are a lot of white spec ops men with athletic backgrounds in the world."

"Hello!" Jesem said, getting as much volume as he could out of his raw throat. "Who's there? Who's on the phone? Is that the embassy?"

Rapp looked down at him. He stared back defiantly. Like Kennedy said, the clock was ticking. It was time to act. Rapp nodded toward Maslick and ran a finger silently across his throat.

Jesem clearly understood the gesture and immediately started jerking back and forth, trying to free himself. "Stop!" he yelled as the two-hundred-twenty-pound Delta man walked up behind him. "I'm an American citizen, you can't do this! You can't—"

Maslick grabbed his long hair with one hand and his chin with the other, twisting the young Coloradan's head a full one hundred eighty degrees before kicking over the chair and spitting on his corpse. Normally, Rapp would have con-sidered the last part a little unprofessional, but under the circumstances, it was hard to criticize.

"Mitch? Are you still there?"

"I'm here."

"That wasn't a television."

"I'll explain later. Look, Irene. I've got an idea. Let me and Mas work on it. In the meantime, I need everything you can get on a man named Eric Jesem from Durango, Colorado."

"Eric Jesem," she repeated. "I'll get our people on it right away."

Rapp disconnected the call and looked down at what was left of the young American—his pulverized face, the severe contusions on arms still secured behind the toppled chair. Finally, he approached and yanked up the dead man's shirt.

"What are you looking for, Mitch?"

"No tattoos," Rapp commented.

"So?"

"So, does he remind you of anyone?"

Maslick snorted. "You, kind of."

When Rapp started pulling off the man's clothes, Maslick took a hesitant step back. "Now, hold on, Mitch . . ."

"Shut up and get his pants."

Unwilling to defy Rapp's orders, he knelt and started unbuckling Jesem's belt. "I got a really bad feeling about this, man."

"It worked for Joe Rickman."

"What the hell are you talking about? You blew the back of his head off. How is that working out?"

There was no key for the cuffs, so Rapp broke the bones in Jesem's hands to get them off. When the battered body was completely stripped, Rapp changed into the dead man's clothes. A little loose in the waistband but nothing the belt couldn't handle.

"Did you see the garbage chute in the corridor on the way in?" Rapp asked.

"I saw a metal hatch in the wall. But I'm not sure it's a garbage chute. It might lead to their fucking break room."

"Pick him up," Rapp ordered and then went to the door, opening it far enough to allow him to peer outside. As expected, the passage was empty. Shirani was probably waiting in one of the air-conditioned vehicles. His men would be busy keeping an eye on the presidential guard that Maslick had stationed throughout the facility.

Rapp motioned for Maslick to follow and then padded out into the hallway. He moved quickly to the hatch and pulled it open. The rotting stench suggested he'd guessed right about its purpose and he tossed his clothes into the hole. Jesem took a little more effort, but after thirty seconds or so of pushing he fell through the darkness to the burial he deserved.

When they returned to the cell, Rapp kicked the overturned chair into a corner and faced Maslick. He'd never really paid much attention to how massive the man was, but now it was impossible to ignore the thick shoulders, powerful chest, and dinner-plate hands.

"Has Dr. Kennedy signed off on this, Mitch?"

"Shit. We both know you've been waiting for this moment for years."

"No lie there."

With that, he threw a right cross that connected just below Rapp's cheekbone. He was spun around by the force of the blow and slammed face-first into the wall behind him. It was all that kept him upright as blood started to flow from his nose, mingling with Jesem's as it soaked into the man's T-shirt.

Steadying himself with one hand, he turned to face the Delta man again.

"Is that all you've got?"

Chapter 29

East of Moscow
Russia

Grisha Azarov glanced at the map reading out on his phone and turned left at the end of a half-constructed apartment complex. The traffic was almost nonexistent, giving him an opportunity to examine the crumbling structure.

A number of makeshift tents had cropped up beneath the graffiti-covered concrete that made up the first floor. The inhabitants were a perfect example of Maxim Krupin's subjects. Cold and hungry, but still loyal. Still waiting for him to deliver on his promise to once again make the world tremble at their feet.

The basset hound in the passenger seat spotted something of interest and barked joyously as they moved onto a broad avenue. Azarov had requested that the bomb-sniffing dog be waiting for him when he landed. Fortunately, it had turned out to be an unnecessary precaution. The animal's well-trained nose had turned up nothing in its examination of the car Krupin had provided.

Another four kilometers brought him to a non-descript glass-and-steel building on an even more nondescript side street. He passed by the entrance leading into the parking garage, driving another block before parallel parking next to the side-walk. The hound's tail wagged excitedly when Azarov opened the door but then went still when he frowned and shook his head. "You have to stay here. I won't be long."

It seemed to understand his words and curled up on the seat, closing its eyes. He'd never owned an animal before, but it was hard not to acknowledge the appeal of having a friend that would never turn on him, spy on him, or try to kill him. Now that Olga was gone, maybe it was something he should look into. He could pay Cara to take care of it when he was gone. Another excuse to see her without exposing his feelings.

Azarov traversed the sidewalk and entered the lobby he'd driven past. As always, the front desk was empty and he went directly to the lone elevator at the rear. It opened automatically at his approach and he stepped in. There were no buttons, so he just stood there, moving a hand subtly toward his gun as he began to descend.

The elevator had been designed as a death trap. It could be dropped, filled with gas, or simply fired upon when the doors opened. Unfortunately, he had no choice but to hope that none of those options were currently on the table.

When he came to a stop and the doors slid back, the spec ops unit he half expected to find was absent. Instead, he saw nothing but the familiar gray corridor broken by a single door on the right. He listened to the sound of his footsteps and the hum of the cameras tracking his progress as he approached the door. It, too, slid open and he entered, but then stopped short before fully crossing the threshold.

The large conference table that normally dominated the room was gone and a massive desk had been placed near the rear wall. Sitting behind it was Maxim Krupin.

"Mr. President," Azarov said, not bothering to hide his surprise at the man's presence. "I wasn't expecting you to conduct this meeting personally."

Azarov studied the room as he spoke, looking for any hint that this was a trap. But there was nothing. In light of that and the fact that he hadn't been relieved of his firearm, it seemed that no attack was imminent. Whether this would be a positive development in the long run remained to be seen.

The Russian president's physical presence suggested that the situation was even more dangerous than Azarov's worst-case projection. The fact that Krupin would agree to leave the security of Moscow and resurface in a forgotten FSB outpost was extremely telling. Not only was he unwilling to include his most trusted advisors in this meeting, he didn't even want to give Azarov his orders inside the walls of the Kremlin.

"Sit," Krupin said simply.

Azarov took a chair in front of the desk and the president turned a laptop toward him.

"Do you know what this is?"

The image on screen was immediately recognizable. "A map of Saudi Arabia."

"And the highlighted area?"

"The country's most significant oil-producing region. The majority of Saudi Arabia's oil comes from there."

"Historically, the Saudis have acted as swing producers," Krupin said, lecturing Azarov on matters he was fully aware of from his cover as an energy consultant. "But they've ceased acting responsibly in that role. They insist on producing at full capacity, depressing energy prices worldwide."

"They're committed to keeping renewables economically nonviable and American production unprofitable."

Krupin tapped a key, switching to a photo of a room with a floor covered in bomb-making equipment. "And this?"

Along one wall were six medium-size wooden crates. It wasn't hard to guess what was in them, and Azarov felt his mouth go dry. "I assume that your operations in Pakistan were successful and that the boxes contain fissile material from Pakistani nuclear warheads. It appears that the material is being used to build dirty bombs."

It could have been much worse, Azarov tried to

remind himself. At least these weren't the sophisticated nuclear bombs he had feared Krupin was building. "Beyond that, I can only speculate."

"Please do."

"You'll place them at strategic points in the Saudi oil fields and detonate them. It will completely shut down extraction and refining in the area for the foreseeable future."

"Very good, Grisha. But you make one mistake. It won't be me placing the bombs, it will be you. Our military forecasters say a front is coming in that will create ideal wind conditions."

"Of course," Azarov said numbly.

"With the exception of your failure to kill Mitch Rapp, you've served me well. This will be your final task. When you return, I'll give you a position of power in my administration. Or, if you prefer, I will make you an oligarch. Dmitry Utkin's assets are still under my control. Since you were the one who killed him, it would be fitting for you to be the one to inherit his empire."

"I'm not sure I'm the wisest choice for this operation, Mr. President. After my confrontation with Scott Coleman, it's possible that the CIA knows my identity. Surely you have access to skilled men that the Americans are unaware of."

Krupin nodded thoughtfully. "It's possible that they know who you are. But it's also possible that Irene Kennedy's suspicions go well beyond the matter of your identity. Russia's future turns on this single event, Grisha. Will we be great again or will we rot and fade into irrelevance? I can't trust something this important to anyone else."

"But if the Americans have suspicions, they may be able to trace this back to you. Certainly the fact that spiking oil prices will benefit Mother Russia won't be lost on the rest of the world."

"And what will they do, Grisha? With Saudi Arabia's reserves largely inaccessible, our production capacity will become even more critical to the world economy. And our nuclear arsenal precludes any military action against us. With the money that comes flooding in, I'll be able to retake the breakaway states that were stolen from us. I'll restore Russia to its rightful place in the world order."

"Mr. President, I must—"

"Do you know what the people want?" Krupin said, cutting him off. "Not full bellies. Not warm beds. They want glory. They want power and respect. They want to be part of something great so that they can tell themselves that their pathetic little lives matter."

The bizarre truth was that Krupin was probably right. The Russian people hated the breakaway states—their perceived indifference to Mother Russia, their halting steps toward the West. But most of all, the Russian people hated their success. The loss of the superiority they'd once felt as they gazed out over their empire.

Even if Krupin's actions were at some point discovered, it was possible that the Russian people would see them less as a crime against humanity and more as a bold move on the international chessboard. Decisive action against a terrorist-sponsoring Saudi regime bent on keeping Russia weak.

And he was most definitely correct about Russia's oil and gas production becoming critical. Without the flood of money that propped up the corrupt and hopelessly incompetent Saudi government, the royal family would collapse. ISIS would overrun not just Saudi Arabia but also Kuwait and the UAE, to name just a few. Energy prices would skyrocket and Russia would go from being a decaying nation with an economy smaller than Italy's to a world power with the ability to break its enemies by simply turning off the spigot.

Azarov suddenly regretted the understanding of economics and politics that he'd gained over the years. It was impossible not to see a future of millions dead in the Middle East. Of a world held hostage by a megalomaniac with a nuclear arsenal and natural resources that he used not for the greater good—or even for profit—but as a tool to maintain his own position.

The gun hanging beneath Azarov's arm started to make its weight felt. He had the power to end this. To put a neat hole between Krupin's eyes and to save the world from the horrors he would inflict.

It was an interesting thought but, in the end, a fleeting one. Saving the world wasn't his responsibility. And even if it was, what would be the point? If not Krupin, then it would be someone else. The human race's fate was to sow the seeds of its own destruction. Let deluded patriots like Mitch Rapp risk their lives to save a world that neither wanted nor deserved saving. Azarov's only responsibility was to himself.

"My team?" Azarov asked.

"Men hand-picked by me from the ranks of ISIS."

"They're unreliable and poorly trained," he protested. "At a minimum I should be provided soldiers or former soldiers. Preferably from the Russian special forces."

"Out of the question."

"Then this operation may end up the same way the action against Rapp did."

This was the kind of insubordination that would normally cause Krupin's anger to flare, but in this case the man was doing an admirable job of keeping his infamous temper in check. It was another indication of how critical this operation was to him. If his plan failed, it was likely that Russia's slide would become irreversible. The people would eventually turn against him. And when they did, it would be with the same speed and violence as they had against the czars.

"I don't think so, Grisha."

"May I ask why?"

"I would be concerned if you didn't. My plan is not complicated. You will accompany the weapons to Al-Hofuf, a Saudi city I imagine you're familiar with. There you will distribute them to six two-man teams who will take them to coordinates our people have designated as being optimal. Your men's ability to blend in is far more critical than any specialized military training they might have."

He tapped a few keys on his laptop and brought up markers for those locations before continuing. "You'll accompany one of those teams to an abandoned oil-production facility. From that central location you'll command the operation."

"There appear to be seven markers."

"One backup team, should problems arise."

Azarov nodded silently. "Can I assume, then, that you plan to wait until all the weapons are in position before detonating?"

"It seems prudent. The location farthest from Al-Hofuf will take an estimated fourteen hours to reach, while the closest will be a journey of only about three and a half hours. The teams will be staggered so they all reach their destinations at the same time. We don't want the Saudis and Americans to know what's happening until it's done."

"Then why not detonate the bombs remotely when you see that everyone is in position? What is the point of having me on location?"

"Two reasons. First, with the storms we're predicting, satellite communications are likely going to be unreliable. And second, while we've trained the ISIS teams as thoroughly as possible, they can't be relied on to handle any significant problems. For that, only you can be trusted."

"So, I will have the ability to remote-detonate the weapons?"

"No. We couldn't create a foolproof system for that. Each man will have his own detonation code. When they are cleared to do so, they will enter them in within thirty seconds of each other."

"And be vaporized."

"Of course."

"What about the bomb that I'm being asked to detonate?"

Krupin's irritation at being interrogated like this was beginning to show, but still he answered. "You will leave in the vehicle you arrived in. When you're at a safe distance, the two men you left behind will detonate the bomb. Should they be unable to, you will be provided with a code that has a twenty-minute delay."

"But what if—"

"All the operational details are here," Krupin said, cutting him off and holding out a thumb drive. "Review them and, as always, if you have any concerns, contact me."

Azarov accepted the drive and just stared down at it.

"Do this, Grisha, and you will have anything you want. Unlimited wealth. Unlimited power. You—"

"I want out," Azarov said, without looking up from the innocuous piece of plastic in his hand.

"What?"

"I want to never return to Russia. I want you to forget I exist."

Krupin leaned back, his narrow lips spreading into a smile. "Are you going to retreat to Costa Rica? Return to the farming of your youth?"

"That's my affair."

Azarov's tone registered in Krupin's eyes but nowhere else. "And if I refuse?"

"Then I'm sure the ISIS team you're so confident in can handle the operation without me."

"You may not be as indispensable as you believe, Grisha."

Again, the gun beneath Azarov's arm made its presence felt. This time there must have been some hint of it in his body language because, for the first time in their relationship, the Russian president became visibly nervous.

"If you want to turn your back on everything I'm offering you to live a life with no value, Grisha, then so be it. As you say, that's your affair."

Chapter 30

Near Bhakkar
Pakistan

Joe Maslick adjusted his grip under Rapp's arm, dragging him down the hallway with the help of one of Saad Chutani's men. Rapp wasn't moving at all, his bare feet just dragged lifelessly across the concrete floor. Maslick was actually a little relieved when he started to cough, despite the fact that every successive convulsion sprayed blood from his grotesquely swollen lips. When a pink tooth dislodged and skittered across the floor, though, the sweat running down the former Delta operator's back turned cold.

Had he gone too far? The goal was to mimic the damage Jesem had suffered and obscure any differences between his and Rapp's features. It had been no small task. The Pakistanis had gone to town on Jesem, and his nose had been significantly different from Rapp's in both size and shape. Trying to make the switch convincing without doing damage severe enough to hinder Rapp's operational ability had been impossible.

Rapp had survived his years in this business because he was just plain faster, stronger, smarter, and more accurate than everyone else. There was no way that was true any longer. If he never came back from this mission, Maslick would spend the rest of his life wondering if it had been the result of one too many uppercuts to the chin for him to see straight. A kick to the ribs that was a little too hard to allow him to move effectively. Internal bleeding created while trying to match the bruising on Jesem's stomach.

General Shirani appeared at the end of the hallway with two of his men, effectively blocking it. Just like Rapp had said he would.

"What are you doing with my prisoner?"

Maslick took in a breath and let it out slowly. This was going to be the hard part. He'd never been much of a talker, even when he was a kid. But that was okay. His job was shooting, not making speeches. He said what needed to be said and then killed the people who needed to be killed. Unfortunately, his orders in this situation were somewhat different.

"Get the fuck out of the way," he said.

Good use of vulgarity, but too quiet. Too hesitant. Shirani was a useless Pakistani piece of shit, but he was still a four-star. And that was a rank Maslick had spent most of his life being taught to respect.

"Where is Mitch Rapp?"

"He went out to one of the trucks. Said he needed to talk to—"

It turned out that Rapp wasn't really unconscious. Maslick felt a painful jab in the small of his back.

"I mean, he said he needed to get out of this shithole."

"Our nuclear facility isn't luxurious enough for him?"

"I think he meant your whole fucking country."

The sharp edge of Rapp's thumbnail was replaced by a couple of encouraging pats.

Both Rapp and Kennedy believed that General Shirani had an open communication channel with ISIS. He denied any connection, but the truth was that he'd get in bed with anyone interested in weakening the civilian government.

The idea now was to piss him off. To make him so mad that he'd forget his fear of Rapp and do anything he could to screw over America in general, and the Agency in particular.

"Answer my question," Shirani said through clenched teeth. "Just where is it you think you're taking my prisoner?"

"He's our prisoner now," Maslick said, following the script Rapp had given him. "I'm taking him to our base outside of Awaran. So why don't you get the fuck out of my way?"

Shirani's cheek twitched visibly. His men moved their hands a little closer to their weapons, waiting for the order to kill the insubordinate American standing in front of them.

"You're not taking that man anywhere."

Maslick hesitated and Rapp gave him an encouraging nudge.

"Hey, if you want to talk to Mitch, I can go out and get him. But if he has to come back in here, I can guarantee you he's going to kick your fat ass up and down this hallway. I'll bet that won't play too good on your campaign posters."

He'd finally pushed the man to the point that he was pretty much mute. Whether that was a good thing or not remained to be seen. What was certain, though, was that he was succeeding in the mission that Rapp had charged him with. He'd made the old soldier so mad that he couldn't think straight.

As Maslick started forward again, Shirani, in a pathetic effort to save face, grabbed the man he thought was Eric Jesem and looked into his swollen face. "Take him if you want him. He's given me what I need."

Maslick's normal strategy would be to call that a win and get the hell out of there before everyone started shooting at him. But that wasn't what they were after here.

"He didn't give your punk-ass interrogators shit."

Maslick pulled Rapp away from the man and began dragging him toward the front of the building. "Now tell your people to get out of the way so Chutani's guys can get a transport in. This man needs to be in Awaran by zero six thirty and Mitch and I want to be on a plane out of here in an hour. Is that understood?"

When they came out into the blinding sunlight, Maslick half expected to find fifty guys with M4s pointed in his direction. Instead, there was an armored van and a couple of men from Chutani's elite guard. He handed his limp prisoner off to them and they literally threw him into the back. Maslick watched as Rapp slammed down on his cuffed hands and rolled into a bench. A moment later, the doors were locked and Maslick was standing in the cloud of dust left by the vehicle's spinning tires.

He watched it pass through the gate and recede up the road for what was probably too long, then started toward a vehicle that would take him to a commercial airport. Apparently, the G550 was cooked. Rapp had trashed the landing gear with his little excursion into the desert.

Out of the corner of his eye, he could see Umar Shirani standing in the doorway of the building's tiny office. The man looked like he wanted to carve someone's heart out.

Mission accomplished.

Chapter 31

The van doors slammed shut but Rapp remained motionless, lying on the steel floor with his hands secured behind him. The motor came to life and the vehicle began bouncing painfully along the dirt road that led to the missile site's outer gate. He rolled on his side, closing his eyes to keep blood from flowing into them. Maslick had done a skillful job matching the look of Eric Jesem's injuries without crossing the line. As near as Rapp could tell, he had no significant damage to his ribs or joints, and his eyes were badly blackened but not so swollen as to interfere with his vision. Bruising on his torso was impressive, but no obvious internal injuries or slipped disks.

On the downside, he'd lost one tooth and a few more were clearly on their way out. The damage to his nose was severe enough that he wondered if he would ever breathe out of it again. And, finally, he was bleeding badly from a cut Maslick had carved into his forehead. An admittedly artistic job, though. It matched the one Jesem had in every detail.

The van jumped onto the pavement and the ride smoothed out as it accelerated. When Rapp was certain they were past any residual guards who might want to look in on him, he pulled off his cuffs. Maslick had used the tips of Jesem's shoelaces to jam the locking mechanisms while Rapp recovered from a slightly overzealous kick to the stomach. Low-tech but effective.

The back of the van was brutally hot, probably close to one hundred twenty Fahrenheit, with ventilation limited to a few holes drilled through the sides. Soon, though, the sun would go down and the unbearable heat would turn to bitter cold. A good twelve hours of it, if they made it to the CIA black site that was ostensibly their goal. If everything went to plan, though, his trip would last nowhere near that long.

Maslick had done a solid job of winding up Umar Shirani—better than Rapp had imagined the former soldier capable of. The general would be blind with rage at being castrated like that in front of his men, which was exactly the reaction Rapp was looking for. It was unlikely that the old soldier would let that kind of humiliation go unanswered.

At this point, though, his power to retaliate was limited. The best he could do without exposing his role was to get in touch with his contacts at ISIS and give them the route of the van carrying their American compatriot. Shirani would deny the CIA their prisoner and any information he might have.

Rapp closed his eyes and did his best to drift off despite the pain radiating from virtually every part of his body. The heat and lack of water were going to do a job on him and it was critical to conserve as much strength as he could. If he was right about what would come next, he had to maintain as much of his physical and mental capacity as possible.

Rapp awoke just as the van's driver slammed on the brakes—a split second too late to keep from sliding forward and smashing his head. Automatic gunfire erupted a moment later and he flattened himself against the steel floor as a few errant rounds rang off the vehicle's exterior. The barrage grew in intensity, turning deafening when the men in the cab started to return fire.

Rapp's head was still foggy as he crawled toward the doors and retrieved the discarded handcuffs. Opening one of the shackles so that it could be used as a claw, he slithered the rest of the way toward the rear. Shouts became audible outside and he threw his arms protectively over his head as rounds stitched themselves across the vehicle's door.

They were clearly intentional. Chutani's men would do what they could to make sure Eric Jesem didn't live long enough to be rescued by his ISIS companions.

Rapp heard the handle rattle and he pushed himself to his knees. A moment later, the doors were yanked open and one of Chutani's men was there, holding a Beretta in his hand. With nothing but two feet of air separating them, this time he'd get the job done.

The pistol rose and Rapp lunged, swinging the open handcuff toward the guard's neck. By the time they collided, though, the man was already dead—hit by a bullet that entered his right side and exited the left in a cloud of blood and bone. They landed gracelessly on the road and Rapp rolled the corpse on top of him as guns opened up from a chase car stopped twenty-five yards back. The sun was beginning to dip below the horizon, reducing visibility but not the temperature of the asphalt. Sticky tar penetrated his shirt, burning the skin on his back badly enough to force him to cast off the man's body and run in a crouch for the road's shoulder.

Bullet impacts sounded to his left and he adjusted his trajectory away from them. The blow to the head he'd suffered when the van stopped would have been enough of a disadvantage on its own. Combined with the heat and the beating he'd take from Maslick, his legs felt like they were going to collapse beneath him.

The rounds continued tracking, getting closer as Rapp ran. He cleared the edge of the road and tripped in the glare of the setting sun, slamming into a pile of jagged rocks before sliding down a steep embankment. When he stopped, he tried to get up, but his body refused to obey. Naked willpower got him to all fours, but then he collapsed and rolled onto his scorched back in the gravel.

Consciousness came and went as the sound of the battle raged around him. Gunfire. Shouts. The screams of the wounded. When he finally managed to open his eyes, he saw the silhouettes of armed men standing over him. One of them unwrapped the scarf hiding his face before putting a bottle of water to Rapp's split lips.

"What have they done to you, brother?"

Chapter 32

Location Unknown

Rapp regained consciousness in frustrating fits and starts. Sound came first—the mechanical growl of distant vehicles, wind whistling through cracks in walls. Muffled voices. Then came the pain. Oddly, the worst of it emanated from the part of his back that had been burned by the road. His head was a close second. Dull instead of sharp, but pounding with impressive intensity.

He let his eyelids rise slightly, adjusting to the glare before fully opening them. The woman hovering over him was in her early thirties, with hair covered by a scarf and a pretty face marred by a prominent black eye. She was dabbing at his forehead with something but scurried off when she saw that he was awake.

Rapp was lying on a bed wearing nothing but Eric Jesem's shit-stained boxers. The wounds he'd suffered all appeared to have been cleaned, stitched, and bandaged. His nose was of little use but he could taste rubbing alcohol in the air.

The room was small, consisting of nothing more than four concrete walls that had seen better days. Not a cell, though. While there were no windows, there was a threshold with a missing door leading to an outer room. He could hear men speaking Arabic, but their voices were too quiet to make out much more than a few individual words.

A moment later, a young man entered and stood over him, gazing down at his damaged face. When he spoke, he used mangled English.

"Eric. Friend. You awake. You can move?"

Rapp nodded and pushed himself into a sitting position on the bed. Best to keep his social interactions minimal. Irene had managed to provide him with some background on Jesem, but that was after a lot of hard blows to the head and he didn't remember a lot of it. Even if he did, he would still have no idea who the asshole standing over him was or what his relationship with Jesem had been. He did remember, though, that the Coloradan wasn't an Arabic speaker.

"The general asks for you. Eric, you come? You are strong?"

Rapp gave another silent nod and the man helped him to his feet. They walked into the outer room, where the woman who had been helping him was cowering in a corner. He didn't acknowledge her as he passed, following the man down a set of stairs and out into the sunlight.

They walked up a dirt street that was virtually abandoned. From what he could see, the area had once been a commercial center, with shops and stalls that were now burned or gutted by bombs.

Rapp glanced at what was left of a few signs, making sure not to give away that he was reading. They contained only enough information for him to determine that he was somewhere in Iraq and not Syria. Good for him because of his more extensive history operating in this theater.

Since the man with him was clearly ISIS and walking around with impunity, it was fairly certain that they were in an area controlled by the terrorist group. At this point, that narrowed it down to north-central Iraq.

He continued his subtle search but could find nothing that contained a city name and he couldn't risk asking. While it was possible that Jesem had never been there, it was also possible that they'd just left his apartment. Rapp would have to keep his questions limited to things that the American terrorist definitely wouldn't know.

"How long was I unconscious?"

"Four days, brother."

Too damn long. The stolen fissile material could have been transported almost anywhere by now.

"How did I get here?"

"We fought the men taking you to the Americans. You do not remember?"

"No."

"You hurt your head. We thought you die. But Allah is not taking you. He wants you to stay. To fight."

They turned onto a wider avenue and a pickup full of young armed men passed them, whooping and calling out as they did. Rapp ignored them, focusing instead on the building they were approaching. It had a governmental look to it but the sign had been ripped off and dumped facedown in a pile of refuse. So, still no city name.

The interior showed a significant amount of damage from small arms fire but the stairs to the basement were in good shape. After being led past a few wary guards, Rapp found himself standing in front of a man wearing the uniform of one of Saddam Hussein's generals.

"I was told what the Americans did to you, Eric, but now that I see it, I'm shocked," the general said in respectable English. Rapp couldn't put a name to him, but there was something familiar about his face. Had it been on one of the playing cards they'd handed out to U.S. troops? Had they met when the Agency was trying to get its arms around the tangled web of religious, political, and tribal alliances that plagued Iraq? Back when the politicians in Washington still thought there was some hope of sorting the good from the bad?

"My sources say you faced the CIA's Mitch Rapp."

Rapp nodded. "Sources" almost certainly meant that piece of shit Umar Shirani. Fortunately, the man was as predictable as he was corrupt.

"I'm also told that you said nothing. I'm impressed. Rapp has broken great men. Devout men."

Rapp nodded a silent acknowledgment of the compliment.

"What can you tell me, Eric? What do the Americans know? What do they suspect?"

Now the truly dangerous game started. How much to say? He needed to draw the man into conversation, but it would only take one slip to guarantee a summary beheading.

"They said that we've taken fissile material from Pakistan's missiles."

"How many?"

"They believe six."

"So they know of all of them," the general muttered. "Do they know anything of our plan?"

"They believe that we're building nuclear weapons and that we're going to smuggle them into the United States."

"Fools. How I would love to see the look on the American president's face when he learns the truth."

What truth?

"Yes, sir."

"The nurse who examined you said that none of your injuries are life threatening. You will recover. But, I'm afraid, not quickly enough to play a role in our operation. I'm sorry."

The expression of deep disappointment that

settled on Rapp's swollen face wasn't entirely manufactured. It was unlikely that anyone knew where he was or even if he was still alive. With no way to communicate with the outside world, he had no choice but to handle this himself. And that wasn't something that was going to happen from the bleachers.

"Please, General. I'm already healing. Test me. I can still carry out my part."

"I admire your devotion, Eric. And you're right. You will heal and play an important role in spreading God's law across the world. But not over the course of the next three days."

So now Rapp had a time frame, but no plan. And still no way to tell anyone even if he did.

"Sir, I beg you—"

"No," the soldier said, displaying a hint of anger at having his orders questioned.

There was nothing Rapp could do but bow his head submissively.

"I'm truly sorry we can't use you in this, Eric. But there are more ways than one to reward your courage and devotion."

Chapter 33

Rapp stayed a pace behind the unnamed general as they started up a street occupied by only a few armed men posted on corners. The Iraqi glanced up at the hazy sky and Rapp emulated the familiar tic. People in this region had a well-founded fear of American drones and he now shared it. Standing too close to this piece of shit created the very real danger that he might be vaporized by someone he was on a first-name basis with. Fortunately, the winds had picked up to the point that U.S. drones would be grounded and satellites would be blinded by blowing sand.

The general turned down a bombed-out alley and Rapp followed, glancing back at the man who had rousted him from his bed earlier that day. The three of them were now alone in the narrow corridor, obscured by walls rising up on either side and the howl of the wind. It would be so easy. A quick turn on his heel followed by a throat strike. The general, lost in his own thoughts, wouldn't notice anything until Rapp clapped a hand over his mouth and dragged him into one of the collapsing buildings around them.

How long until he was discovered, though? Generals might occasionally stroll through the streets with only a single guard, but their schedules were always tight. It was unlikely that much more than a few minutes would pass before someone came looking. Nowhere near long enough to get any actionable intelligence. And then there was still the problem of getting word out to someone in a position to take that action.

Rapp heard the mob before he saw it. Cheers, loud enough to drown out the wind, rose and fell in an unpredictable rhythm. Less than two minutes later, they entered a large plaza containing a gathering that, under clear skies, would have been immediately targeted by the U.S. There were probably two hundred men, almost all pumping assault rifles in the air. At the north end of the square was a raised stage, hastily constructed of wood planks. And on that stage stood a man holding two girls.

One was probably sixteen and the other no more than thirteen. Both had been stripped naked and looked nearly catatonic. They'd spent their postadolescent lives covered from head to toe and under the watchful eye of their families. Now everyone they knew was dead and they found themselves exposed and alone. Livestock in a sex slave auction.

"If one of these pleases you, you're welcome to her," the general said. "But I'll warn you. Neither is a virgin."

That explained the bruises that were becoming increasingly evident as they approached through the parting crowd. The girls were being sold for the second or third time by masters who had become bored with them.

A winner in the bidding emerged and leapt onstage. After a careful accounting of his payment, he dragged off the younger of the two girls while the auctioneer tried to drum up enthusiasm for the older one.

Rapp had seen a great deal in his time, but this was something new. As twisted as al Qaeda was, it had a goal, a rationalization for that goal, and a strategy to achieve it. The same could be said for Hamas and Hezbollah. ISIS wasn't playing to win. Their only goal was to leave nothing but scorched earth when they were finally destroyed.

He felt his rage building as he looked at the faces of the men around him. Their bodies pressed against his and his anger quickly grew to the very edge of his control. He turned toward a terrorist dressed entirely in black and fixed his gaze on the AK-47 slung over his shoulder. It looked well maintained and there were spare magazines affixed to the man's belt. How many of these pricks could he kill before he himself went down? Twenty? Fifty? A hundred?

The general stopped and threw an arm around Rapp's shoulders. The sudden weight of it pulled him from his violent fantasy, forcing him back into the present. The older girl was finally carried offstage as another was forced up the stairs.

Unlike the two before her, she was wearing a chador. A little mystery to whip up the crowd.

In an impressive piece of showmanship, the auctioneer grabbed her and tore off the chador in one deft motion. The mob erupted, but then settled down when they discovered she was wearing jeans and a T-shirt underneath.

"She's a bit old," the general commented. "Her family allowed her to go to university instead of marrying. But it's been confirmed that she's a virgin and I think you'll agree that she's quite beautiful."

They were now standing only about ten feet from the base of the stage, and there was no denying it. She had long black hair and flawless skin, with eyes that held less terror than Rapp would have expected under the circumstances.

"Do you want to see more?" the auctioneer shouted.

The cheers that rose up were powerful enough that they reverberated in Rapp's chest.

The man grabbed the front of the young woman's shirt and was going to rip it off when she jammed a thumb in his eye. And not just a little bit. She drove it in nearly to her knuckle.

The crowd fell into a stunned silence and Rapp fought back a smile as the auctioneer let out a high-pitched scream. Two men charged up the steps and grabbed the woman, whose thrashing was accompanied by an impressive string of obscenities in at least five distinct languages.

The auctioneer managed to get hold of himself and shouted something unintelligible to a man near the base of the stage. A moment later, he was scurrying up the stairs with a gas can clutched to his chest. The partially blinded man grabbed it and took the cap off. When he started lurching toward the captive woman, Rapp pointed and shouted over the noise. "I'll take her."

The general looked over at him and grinned. "Spirited women! I agree."

He pulled his sidearm and fired into the air, stopping the advancing man in his tracks. All attention was now on them.

"This is our American brother Eric Jesem," he yelled. "The man who was tortured by Mitch Rapp but said nothing!"

This time the whoops of the mob were accompanied by sporadic automatic fire. The general held up his hands for silence. "He wants this woman and we will grant his request. A reward for his courage and his devotion to jihad."

Rapp ascended the steps to the roar of the crowd and the angry one-eyed stare of the auctioneer. He told himself that his decision had been tactical —that this woman had guts, local knowledge, and no love for ISIS. But was that all of it? Or were the years starting to make him soft? Did he really believe she could help him or did he just not want to stand there and watch her burn?

When he closed to within a few feet, the men holding her let go. She didn't try to escape but instead charged him, swinging red-painted nails toward Rapp's damaged face. He grabbed her by the throat, stopping her with a violent jerk. She continued to fight, trying futilely to get to him as he increased the pressure around her neck. Finally, she blacked out and crumpled to the ground.

Rapp scooped her into a fireman's carry and walked offstage, to the noisy approval of his audience.

Chapter 34

Walter Reed Medical Center
Bethesda, Maryland
U.S.A.

Irene Kennedy pushed her reading glasses onto her head and looked at the walls of the hospital break room. The space had been swept for listening devices and she had her secure laptop, but there was still only so much she could do from Bethesda. As desirable as it was to stay close to Scott Coleman, she needed to get back to Langley.

A quiet knock sounded on the door and a moment later Mike Nash poked his head in. "You have a minute, Irene?"

Nash had recently turned forty, but there was little sign of it. The former Marine had been understandably angry when Mitch Rapp had ended his ops career. Since then, though, he'd come to terms with his new life and was performing admirably in his role as one of her top executives.

With no real need for physical speed or endurance anymore, he'd gained a fair amount of weight—every ounce of it muscle. The primary purpose of the new physique was to stabilize the damage his spine had suffered in an explosion in Afghanistan. It had the additional benefit of making him even more physically attractive, which, combined with his natural charm, made him quite popular on Capitol Hill. Even the most odious members of Congress never missed an opportunity to slap Nash on the back and get their photo taken with a bona fide American hero.

Increasingly, Kennedy found herself begging off political meetings and sending him in her place. As good as he'd been at ops, he was even better at handling the egos in Washington—an activity that she found more difficult every year.

"What news do we have on Mitch?" she asked.

"None," he said, taking a seat directly across the table from her.

"What do you mean, none? We must—"

"I mean none. Winds across the region are kicking up and we lost the vehicle he was being transported in when visibility went to shit."

"What about informants?"

"We're afraid to use the few we have. We don't want anyone asking questions about Eric Jesem. People might start paying too much attention to him."

Kennedy took a deep breath to obscure her anger at the lack of progress. She'd already been too hard on Joe Maslick. He'd contacted the Agency in time for them to get surveillance in the air, but there had been nothing else he could do. Even her own ability to insinuate herself into Rapp's plans was spotty. Particularly when he went completely insane and decided to go alone and injured into ISIS territory.

"What about the man who attacked Scott?"

"I have better news on that front," Nash said, tapping the briefcase he'd placed on the floor next to him. "We've got some solid suspects and our people are working to flesh them out."

His tone was typically upbeat but his face was etched deep with worry. While he and Rapp had suffered more than their share of conflict over the years, they were still close. And Scott Coleman was probably the best friend Nash had. Fortu-nately, she, too, had some good news.

"I'm told that Scott's fighting off the infection."

Nash's eyebrows rose perceptibly, but he had learned over the years to be cautious with his optimism. "So . . . there's a chance? He could make it?"

"Actually, he's awake."

Nash ran a hand over his mouth, wiping away the sweat that was glistening over his lip. "Can I see him?"

Kennedy stood. "I think that can be arranged. But we've been warned not to upset him. He's extremely weak and very lucky to be alive."

Nash bolted for the door, but then managed to stop long enough to hold it open for her. She had to admit that despite the fact that everything else was falling apart, being the bearer of good tidings was a real pleasure. It was an unusual role for someone in her position.

Nash stood a few feet from the glass, taking a moment to adjust to the reality of the man on the other side. Coleman was propped in his hospital bed with bandages covering most of his head and half his face. One of his arms contained multiple IV needles and the other was immobilized in an elaborate harness. His heavily bandaged leg was elevated in a sling and there was a drain tube inserted between his ribs.

His eyes were open, though. Fixed on a sunny window with a thousand-mile stare.

Finally, Nash gave his head a violent shake, squared his shoulders, and pushed through the door.

"How's the taxpayer-funded vacation going?"

Coleman turned his head carefully, tracking Nash as he dropped into an overstuffed chair.

"It's going okay, asshole."

Kennedy entered and took the only other seat. "How are you, Scott?"

"You tell me."

His voice sounded strange, something that could only partially be explained by the recent removal of his breathing tube. Beneath the hoarseness was a mix of emotions the former SEAL was normally immune to: anger, disappointment, embarrassment. Kennedy knew that he was questioning his abilities, telling himself that he'd let his team down. It was all complete nonsense, of course, but she'd learned that it was unavoidable nonsense in men like him.

"The doctors tell me it's going to be a long, difficult process, but that you're going to make a full recovery."

Not really a lie, but a statement dressed up with a fair amount of positive spin.

"Did we get the nuke?"

"Yeah," Nash said. "We even flew it back here and let Craig tear it apart. Got a lot of good intel."

"Where's Mitch?"

"He and Mas had to take the warhead back. The Pakistanis were getting their panties bunched up about us having it."

They would say nothing about Rapp's current status, the missing fissile material, or the other compromised nukes. Until Coleman was in far better condition, the message was that the operation had been a complete success.

"And the guy who did this to me?" he said, shifting his gaze back to the window.

"We don't have to talk about that now, buddy. It can wait."

"Do you know who he is?"

Nash glanced at Kennedy, who nodded subtly. If Coleman felt up to it, they needed his help.

"We've been spitballing a few ideas. You want to take a look?"

"Yeah," came the expected reply.

"Do you remember his face?" Kennedy asked.

Coleman went deathly still for a moment. "I remember."

Nash pulled a tablet from his briefcase, arranging the photos of nine men on screen before carrying it to his injured friend.

"You think it's one of them?" Coleman asked.

"Maybe. There aren't that many choices based on the description of . . ." Nash's voice faltered for a moment. "You know. Of what happened."

"You mean me getting my ass kicked like I was from the fucking typing pool?"

Nash let out a long breath. "No one blames you for this, Scott. Not me, not Mas, and most of all, not Mitch."

Coleman wasn't buying. "Maybe it would have been different if it had been you out there."

"Yeah, I'd be dead. Look, Scott. I was a good soldier. But as much as I hate to say it out loud, I wasn't as good as you. So let's forget all this bullshit, okay?"

When Coleman didn't respond, Nash tapped the tablet. "What do you think? All we got from Mitch was white, around six feet, and between thirty and forty years old. Do any of these guys ring a bell?"

"Who are they?"

"Top foreign spec ops guys we've lost track of."

The former SEAL scanned the faces. "The one on the lower right. It doesn't really look like him, but there's something familiar. Is it possible I know him from somewhere else?"

"I doubt it," Nash said, retreating back to his chair. "His name's Grisha Filipov."

Coleman just shook his head as Nash went to work on the photo, darkening the hair, smoothing the cheeks, and lifting the eyelids.

"Describe his nose, Scott."

"I don't know. Not real big. Kind of sharp."

Nash brought up a selection of noses from a drop-down menu. It was a common change for a plastic surgeon to make—easier to take away flesh than to add it.

He chose the best match and then used a commercial software program to age the man to his midthirties. Finally, he walked the tablet back to Coleman.

This time there was no need to ask him what he thought. The rhythm of the heart rate monitor he was connected to accelerated audibly.

"Grisha Filipov," Coleman finally managed to get out.

"I didn't want to say anything to influence you, but this was our top pick."

"Russian?"

"Yeah. Spetsnaz. He was identified as an

exceptional athlete when he was a kid and put into the Soviet athletics machine. Interestingly, he ended up in a sport you're a fan of—biathlon. Turns out he had a minor heart murmur. The system spit him out and sent him back to the family farm. A few years later, he joined the military. Apparently, he strolled through spec ops training without breaking a sweat and tested extraordinarily high on intelligence tests. After distinguishing himself in a few operations, he left the military and disappeared. Our guess is that he caught the eye of Russia's new president."

"Krupin," Coleman said.

"It makes perfect sense," Irene Kennedy interjected. "Krupin was consolidating his power at the time and Filipov would have been just the kind of person he would have needed—young, talented, and relatively anonymous."

"Do you know where he is?" Coleman said.

"Not yet. But we'll find him."

"When you do, don't get anywhere near him, Mike. Take it from me. Drone that asshole from the stratosphere."

"That's up to Mitch."

Coleman opened his mouth to say something but fell silent when a timid knock sounded on the door. Irene Kennedy glanced at the glass wall and saw Claudia Gould peeking through. She waved her in.

"Are they bothering you?" Claudia said, taking

a position by Coleman's side and adjusting his pillows.

"Definitely," he said. "I think you should throw them out in the street."

She frowned at them. "Are you talking business? You know the doctors said not to upset him. He needs rest."

Kennedy rose and motioned for Nash to do the same. "You're right. We've overstayed our welcome. Claudia, I have to get back to the office. You have my personal number as well as Mike's. If there's a problem—any problem at all —you should call one of us immediately."

"I understand."

The young woman reached for the tablet but then froze with her fingers still a few inches away.

"Claudia?" Kennedy said. "Are you all right?"

"Grisha Azarov," she said, sounding a bit startled. "Was it him, Scott? Did he do this to you?"

"What did you say?" Nash asked. "Azarov? We have his name as Filipov."

"No," Claudia said. "Not Filipov. Not for many years."

"You know this man?" Kennedy said.

She suddenly took on a bit of a deer-in-the-headlights expression. "No . . . No, I—"

"Calm down," Kennedy said. "You're among friends. Everyone in his room knows who you are."

"I'm not that person anymore."

"I'm sorry. You're right. Who you *were*. Now, do you know this man?"

She chewed her lower lip for a moment and nodded. "Louis ran into him years ago in Belarus. He never told me the details of what happened, but I know this: There are only two men in the world my husband was afraid of. Mitch and Grisha Azarov."

"Did you create a file on him?"

"Of course. Louis wanted to know everything in case they ever met again."

"And can you still access that file?"

"Yes. From my computer. It's in Mitch's apartment."

Nash grabbed the tablet off the bed and put a hand on Claudia's back. "Why don't we head on over to Mitch's place, then? You probably need to pick up a few things anyway."

"But what about Scott?" Claudia protested as Nash pushed her toward the door.

"No need to worry," Kennedy called after her. "I won't leave until you get back."

Chapter 35

Location unknown

Rapp shifted the limp woman to a more stable position on his shoulder and pushed through the door to Eric Jesem's apartment. He'd been careful when cutting off her air, doing just enough to put her down and keep her from going completely nuts on their way back through the crowd. At this point, it was almost certain that she was faking unconsciousness. Patiently waiting for an opportunity to take his head off.

"Hello?" he called.

No answer. The woman who'd patched him up must have belonged to someone else.

Rapp went straight to the bedroom—as the girl he was carrying would have expected—but then just dumped her on the bed and headed for the kitchen. He couldn't remember the last time he'd eaten and it'd be nice to take in a few calories before she started chasing him around the apartment.

The kitchen was barely big enough to walk through sideways, but a cursory search turned up a few packages of the Middle East's answer to ramen. Good in a pinch, but not his first choice. A little more effort rewarded him with a stash of

American-supplied MREs hidden beneath a broken stove. Normally, finding U.S. supplies in the hands of terrorists irritated the shit out of him, but today he wasn't complaining. He dug through the packages, finally locating the Mexican chicken he was hoping for.

Surprisingly, the sink worked, so he put some water in the heater bag and then made himself a PB&J. Chewing it carefully so as not to dislodge any more teeth, he walked back into the main room. Furniture was limited to a couple rickety chairs and a TV sitting unplugged on the floor. Rapp flipped a wall switch and got the expected nothing. There were two lamps in a corner, one battery-powered and the other hooked up to a gas canister. More interesting was the cell phone plugged into a solar charger on the sill of the apartment's only window.

He turned it on and confirmed that there was no signal. A lot of the area's cellular capacity had been taken out in the fighting and what was left was being jammed by the U.S. military. A quick scroll through Jesem's emails and texts turned up nothing of interest. Phone records were completely blank. It was likely that Marcus Dumond back at Langley could dig up all kinds of useful information on the device, but Rapp's techno-logical skills were limited to the basics.

There was a box under one of the chairs and he went through it, finding Jesem's U.S. passport, a few personal effects, and some porn. Not exactly a treasure trove of actionable intel. Nothing about his life, his mission in Pakistan, or ISIS's plans for the fissile material they had stolen. And Rapp still didn't know where the hell he was.

The drawers in the bathroom contained little more than a toothbrush and some paste. He closed the warped door as best he could and leaned into a cracked mirror. The face staring back at him was about what he'd expected: split lips, blackened eyes, and a battered nose beneath a stitched forehead.

It wasn't as bad as it had been when Maslick originally did the job, though. One of Rapp's many strengths was his ability to heal. In this case that talent was working against him. The comic-book puffiness around his eyes had already subsided appreciably and the discoloration where his cheeks emerged from his beard was fading.

Worse, though, was the nose. His looked nothing like Eric Jesem's and Maslick had been forced to break it to obscure that fact. Unfortunately, the woman who had done such a thorough job cleaning up Rapp's wounds had done an equally thorough job straightening his nose. Another few days and anyone who knew Jesem would start to see through the damage.

His experience with purposely injuring himself was pretty limited and he looked around the bathroom, trying to find something he could use.

The toilet seat seemed promising initially, but it turned out to be too light and flimsy. The sink also captured his attention for a moment, but the wall overhung it in a way that would limit his momentum. And then there was the issue of explaining why his face was getting worse instead of better.

A moment later, the solution to his problems kicked open the bathroom door. He ducked instinctively and the battery-powered lamp went arcing over his head, slamming into the wall above an empty towel rack. The young woman pulled it back for another attempt and Rapp started to recognize the opportunity she represented.

When she swung again, he only partially blocked the blow, allowing the lamp base to land a painful blow to the right side of his face. It lacked the knee-shaking force of one of Maslick's fists, but it was a step in the right direction.

Rapp slipped past her and into the main room to give himself space to maneuver. She didn't hesitate, chasing after him and taking another vicious swing. Hate and rage had transformed her beautiful features into something that would have startled even Stan Hurley—a man who had done hate and rage better than almost anyone.

Instead of retreating, Rapp moved closer. The shaft of the lamp hit him in the left eye, knocking him back a few steps. He blinked a few times to confirm that he could still see out of it as she came at him with an ear-splitting scream. This would be the money shot and he had to admit that he wasn't looking forward to it. A surge of adrenaline coursed through him when he turned and let the lamp hit him square in his broken nose.

"Fuck!" he shouted, staggering back as blood began pouring into his beard.

She pressed her advantage, undoubtedly thinking she was on the verge of finishing him off. This time he caught the lamp and swept her feet out from under her. She landed flat on her back on the concrete floor, knocking the wind from her lungs.

Rapp threw the lamp into a corner and went back into the bathroom to examine his face. No chance anymore of anyone differentiating his nose from Jesem's. In fact, it was hard to recognize the thing in the center of his face as a nose at all. If he managed to survive long enough to get back to the States, Irene Kennedy was going to be writing a serious check to the Agency's plastic surgeons.

He shoved some toilet paper in his nostrils to stop the bleeding and passed back through the door. The woman had made it to her knees and she looked up at him. The beating she'd just doled out had clearly done nothing to diminish her burning hatred.

"Do you speak English?" he asked, unwilling to reveal his language skills.

"If you touch me, I'll kill you."

Not only did she speak English, she spoke it pretty well.

"What do you say we call a temporary truce? Dinner should be ready."

He retreated into the kitchen and came out with the Mexican chicken. She rose to her feet, but seemed unsure what to do. Undoubtedly she was wondering why she hadn't been raped the moment she'd hit the bed.

"It's drugged," she pronounced.

He shoved a heaping spoonful into his mouth and then held the package out to her. She took a hesitant step forward and then snatched it from his hand. He watched as she wolfed it down like she hadn't eaten in a week—which was probably the case.

"What's your name?" he asked.

"I don't have to talk to you," she said, trying to get the last piece of chicken from the bottom of the container.

"You might want to think about your situation a little more carefully."

"If you come near me, I'll kill you."

"You already said that. Tell you what. I saw a package of Asian beef in there. Answer a few simple questions and I'll make it for you. Now, what's your name?"

She backed away a few steps. "Laleh."

"Are you from this area, Laleh?"

"Yes."

"Where are we?"

"I don't understand the question."

"What city? What country?"

Her eyes narrowed as though she thought she was somehow being tricked. "Al-Shirqat, Iraq."

Rapp nodded silently. North-central Iraq. Dead in the middle of ISIS-held territory.

Chapter 36

The White House
Washington, D.C.
U.S.A.

"You can go right in, Dr. Kennedy."

"Thank you, Gloria," she said, passing through a door that led directly into the Oval Office. Predictably, President Alexander was on the phone, but he stood and pointed to a chair in front of his desk. A small table next to it contained a steaming cup of tea.

She immediately recognized his conversation as a meaningless political strategy session and tuned it out. It was much more interesting to just watch the man as he twirled a pencil across the back of his knuckles and tried to hide his impatience.

Joshua Alexander was barely over fifty, but his brown hair was quickly turning gray. The dimpled smile and playful eyes that had so effectively ingratiated him with voters were still there, though. More importantly, he had proved to be something of a backroom realist. He knew what needed to be done to keep the country safe and while he tended to dislike being directly involved, he was often willing to look the other way. In the end, it was probably the best she could hope for from any politician.

Alexander finally managed to extricate himself from the call and laid the handset in its cradle.

"Irene. You look like shit," he said, and then caught himself. "I'm sorry. That was rude, wasn't it? How's Scott doing?"

"Much improved, thank you for asking."

"Normally I'd take that to mean you're finally going to get some sleep. But you never call emergency meetings with me to talk about how well everything's going."

"I'm afraid not, sir."

"Look, I'm sorry, but you've only got five minutes. I have the Turkish ambassador coming in and I don't have to tell you the mess they're dealing with."

"I understand, sir. I'll get directly to the point. We've learned that the fissile material missing from the Pakistani warhead we examined isn't an isolated incident."

"What do you mean not 'an isolated incident'?"

"We have confirmation that a total of six warheads have been compromised."

Alexander just sat there for a moment, staring at her. "Do you know who has it?"

"We think ISIS, but it may be more complicated than that."

"ISIS! Now hold on, Irene. You're telling me that the most violent bunch of psychopaths to walk the earth in the last five hundred years have the fuel to build six nuclear weapons?"

"I'm afraid so, sir."

"Can they do it? Do they have the resources?"

"On their own, it's doubtful. Building a weapon would take sophisticated materials, expertise, and machining capability—most of which has been destroyed in the area they control."

"Dirty bombs, then."

"That would be well within their capability. They could also sell it—to other terrorist groups, to the Iranians, or any other country interested in building a nuclear capability."

Alexander's secretary knocked and poked her head in. "Sir, the Turkish—"

"Reschedule him, Gloria."

"You're booked until eleven thirty this evening, Mr. President. I—"

"Then tell him midnight!"

"Yes sir," she said, immediately withdrawing and closing the door.

"I'm afraid there's another complication," Kennedy said when they were alone again.

"*Another* complication? You've got to be kidding me."

"We have mounting evidence of Russian involvement."

"Krupin? Why would he get mixed up in something like this? He has personal control over the world's second largest nuclear arsenal—

317

something he reminds me about every time we talk. He doesn't need to steal fissile material from the Pakistanis."

"Our people have done a full analysis of the decoy fuel canisters they found in the warhead. They've also been in touch with the Pakistani engineers examining the five other compromised weapons. All the containers appear identical. The metals originated in China, but evidence is strong that they were manufactured in a Russian facility. One controlled by the government."

"And how was that determined?"

"Microscopic pollen and industrial soot found in the welds."

"That's all you have?"

"No, sir. The man who attacked Scott Coleman appears to be a former Russian soldier who disappeared over a decade ago."

"Can I assume you have him in custody?"

"That would be an incorrect assumption."

"Then you're going off prints and DNA?"

"I'm afraid not, sir. Scott identified him from a photo."

"So you have a clear photo of the man?"

"We had to digitally enhance it to account for age and plastic surgery."

He just stared over the Resolute Desk at her. "And let me guess. Craig Bailer is the man who examined the nuke."

"That's correct, sir."

"To summarize, then, we have a guy who used to work on cars in your motor pool saying that some dust in a Pakistani warhead looks Russian."

"Sir, Eric has PhDs in—"

Alexander held up a hand, silencing her. "Please, Irene. I'm the one who approved the funding for his little playhouse out there in Virginia. But what do you want me to do, mass our military on the Russian border? Imagine this with me for a moment. Eric Bailer testifying to the UN about Siberian pollen while spitting tobacco into an empty beer can. Then, to corroborate his story, you pull out a picture of a Russian agent that you admit you Photoshopped the hell out of."

"I understand your position—"

"Do you? Do you really?"

"The intel is solid, sir."

"That's what scares the shit out of me, Irene. I know you wouldn't bring this to me if you didn't believe in it."

He pushed his chair back and folded his arms across his chest. "Krupin's a card-carrying sociopath, and he's backed himself into a corner. His economy's cratering and he's not going to be able to keep his people distracted with pointless military adventures for much longer. He knows that better than anybody. And he also knows that if he ever loses his grip on power,

319

someone's going to either throw him in prison or put a bullet in the back of his head."

Alexander was exactly right about his Russian counterpart. Most Americans worried about Russian strength, but the real thing to fear was its weakness. Russia had lost its empire and was now being further punished by low energy prices and economic sanctions. Krupin, despite his posturing in Russia's state-controlled media, was a desperate man. So much so that the CIA had actually quietly helped him over the past few years. Such was the tangled web that made up her world. While having a ruthless dictator running roughshod over Eastern Europe was less than ideal, a power vacuum was the surest way to chaos.

"How does getting involved in something like this help him, Irene? What's his play?"

"We can only speculate at this point, Mr. President."

"Then do it."

"As you say, his grip on power is slipping, and the reason for that is almost entirely economic."

"But how does giving ISIS the ability to nuke Chicago improve his position?"

"I'm not sure Chicago is the goal. There's no question that ISIS wants to draw the U.S. into a fight, but their primary goals are regional. Given this kind of capability, we think it's likely that their strategy would be to strike within the confines of the Middle East."

"So Krupin nukes Riyadh, Tehran, Tel Aviv, and God knows what else. He denies any involvement and then sits back while ISIS rolls across the world's main energy-producing region."

"That would certainly accomplish his goals. Oil prices would go to hundreds of dollars a barrel and the major world economies would be shaken to their foundation. Russia would become both extremely wealthy and extremely powerful because of its reserves. But I wonder if he would need to go that far? He wants high prices, but the kind of destruction you're talking about could blow back on him. Particularly with respect to his oligarchs, who have diverse interests all over the world."

"Then what?"

"We're still working on that problem, sir. The Middle East is so fragile right now, it wouldn't take a great deal to tip it. If a few of the more established governments fell, it's likely that we would see a domino effect."

"Like the Arab Spring."

"Yes, sir. But on a much more disruptive scale."

"What do we do, Irene? Have you created some kind of action plan?"

"Mitch is working on tracking the material."

"Working on it how?"

"He's posing as an American ISIS recruit."

"Has he found anything?"

"We aren't certain."

"What do you mean, you're not certain?"

"We don't actually know where he is at this moment. We assume in ISIS-controlled Iraq, but we haven't been able to verify that."

"Are you certain he's even alive?"

She picked up the tea mug and let the ceramic warm her hands. "Certain? No, sir. But we have every reason to believe he is."

"Why?"

"Because he always has been before."

Chapter 37

Al-Shirqat
Iraq

Rapp tried to curl into a more comfortable position on the worn mattress, but finally had to admit that there was no hope. Between the burns on his back and the damage Maslick had done, he'd probably be better off trying to sleep standing up.

Not that it was just the pain keeping him awake. It was also thoughts of Pakistan and his failure there. That fissile material was in the wild because he'd allowed himself to lose focus and be lured to South Africa. The question now was what he was going to do about it.

Options were limited. The most obvious was to convince the Iraqi general to put him back on his team. Unfortunately, that was easier said than done. Rapp would have to prove his physical abilities in front of witnesses, and the only way he could think to do that was to find the biggest, meanest son of a bitch in town and pick a fight with him.

As plans went, though, it was complete crap. For all he knew, Eric Jesem couldn't fight his way out of a paper bag. Winning could easily blow his cover and end with him enjoying a starring role in the next ISIS execution video. A lot of risk for not much hope of reward.

His second option was to figure out a way to contact Kennedy. Maybe she had some intel that could help him. Hell, maybe he could just bring down a wrath-of-God bombing raid on the city and flatten everything taller than a curb. The problems with that plan were even worse. With the U.S. military jamming, there was no way to get a line out and he had no way of knowing if the fissile material was even within a thousand miles of Al-Shirqat.

In the other room, Laleh murmured something in her sleep. He'd left her on the floor near the kitchen with a wool blanket and a full stomach. She'd answered a few of his questions but turned out to be the master of the reluctant one-word response.

Building trust between them could turn out to be harder than securing the missing fissile material. Just because she hated ISIS didn't necessarily mean that she had any love for Uncle Sam. It was entirely possible that she despised the idea of America even more than the reality of the men tearing her world apart. He'd seen it a hundred times before.

A nearly inaudible click sounded in the front room and Rapp raised his head from Jesem's filthy pillow. The rhythm of the girl's breathing continued, just loud enough to be heard over the howl of the wind outside. He was starting to settle back in when the creak of ancient wood reached him.

Rapp rolled out of bed and padded silently to the bedroom's empty doorway. A sliver of desert moonlight gleamed around the old towel hanging over the window, making it possible to see the hazy outline of Laleh on the floor but not much else.

The next sound was hard to mistake—the dull scrape of the front door sliding against an uneven floor. He moved quickly across the room, keeping to the edges where the floorboards had the most support, finally halting next to the apartment's only entrance.

The door moved slowly inward, finally stopping when the gap was large enough for a person to squeeze through. Rapp remained motionless as a man with an AK-47 entered. A moment later, a second man appeared and carefully pushed the door closed. Now that they were inside, Rapp expected them to spread out—one going for the bedroom while the other cleared the kitchen and bathroom. That didn't happen.

He watched with momentary confusion as the two men just stood there, crouched and frozen. After a couple seconds, he figured it out. They'd used too much light getting up the stairs and were now waiting for their vision to adjust.

That brought Rapp to an obvious question:

What were a couple of amateurs doing creeping around Eric Jesem's living room at three in the morning?

He stepped forward and slammed his fist into the back of the trailing man's head, dropping him like a sack of potatoes. The other turned toward the sound, but Rapp twisted the assault rifle from his grip and arced the butt toward his head. He only needed one of them alive for interrogation. Two would just double the chances of a problem.

"No!"

Laleh's shout was accompanied by her throwing herself in front of the man. Rapp barely avoided caving in the back of her head, redirecting the weapon's trajectory at the last second.

He flipped it around and slid a finger through the trigger guard before lighting the kerosene lamp. "Do you know them?"

When she didn't answer, he raised the rifle butt to his shoulder, taking aim at the head of the man behind her.

"Stop!" Laleh said immediately. "They're my brothers."

She moved to the unconscious one, rolling him on his back and cradling his head in her lap. Rapp kept the AK trained on the other.

"What are they doing here?"

The man in his sights answered in Arabic. "Coming to save our sister and kill a godless ISIS pig."

"What did he say?" Rapp said, deciding to keep playing dumb on the language front.

"That they weren't going to harm you. That they just came to take me home."

In a lifetime of being lied to, that may have been the least credible one he'd ever heard. Setting aside for a moment the unvarnished hate in the man's voice, he was rocking from side to side, apparently trying to decide whether running straight into automatic fire was worth the possibility of getting his hands around Rapp's neck.

"Are they part of the resistance to ISIS?"

"What resistance?" she responded. "They are devout Muslims who welcome the coming caliphate. They were just protecting our family's honor."

Rapp tightened the butt on his shoulder and centered the man's face in his sights. "I'm going to count to three, Laleh. Either you start telling me the truth or you're going to spend the rest of the night scrubbing your brother's brains off the wall."

"Please!" she said, the panic rising in her voice. "They fought when ISIS first came, but they're doing nothing now. They're in hiding. We've lost. You've taken everything from us."

Rapp lowered the weapon to his hip but kept the barrel lined up on the man. "Whether your brothers are part of it or not, is there an active resistance?"

"No. Not anymore."

"Tell this animal nothing!" the man said in Arabic. She responded in the same language. "I'm not telling him anything he can't see with his own eyes, Mohammed. You are no threat to him and his army."

She switched back to English. "My brothers and the men loyal to him talk. But that's all they do. Talk."

It was likely true. The combined forces of the entire world weren't sure how to fight ISIS. A small group of untrained men huddled in a basement weren't going to be able to do much more than get themselves killed. With the right mission and the right leadership, though, a compact, inexperienced force might be able to make a difference.

"I'm an American agent tracking nuclear material stolen from Pakistan," Rapp said, deciding that there was no more time for caution. "I believe that ISIS is going to use that material in an attack and that the attack is being run out of Al-Shirqat."

The man in front of him clearly understood and looked at Laleh. She shook her head slowly and spoke in Arabic. "I don't know, Mohammed. He saved me from being burned. And I can tell you that he hasn't touched me."

"He's lying," her brother responded. "We know all about Eric Jesem. About the things he's done.

He's not an American agent. Even CIA men have lines they don't cross."

"My brother doesn't believe you're an American agent," she said.

"You mean he doesn't believe that Eric Jesem is an American agent."

"I don't understand."

"What do you know about him? About Jesem?"

This time her brother answered directly. His English wasn't as good as Laleh's but it was easily understandable.

"We know that he's a butcher of women and children," he said, his eyes scanning the room.

Rapp would have smiled if his lips hadn't been so badly damaged. Despite no hope of closing the distance between them, the man still seemed to be searching for an opportunity to attack. Not well trained, but motivated. That was better than nothing.

"I had one of my men snap Eric Jesem's neck and then we stuffed his body down a garbage chute."

Laleh's brow knitted for a moment and then she started to understand.

"He asked me what city this was," she said in Arabic. "And the lamp! He let me hit him in the face over and over before he took it from me. He wanted me to do it! He wanted me to damage his face!"

Her brother just shook his head. "No. He's

clever. We know about him. He's from a rich family in America. He went to college. Then he came here to kill people who have nothing to do with him. Don't believe him, Laleh. He's the devil."

"Did Eric Jesem speak your language?" Rapp said, switching to flawless Arabic.

They just stared silently up at him.

"Like you say, he was a thirty-two-year-old American who grew up in Colorado, went to college, and then took a job as a Realtor at his father's company." Rapp pulled up his shirt, revealing not only the recent damage done by Maslick but years of healed battle wounds: puckered bullet holes, jagged knife scars, and the more precise lines created by surgeons' scalpels. "Do men like Jesem look like this?"

They were too stunned to respond.

"What's the name of the general who brought me to the square?"

Laleh finally found her voice. "Mustafa. Ali Mustafa."

Rapp vaguely recognized the name. Not one of Saddam Hussein's inner circle, but still high up in his army. Artillery, if he was thinking of the right man.

"Do you know anything about an operation being run out of here by Mustafa? Something big?"

"There's been talk," Mohammed said finally.

"No details, but we know it has something to do with a facility outside of town. Mustafa brought men there to train. Eric Jesem was one of them."

"How many men in total?"

"Fifteen. Maybe twenty."

It seemed like about the right number. Six weapons handled by two-man teams so as not to raise suspicion. Then some backups in case there were problems.

"Do you have access to outside communications?"

"No. The hard lines have been destroyed and the Americans are jamming cell signals."

Rapp nodded. "Can you get me to that training camp?"

"Yes. It's not far. But for what reason?"

Rapp tossed the man back his weapon. "To kill as many of the people there as I can."

Chapter 38

Langley, Virginia
U.S.A.

Irene Kennedy sat down at her desk for the first time in days. She'd barely reached for her briefing file when Mike Nash entered waving a manila envelope. It looked distressingly thin.

"You found him?" Kennedy said hopefully.

Nash fell into one of the chairs in front of her and tried to find a comfortable position. She'd purposely chosen furniture with backs too straight and padding too thin in order to discourage long, unproductive meetings. There were some even less comfortable ones in a storage closet that were brought out during visits by members of Congress.

"Not exactly found. But with Claudia's data to work with, we've made progress."

"I don't need progress, Mike. I need success."

"I know. The machine is running, but this guy isn't exactly an amateur."

He pulled an eight-by-ten photo from the envelope and placed it on her desk. Grisha Azarov apparently didn't share Rapp's uncanny ability to avoid being caught on camera. He was staring straight into the lens as he strode across a stage with a microphone in his hand. The dark hair and sculpted nose were close matches to the composite Nash had created. His skin was more tanned, though, and his eyes leaned a bit more toward Asian. The pinstripe suit he was wearing seemed a bit too large, as though it had been tailored to obscure the physique beneath.

"That's Azarov—or Filipov, if you prefer—speaking to almost a thousand people at a conference last year in Abu Dhabi."

"What kind of conference?"

"Extraction industry. This guy is taking the concept of hiding in plain sight to a whole other level. He's the head of a well-known oil and gas consulting firm that operates all over the globe. His clients include Exxon, BP, and Aramco, just for starters. Hell, they're so good, even we've used them a few times."

"That would allow him to move around Russia and the Middle East without attracting attention."

"And he takes advantage of that ability. A lot. Our information on his travels is still spotty, but we have entry and exit dates putting him in Pakistan when Scott was attacked. He flew in on his company jet and was staying in the nicest suite the Islamabad Marriott offers. He has condos in London and New York, but doesn't seem to have been to either for years. We were able to infiltrate the management companies caretaking them and get people inside, but they didn't find anything."

"He must live *somewhere*."

"Agreed. His permanent address is listed as the offices of his company in Moscow, but I think we can do better than that."

He pulled a colorful map of the world from the envelope and unfolded it on her desk.

"This is a graphical representation of his private jet's trips?" she asked, examining the hundreds of arcing lines between countries and continents.

"Not exactly. We suspect that his plane is putting in a lot of hours empty."

"He's trying to throw off anyone who might be watching."

"Like I said, this guy's no amateur. But we know he doesn't fly commercial, so what you're seeing here is a representation of charter flights coming and going from locations where we could place him and with passengers whose identities we couldn't verify. Three hundred and twelve in all over the course of five years. Notice anything unusual?"

"There seem to be an unlikely number of flights going to Central America."

"Nicaragua, Costa Rica, and Panama, to be precise. Our statistics guys say that there's less than a ten percent chance that the pattern is a random occurrence."

Egypt, and the UAE are different. They're protected by either their stability, their military capability, or both.

"So nuke Dubai, Cairo, Riyadh, Tehran, and Jeddah. Throw in Tel Aviv, just to get the shit storm really rolling. Then ISIS moves in and oil prices spike to record levels. Krupin would have the money to pay off every corrupt bureaucrat from Moscow to Siberia and to drown the average citizen in new entitlements."

Kennedy didn't respond, instead pulling off her reading glasses and setting them on the desk.

"You don't agree, Irene?"

"I don't *disagree*. Anything is possible at this point. But Krupin is a sociopath, not a madman. He's not motivated by God or illusions of world domination. He just wants to maintain power. Your scenario has so much potential for blowback. Retaliation from the West, unforeseen economic consequences. Even an increase in terrorist attacks inside Russia. It seems to me that he'd do as little as possible to get the effect he needs."

"So Saudi Arabia. That's where you get the biggest bang for your buck."

She nodded noncommittally.

"It's frustrating, isn't it, Irene? I have this nagging feeling that Mitch knows the answer to all our questions, but he has no way of getting us the information."

She had the same feeling, though her confidence was beginning to falter. Earlier that day, she'd had a conversation with Joe Maslick in which he admitted to downplaying the beating he'd given Rapp. Further, analysis of satellite images depicting Rapp's "rescue" from the transport van suggested that he'd fallen down a fairly steep incline. Whether that fall had been caused by a bullet to the back was a question of significant debate. The bottom line was that there was a very real possibility that Mitch Rapp was dead or incapacitated.

The phone on Kennedy's desk buzzed and the voice of one of her assistants came over the speaker. "I have General Templeton returning your call on a secure line."

Nash's eyebrows rose at the name of the chairman of the Joint Chiefs.

"Put him through."

She pushed a button and put him on speaker. "Thank you for getting back to me so quickly, James."

"Not a problem, Irene. What can I do for you?"

"It's my understanding that you've been briefed on the items that recently went missing from Pakistan?"

"Yes."

"We have an operative who we believe has infiltrated ISIS and is now somewhere in territory held by them. It's possible that he has information on those items and how they're going to be used."

"I see. And how does that involve me?"

"I want to recommend to the president that we shut down our electronic jamming operations in the area, and I'd like your support."

There was a stunned silence over the line. "Let me get this straight, Irene . . . You want me to let the most technologically sophisticated terrorist group in history plug back into the grid because you think one of your guys *might* have infiltrated ISIS and *could* have useful information? Look, you know I have nothing but respect for you, but are you out of your mind?"

"The operative I'm talking about is Mitch, James."

This time the silence went on for quite a bit longer. Finally, the general spoke again. "I'll get behind eight hours, Irene. Not a minute more."

Chapter 39

Al-Shirqat
Iraq

The wind had continued to strengthen and now seemed to be steady at fifteen knots, with gusts coming in above thirty. The darkness and the hiss of dust blasting the surrounding structures created a disorienting environment of sensory deprivation. It was all Rapp could do not to wander off the street and run into one of the buildings lining either side.

Laleh's directions had been impressively detailed, but following them in the prevailing conditions was challenging. A set of headlights appeared at the far end of the street and approached. He shaded his eyes, memorizing every detail of the newly illuminated terrain— the bullet-ridden stone façades, the narrow alleys, the blackening corpses hanging from a disused power line.

When the vehicle got close, he turned toward it, raising a hand in greeting. The armed men in the back looked on suspiciously but then quickly recognized him as the American who had gained General Mustafa's favor. The man who had defied not only the CIA but the infamous Mitch Rapp.

They shouted unintelligibly as they passed, saluting him with their assault rifles. Rapp continued along the street, navigating by mental map as his eyes readjusted to the darkness.

He ran a hand along the front of a building to his right, using his fingers to locate the alley he had seen moments before. It was the one Laleh had told him about, but it was less than five feet wide, creating an even deeper darkness. It took almost a minute, but Rapp found the door handle he'd been assured was there and used it to enter a building that smelled of charred wood. He ascended the stairs, aiming for a dim sliver of light bleeding around a door at the top.

Knocking turned out to be unnecessary. The door was pulled open and he was yanked inside. The man closing it behind him was immediately recognizable as Laleh's brother Mohammed. The other four men in the room were armed and standing against the far wall. Weapons ranged from AKs to a Smith & Wesson SD40 pistol, and all were aimed at him.

"These are your men?" Rapp asked in Arabic.

"Yes," Mohammed said, moving to take a position with them.

Rapp let out a long breath and squinted his swollen eyes against the glare of a single overhead bulb. Laleh's other brother was there, still looking a bit shaken by the blow Rapp had delivered. The two men to his right were both thin and wearing glasses that looked fairly thick. Rapp had met hundreds like them in his time operating in the Middle East—secular intellectuals prone to endless political philosophizing but good for little else. The last man was a beast, nearly Maslick's size, with a thick beard and eyes full of hate.

"*All* of them?" Rapp said.

Mohammed nodded.

So, two guys who looked like they used inhalers, one he'd obviously hit a little too hard, and one who was staring at him like he wanted to carve his heart out with a sharp rock. Outstanding.

"How did you learn to speak Arabic so well?" the big one said.

"My mother emigrated from Iraq in the fifties. She taught me."

It was a reasonable cover story that explained both his dark complexion and his accent.

"You're a liar. You're one of the CIA men who has been killing our people for decades."

Rapp shrugged and waved a hand in the general direction of the blacked-out windows. "What has the CIA ever done to you that can compare with this?"

The other men had lowered their weapons, but the big one talking kept his aimed at Rapp's chest.

"Why should we help him?"

"We've already discussed this," Mohammed said. "The Americans are the only people with the power to defeat ISIS and free our country. But they hesitate. Why, Gaffar? Because they see us squabbling endlessly among ourselves. They see no hope."

Mohammed grabbed a rolled up poster-size piece of paper and spread it out on the floor. Rapp knelt next to him and immediately recognized it as a map of Al-Shirqat.

"We're here," Mohammed said, pointing to the northern part of the city while the others gathered around. He ran his finger toward the western edge. "The building housing the training facility you're looking for is here."

"Outside of town."

"Barely. Perhaps half a kilometer. The Americans built it as a school but the instructors have all been executed. Now the building is used to hold girls being sold and used by ISIS. Three months ago, a group of new men came to live and train there. Eric Jesem was one of them."

"How many men in total?"

Mohammed glanced at one of his bespectacled comrades, who answered in a voice quiet enough that it was difficult to hear.

"At first, maybe fifty. Most, including Jesem, left about a month ago. Some returned but most haven't. Now our best estimate is twenty-three men."

That made sense. Mustafa had sent teams, including the one Jesem had served in, to get the fissile material in Pakistan. A number of them had been killed; others had likely been posted to other positions within ISIS. The men who remained were the ones who had been chosen to carry out the next phase of the operation.

"Describe the building," Rapp said.

"It's primarily built of concrete, with two stories," Mohammed said. "A fence surrounds it, but the gate was knocked down when ISIS took over and has never been repaired. One guard at the entrance. The children are kept on the upper floor at night. It's accessed by a staircase at the back of the building. The men sleep in various locations throughout the ground floor."

"Are all of your people familiar with the layout?"

He nodded.

"Electricity?"

"They have generators. Some usage at night, but limited."

It was more or less what Rapp expected. They'd put the training facility in a building full of kids to give it cover from U.S. bombing raids, but running full lights at night would be pushing it.

"Weapons?"

"All are armed with AK-47s and a single sidearm. The models of those vary."

"What about you?"

"We have what you see here. A few spare magazines each."

"Any access to more men or arms?"

"No."

"Okay," Rapp said, standing. "Then let's go."

They all just stared at him. Mohammed's brother was the first to speak. "What do you mean? Go where?"

"To attack that facility."

"We can't just attack them. We would need to discuss it. To plan. We would—"

"What is there to talk about? Mohammed said you're all familiar with the facility's layout. We know the strength of the opposition force and we know where the students are."

"No. This is—"

"Silence!" Gaffar said, rising to what Rapp estimated to be a full six foot four. "We will not attack that facility."

"Why?" Rapp said. "Are you afraid?"

In response, he raised the barrel of his SD40, leveling it a few inches from Rapp's ruined nose. "Because I won't follow you. Look at your face. At what you let someone do to you. No. You speak as though you're a great warrior but you smell like a bureaucrat. Like a man who will have piss running down his leg at the first sight of blood."

Rapp considered trying to talk the man down,

but he was clearly not the type to be swayed by conversation. And, frankly, that made him uniquely useful in this group.

Instead, Rapp dodged left, grabbing Gaffar's wrist and yanking his arm straight. A moderate blow to the Iraqi's exposed elbow was enough to get him to drop the gun but not enough to do any damage. Rapp had already made that mistake with Mohammed's brother.

The pistol fell and Rapp caught it as the other men in the room scrambled for their rifles. He drove his foot into the side of the big man's leg to take him down, simultaneously firing four rounds toward the men reaching for their weapons. Each struck less than an inch from their hands.

After the echo of the shots died, everything went completely still. Gaffar was on his knees and the others were frozen near the back wall. Rapp stuffed the pistol in his waistband and pointed toward the door. "Who's driving?"

Chapter 40

Near Jiwani
Pakistan

The man piloting the truck was going too fast, but trying to impose reasonable driving habits on the people of this region was an exercise in futility. Grisha Azarov gripped the wooden crate he was perched atop and tightened the scarf protecting his lungs from the dust.

The young men seated around him seemed to be enjoying their journey through Western Pakistan on the open flatbed. Neither the spine-crushing jolts nor the oppressive heat seemed sufficient to dampen their spirits.

All were members of ISIS, selected by Maxim Krupin for their desirable qualities. They were obviously young and strong. Beyond those traits and their deep well of enthusiasm, though, Azarov wasn't sure what made them so exceptional.

The truck came around a corner at a speed that caused the load to list dangerously. The crates, filled mostly with goods to be traded along the Gulf, had been stacked more than four meters high. Azarov clung to one of the ropes securing the load as the vehicle rocked onto two wheels. He found himself almost hoping for a well-timed wind gust. It would be a fitting end to this twisted enterprise: him lying among the injured ISIS men surrounded by bolts of cloth, canned food, and the fissile material stolen from Pakistan's arsenal.

They crested a hill and the Gulf of Oman became visible in the distance, a blinding mirror under the powerful desert sun. The men around him began to talk excitedly, but he spoke only rudimentary Arabic and had no idea what they were saying.

It was one of the many reasons he should have been a thousand miles from this place. His experience in the Middle East was almost entirely a function of his life as an energy consultant. He was intimately familiar with the region's high-end hotel suites, conference centers, and European-style restaurants. Occasionally, he would be taken to a new extraction facility in the back of an air-conditioned SUV—usually one equipped with a bar.

His mind drifted from the task at hand to his future—a subject that he had never given much thought to until a few weeks ago. Would Krupin really release him? It would be the most reasonable course of action, and the Russian president could generally be counted on to take that path when it was in his best interest. There were a number of notable exceptions, though. Some of which Azarov had been personally involved in.

It would be easy to make the mistake of attributing Krupin's obsession with power entirely to his desire for survival. This was not necessarily the case. There were times when the Russian politician took significant risks to punish some irrelevant apparatchik or low-level criminal who dared to defy him. There was never any profit in it, only an opportunity for Krupin to exercise his rage and sense of superiority.

Would this be one of those instances?

Azarov had served the Russian president for so long that it was hard to remember the modest farmer and soldier he once was. When they'd first met, Krupin had seemed like a god. Bold and cunning, worldly and well educated. Azarov was dazzled—overwhelmed, really—by the man. He'd wanted what Krupin had. To be respected and feared by great men. To wield power and wealth with the same thoughtless ease. To become a man who commanded the attention of the world.

Now, though, he wanted none of those things. And he had learned to see Maxim Krupin for what he was: a desperate and ultimately weak man whose legacy could be only destruction, because it was all he knew.

The truck finally came to a stop where the dirt road disappeared into a sandy beach. A three-masted dhow was anchored just offshore, its angled stern and tapered bow bobbing in the light chop. The men around him immediately got to work, some jumping to the ground and others beginning to free the truck's cargo. Azarov climbed down one of the straps and stood in the shade of the teetering load, gazing across the water toward Oman.

Was Mitch Rapp on the far shore, staring back from a similar beach? Russian intelligence had managed to pick him up at the hospital where Scott Coleman was being treated, but the fools had then promptly lost him. There were reports that he'd been near Bhakkar, but Krupin's agents had only been able to confirm the presence of Joe Maslick.

A confrontation with Rapp was inevitable, but Azarov didn't want it to be here in the blinding sun and oppressive heat. These were Rapp's conditions. In some ways, his home. Azarov would prefer to lure him to northern Russia—somewhere cold, dark, and closed in, where the advantage would be his.

The captain of the dhow waded ashore and pointed at him, shouting something in Arabic. While Azarov didn't understand the words, the meaning was clear: Get to work unloading the truck.

The man had no idea who he was talking to, but he was right. There was no point in attracting attention by standing in the shade while the others ferried crates to the boat. Azarov walked to the back and one of his men pointed to a box marked with a subtle red X. He stacked another on top of it and the Russian lifted them, wading into the water before wedging his cargo into a large inner tube.

He started toward the starboard side of the boat, walking as far as he could before being forced to cling to the side of the tube and kick. He was about ten meters out when he saw a shadow moving in the water beneath him. The diver rose up from the darkness and pulled the marked box through the bottom of the tube. The procedure was even smoother than Azarov had anticipated, resulting in nothing more than minor bobbing. If there had been anyone on shore watching, it was unlikely they would have noticed anything unusual. If the Americans were watching from above, they would be utterly blind to what had happened.

Azarov continued forward as the diver descended to a hidden container attached to the hull.

Once fully loaded, the dhow would take him and his men into the Persian Gulf, where they would unload their smuggled cargo on a remote Saudi beach. It was an uncomfortable and slow mode of transportation, but one unlikely to attract attention.

Azarov arrived at the boat and two men climbed down a cargo net to take the remaining crate off his tube. Once they had it, he swam back toward shore to get another load.

In a few days it would all be over. He would return to Costa Rica and in the worldwide chaos that ensued, he would finally be forgotten.

Chapter 41

Al-Shirqat
Iraq

Rapp slithered up the dirt slope in almost complete darkness. Gaffar and Mohammed were to his left and the two eggheads were on his right. He'd left Mohammed's brother with the car. The man still hadn't completely recovered from the punch to the back of the head, but otherwise he seemed solid.

The moon was full, but the dust in the air had turned it into little more than a smear in the eastern sky. Still, it was enough to see one of the geeks start to rise onto all fours. Rapp shoved his ass down for the fourth time and for the fourth time received a mumbled apology.

Not exactly the team he was used to working with. He'd give a couple fingers in exchange for a few of Coleman's boys, but that wasn't going to happen. What was it Rummy liked to say? "You go to war with the army you have, not the army you might want." And in this case, the army he had consisted of two computer nerds, a man with no combat experience, and a former Iraqi soldier who might put a bullet in Rapp's back the second he turned it.

They crested the slope and went still, looking down on the building a hundred yards away. Detail was hard to see, but Rapp could make out that it consisted of two stories, as reported. Most of the construction did indeed look to be concrete and there was a discernible glint from a chain-link fence. It was probably only seven feet high and had no razor wire—probably built more to keep kids corralled during recess than to fend off an armed assault. A little light was filtering around a poorly arranged blackout shade on the first floor, but that was it. No sign of activity from either the children or the men barracked there. It was 2 a.m. and most everyone would be asleep.

A brief flash near the open gate caught his eye, and he searched using his peripheral vision to maximize light sensitivity. A dim outline became visible through the dust and darkness, a lone guard leaning casually against a sandbag barrier. He would have been invisible if it hadn't been for the reddish glow of his cigarette.

"So you're saying twenty-three men inside, give or take," Rapp said. "Do we have any idea how many kids are upstairs?"

"Perhaps forty?" Mohammed responded. "It's difficult to know. Mustafa's men constantly bring new ones in and auction off others. Most aren't even from this area anymore."

"Ages?"

"As young as six. Maybe a few in their late teens."

That was going to create a complete cluster-fuck. The better part of fifty children panicking and all moving at different speeds, with some of the teens trying to help the younger ones while others just stampeded over them. Not something he wanted to deal with.

"What's our plan?" Mohammed asked.

Rapp scooted back, bringing them all in close so they could hear.

"Mo and I will go in—"

"No," Gaffar said immediately. "I will go with you."

Clearly the big man still didn't trust him.

"I have to have you here," Rapp said. "It's likely we're going to need cover fire when we come out and you're our only experienced shooter."

Gaffar grumbled a bit but seemed to understand that it was the most effective use of their limited manpower.

"What about us?" one of the geeks asked.

"Your job is to protect Gaffar and his position. If anyone comes up behind or to the sides of him, they're your responsibility. I want to be perfectly clear, though. Under no circumstances are you to fire a gun in my direction."

Gaffar let out a quiet laugh.

"What about the two of us?" Mohammed said. "What are we going to do?"

"Just follow my lead. Once we get in, we're going to go straight to the back of the building as quietly as possible. Priority one is keeping those kids contained upstairs. That's your only responsibility."

"And you?"

"Once you make sure no kids are going to get in my way, I'm going to start killing people."

"Alone?" Gaffar said. "With only my pistol?"

"Yes. And if everyone stays calm and does their job, we should be in and out in just a few minutes."

Rapp slapped Gaffar on the back. "When Mustafa's men start coming out of the building, let them. Kill shots at this distance are going to be hard and if you start shooting too soon, you'll just drive them back under cover. Oh, and if the kids manage to get out of the building, remember —they're the short ones."

With that, he pulled Mohammed to his feet and they started strolling casually toward the gate.

The guard turned out to be dangerously inattentive. Rapp and Mohammed approached to within thirty feet and he still hadn't noticed them. Startling the man wasn't ideal, but seemed inevitable in the open terrain. The best they could hope for was to be close when it happened.

Twenty feet came and went. Then fifteen. The man remained focused on getting every last bit of smoke out of his cigarette. Maybe they were going to get lucky. Maybe this would go quiet and easy.

Then again, maybe not. At ten feet, the man picked them up in his peripheral vision and spun, clawing for the weapon on his shoulder.

"Brother!" Rapp called, continuing to approach with empty hands spread wide. Mohammed was a pace back, wearing desert garb and a headdress that revealed only his eyes. Rapp was similarly outfitted but had left his face uncovered so as not to obscure his battered face. He seemed to be at the height of his fifteen minutes of fame. Why not use it?

"Jesem?" the guard said before he could line up the rifle. The pronunciation was completely Arabic, suggesting that he spoke no English. Rapp waved Mohammed forward and put an arm warmly around his shoulders. "Translate for me, brother."

"Of course."

"General Mustafa has given me back my place on the team. I should have waited until morning to come, but I was anxious to rejoin my com-rades."

Mohammed translated his words and then the man's response.

"Welcome back, brother."

Rapp reached into his pocket to retrieve a pack of cigarettes—something he'd learned never to be without when traveling in Muslim nations. At the same time, he slid a knife from his waistband and held the blade flat against his forearm. It was probably more stealth than necessary in light of the fact that the guard was completely hypnotized by the pristine pack of Marlboros. As he leaned in to reach for one, Rapp flicked the knife out and ran it across his throat. The motion was so subtle and the blade so sharp that the man didn't immediately seem to notice.

Rapp guided him to the ground facedown. A foot between his shoulder blades kept him from splattering them as he bled out.

"Are you all right?" Rapp asked Mohammed.

"Yes. Of course."

There was no question that Rapp's companion had seen a great deal in his life. But there was a difference between seeing and participating. He hadn't panicked or run, though, and that was worth something.

"Then let's go."

As they started toward the entrance to the building, Rapp instinctively raised a hand to activate his throat mike but then remembered it wasn't there. Just like his body armor, night vision gear, and, most critically, his silencer. It wasn't quite as bad as going up against a group of well-armed jihadists with a stick and a rock, but it was close. At least sticks and rocks were quiet.

They stopped outside the door and Rapp leaned

into Mohammad's ear. "Remember, we belong here. Until we're sure those kids are locked away upstairs, anyone we run into is our best friend. All you have to do is translate for me just like you did with the guard. If you stay calm, all this will be over in a few minutes."

After a nervous nod, they entered a lobby decorated with a bullet-ridden plaque commemorating the school's opening. Dim, widely spaced bulbs strung together with extension cords provided enough illumination to navigate but not much more. Rapp led, bloody knife still held against his forearm.

They stayed in the center of the hallway, walking casually through a litter of crayon drawings that recalled better times.

"Left just ahead," Mohammed said.

Rapp strode into the narrower corridor, slowing when he noticed that the doors along the right side contained windows. Some had intact glass and others shattered, but all the rooms they looked into were dark. He moved quickly to the first, peering inside at a classroom full of overturned desks.

The next one looked similar, but with one critical difference visible near the center: a lone cot with a man asleep on it. Rapp was about to continue on when he spotted a shadow moving among the desks piled against the far wall. His hand moved subtly toward the gun in his waistband but then his mind identified the vague shape. A girl, probably not much older than Anna, naked and shivering.

Rapp felt his anger building again, but he pushed it aside. There would be time to let it out soon enough.

Footsteps became audible approaching from the west and Rapp turned away from the window, motioning for Mohammed to remain calm.

The armed man who appeared around the corner looked a hell of a lot more serious than the guard at the gate. Rapp computed the distance between them and tried to figure the odds that he could hit him with an underhand knife throw. Before he could finish his calculation, though, the man shouted at him in thickly accented English.

"Eric! I saw you in the square, but I could not reach you in the crowd!"

Rapp was starting to enjoy his newfound fame. Maybe they'd throw him a party and he could pop every one of these pieces of shit while they were cutting the cake.

"Brother!" Rapp said, throwing his arms around the man, despite the AK between them. It was tempting to use the knife, but their joyful reunion was generating too much noise. Someone was bound to hear the commotion and come to see what it was about.

"Why are you here, Eric?"

"General Mustafa has returned me to the team," Rapp said excitedly and then pointed to Mohammed. "This is my new friend. He translates for me when it's necessary."

"God be with you."

"And you," Mohammed replied.

"You really must learn our language, Eric. This is your home now. We are your people."

"I know," Rapp said. "You're right."

The door that he had peeked into earlier was suddenly thrown open and the man who had been sleeping on the cot appeared.

Rapp raised a hand in greeting, but Mohammed was startled by the sound and spun, firing an automatic burst into the man's chest.

Rapp's new buddy, despite having an assault rifle hanging across his chest, hesitated. With no other option, Rapp used that delay to drive his blade into the back of the man's head.

"Get to the girls!" he said, dragging the body toward the open door Mohammed was frozen in front of.

"I'm sorry," the Iraqi stammered. "He scared me. I didn't—"

"The girls!" Rapp said, adjusting the scarf around his neck to cover his face and head. "Now!"

Mohammed started sprinting toward the back of the building as Rapp wrestled the two bodies into the open classroom. He'd barely gotten the first over the threshold when the naked girl shot past him and ran, sobbing, toward the lobby.

The sound of her slamming through the main doors was accompanied by the shouts of men waking up all over the building. What he didn't hear, though, was a gunshot. Gaffar was thankfully less easy to startle than Mohammad. The girl would be allowed to disappear into the night.

"Americans!" Rapp shouted in Arabic. "The Americans are attacking!"

He slid the knife back into his waistband and clamped a hand over his thigh, lurching forward as though he'd been shot. A man appeared in the stairwell to his right and Rapp motioned toward the lobby. "The Americans! They're out front! Hurry!"

More men appeared and ran for the main entrance, checking their weapons, speculating loudly as to the strength of the opposing force, and wondering if the Americans would dare use drones. Rapp's feigned wound gave him an excuse to hang back. Six men were in front of him, none of whom were looking behind them. He reached for Gaffar's Smith & Wesson but then heard the sound he'd been dreading: the screams of young girls mixed with a drumroll of running feet.

His sweet setup went to shit in a matter of seconds. The men ahead started looking back and a moment later he was engulfed in a sea of panicked children. They flowed around him and the ISIS men, trapping them in an irresistible current moving toward the front of the building. The terrorists faced forward again, shouting angrily and swinging their rifle butts. A few connected and the girls went down, but it was useless. The slave trade was clearly better than Mohammed thought, because there had to be at least a hundred of them.

Shooting was pointless. Rapp would be lucky to hit the ground in this environment. He spotted what he needed just ahead and to his right—a three-foot break in the lockers that lined the wall.

With considerable effort, he managed to fight his way out of the flow of escaping girls. Five men were still visible and he braced himself between the lockers, aiming his pistol at a terrorist about to disappear around the corner.

Rapp went for his upper back, not wanting to cause the mess that tended to accompany a headshot. It worked. He went down, but it looked like he'd just tripped in the melee. The gunshot was loud as hell, but in the concrete corridor, it would be impossible to pinpoint its source.

A tall girl with a blanket wrapped around her bumped Rapp's gun hand as she ran past, but he recovered quickly and took out a man who was actually slashing at the children around him with a sword. A man a few feet behind saw him fall and looked back at Rapp, but he didn't have time to raise his weapon before taking a round to the throat.

The last viable target disappeared around the corner just as the tail end of the stampede passed by. Only a few very young girls were left behind, confused and crying.

Mohammed appeared a moment later. Apologizing a little too loudly, but at least not shooting at anything.

"They were already coming through the door when I got there! I tried to push it closed, but it was impossible."

Rapp didn't respond, instead starting to run toward the front of the building. When he came to the lobby, he found close to fifteen men firing blind bursts through the windows.

Rapp went straight for the middle of them, slamming his back into the closed doors with Gaffar's pistol held near his chest. "General Mustafa sent us to warn you that the Americans were planning an attack. But we were too late."

Completely destroying Mustafa's teams wasn't part of his plan, but he needed a few more dead before the night was over.

"We have to get out of here!" Rapp continued. "With the girls gone, the Americans will use their drones. We don't have much time!"

The men nodded their agreement.

"You have to survive to carry out the general's plans," Rapp said. "I'll go out first and draw the

Americans' fire. Follow a few seconds later and run for the desert."

He lurched over to Mohammed and grabbed him by the back of the neck. "Come with me."

They went back to the doors and, with a shout of *Allahu Akbar*, charged out into the night, firing their weapons into the bottom of the hill that Gaffar was ensconced on. Rapp pulled the scarf from his face and hoped to hell that Gaffar was paying attention.

It appeared that he was, because when the flashes from his rifle started up, they were angled safely away from them.

Rapp sprinted ahead, leaving Mohammed on his own and dropping to his stomach about twenty-five yards outside the gate. He aimed through the gloom, tracking the men trying to escape into the night. One to his two o'clock went down, a victim of Gaffar's marksmanship. His companion crouched and skirted the fence, looking for an easy way over. Rapp squeezed off a single round as the man leapt onto the wire and began to climb. The tango jerked visibly before his body folded lifelessly over the top.

Mohammed ran past, unaware that Rapp was lying only a few feet away. He'd follow in a moment. By his count, two more needed to go down before the night's work was over.

Chapter 42

East of Fujairah
Gulf of Oman

Grisha Azarov had taken one of only three hammocks belowdecks. The men assigned to him had commandeered the other two, as well as the limited number of mats spread out below. Crewmembers not on duty were left to sleep among the crates stacked throughout the already claustrophobic space.

By his watch, he had been on the vessel for less than eight hours, but it already felt like days. The captain assured him that they were making good time—the sails were full of the wind so important to Krupin's plans.

Azarov tried to meditate on the details of the operation, but his mind wandered to Mitch Rapp. Was their confrontation approaching? Would the conflict between them be resolved in the coming days? Maybe even in the coming hours?

It was obvious what defeat would bring, but what would victory feel like? Pride at seeing the CIA man's lifeless body at his feet? Relief at having neutralized a threat that otherwise would have kept coming until one of them was dead?

Or maybe nothing more than the same numbness he always felt when he took a life.

A frightened shout drifted down to him from the main deck. The words were in Arabic, but Azarov understood enough of them to tease out a meaning. The Americans had taken an interest in their modest vessel and were moving to intercept.

Crewmembers scrambled for the ladder leading upward while Azarov's men began desperately moving crates. Finally, they managed to expose the relevant section of decking and Azarov pulled up three unattached boards, exposing an electric winch.

He flipped a switch and then glued the boards back down with a bottle of instant adhesive. His men immediately began moving the crates back to their original positions over the winch. As they did, the fissile material attached to the hull began to descend at the end of a hundred-meter-long cable. In less than two minutes, their critical cargo would be resting in the silt at the bottom of the Gulf.

When everything was in order, they ascended the ladder to the main deck. Azarov took an anonymous position near the middle of the line of crewmen anxiously watching the approach of an American Coast Guard vessel.

Charged with contributing to Gulf security, the modern white-and-red Island-class cutter seemed hopelessly out of place against the

Middle Eastern backdrop. That made the situation no less dangerous, though.

It pulled alongside and a boarding craft closed the gap between the two vessels at a speed that suggested a certain amount of urgency. An Arab translator came up the cargo net first, speaking to the captain as uniformed members of the American crew followed.

The dog that appeared next was expected. Though not the Arabs' favorite creatures, they were quite useful in searching for drugs and weapons. The Geiger counter that came up shortly thereafter, though, was definitely not a standard piece of boarding equipment. Of even more concern were the American divers tipping backward into the water.

Russian spec ops had assured him that the size and color of the cable made it virtually invisible when submerged. Further, the Gulf's current would loop it away from the vessel, making it extremely unlikely that a diver would collide with it.

Again, Azarov felt himself being pulled out of the present—a dangerous vice that seemed to get worse as the years dragged on. What would happen to him if Krupin's weapons were discovered? Of course, he and the crew would be taken into custody and the dhow would be put in tow behind the Coast Guard ship. The fact that he wasn't from this region would be quickly

to the entrance of the building he now called home. After confirming that no one was watching, he slipped inside and silently climbed the stairs.

Laleh was pacing across the main room when he opened the door. She jerked to a stop and spun in his direction. "My brothers. Are they—"

"They're both fine," Rapp said, angling toward one of the two chairs in the room. Instead of sitting, he slammed a foot into it, shattering the spindly legs. A few seconds of picking through the debris turned up a wedge-shaped piece that he could shove into the gap beneath the front door. It wouldn't stop a motivated intruder, but it would slow them down.

"What are you doing?" Laleh asked as he tore a long strip of cloth from the blackout shade covering the window.

"We're sharing the bed tonight," he responded. "Get undressed. You can leave your underwear on."

"What? No! I won't let you touch me."

Rapp was in no mood to argue. "Look, I've had about three hours of sleep in the last week and I feel like someone beat me with a baseball bat. We just need to put on a show, okay?"

He went into the bathroom and examined his face. The damage Laleh had done was holding. When he rinsed his mouth, a molar came out with the water, rolling around in the basin for a moment before disappearing down the drain. Damn Joe Maslick.

On the brighter side, no visible pus, weird odors, or fever. That meant no infection. His accuracy had been dead-on and his sprint across the school courtyard felt only about five percent off. So, in the context of his current situation—and his life in general—he supposed this was what passed for a good day.

When he entered the bedroom, Laleh was sitting on the sagging mattress with a blanket pulled up around her neck. Based on the clothes laid out on the floor with OCD perfection, it appeared that she'd actually followed his instructions. He was surprised by the intensity of the relief he felt. Another knock-down dragout with her was more than he wanted to deal with right now.

Her eyes locked on him as he kicked off his shoes and fell into bed. Reaching for the lamp on the floor, he turned off the flow of kerosene and closed his eyes. They shot back open a moment later.

"Laleh?"

"What?"

It was dark, but he could tell that she was still sitting with her back against the wall.

"Don't attack me in my sleep."

"Okay."

"I'm serious, now."

"I said okay."

Her answer seemed sincere so he closed his eyes again and was asleep in less than thirty seconds.

Rapp jerked awake to a loud banging.

"Eric! Open this door immediately!" The voice was muffled but unmistakable. General Ali Mustafa.

"I'm coming!" Rapp shouted, rolling out of bed and grabbing the strip of cloth he'd torn from the shade. At some point in the night, Laleh had allowed herself to lie down, but it was hard to know if she'd slept. Right now she was staring up at him with the exact same expression she'd had before he'd shut out the light.

"Put your hands against the headboard."

"What? No. I—"

"I don't have time to argue," Rapp said quietly. "Do it."

She relented when the pounding turned into powerful kicks accompanied by the sound of splintering wood. "Eric! Open the door!"

"I'm coming!" Rapp shouted while tying her hands to the bed's flimsy headboard. He knew that she'd panic if he did a good enough job to make it hard to escape, so he kept the bonds loose. Just enough to keep the show going.

"Roll on your side with your back to me."

This time she didn't hesitate.

He pulled the blanket halfway down and unhooked her bra, sliding one strap artistically over her shoulder. "Good. Now, stay like that. You're unconscious."

He kicked her neatly arranged clothes across the floor and turned on the lamp before running out into the main room. It would have been more realistic to answer in his underwear but his well-defined muscles and patchwork of healed battle wounds weren't exactly in keeping with an overprivileged prick from Colorado.

"Stop pushing!" he yelled. "It's sticking."

He freed the wedge he'd placed beneath the door and pulled it open, stepping out of the way as Ali Mustafa entered with two armed men.

"Why didn't you—" The general fell silent when he saw the woman tied to the bed. "Ah. I see."

"I'm sorry, sir. I didn't know it was you," Rapp apologized. "Through the door, your voice—"

"It's of no importance," Mustafa said, squinting perceptibly as he examined Rapp's shattered nose. "Your face . . ."

"The bitch attacked me," Rapp said, pointing to the broken lamp lying on the floor.

Mustafa translated and his two bodyguards laughed condescendingly.

"Are you aware of what happened at our training camp?"

"No. Is there a problem?"

"It was attacked early this morning."

"Attacked? By who?"

"It appears that two men killed the perimeter guard and gained entry by saying that I had sent them."

"Have you captured them?"

"Not yet. But I swear to God I will. And when I do, I will make them suffer in ways they've never even imagined."

"How many of our people were hurt? Do you still have enough men to carry out your plans?"

This was where things got tricky—and why Rapp hadn't killed every last one of those pedophile sons of bitches. If he'd completely wiped out Mustafa's team, the general might move on to some kind of half-assed plan B. The fissile material could be split up and disappear into the hands of multiple groups, all with their own capabilities and objectives. The goal had been to take out enough men to once again make Eric Jesem's involvement desirable, but not so many as to make Mustafa's op nonviable.

"Are you all right?" the general said, ignoring Rapp's question. "Are the wounds that whore gave you serious?"

"I can't breathe through my nose but otherwise I'm nearly healed."

Mustafa nodded thoughtfully. "We still have enough men for the primary teams. I'm reinstating you to a position on the backup."

"Sir, really. I feel fine. I can—"

"You will follow my orders!" Mustafa, said, obviously in no mood to argue after the events of that morning. Rapp wondered what pissed the man off more—the deaths of his men or the fact that his underage livestock had scattered.

"Of course, sir. I'll follow your instructions to the letter."

Mustafa gave a short nod and pointed at Laleh, who was still motionless with her hands tied to the headboard. "Enjoy yourself. You leave for Saudi Arabia with the others tonight."

Chapter 44

Persian Gulf
Off the coast of Saudi Arabia

Grisha Azarov watched two men climb down the dhow's cargo net and slip silently into the water. Instead of immediately following, he remained on deck, staring out over the water. As had been predicted by Krupin's forecasters, the region was enjoying a brief respite from the wind before it returned with the sunrise now only a few hours away. Free from the suffocating heat of the vessel's hold, Azarov breathed in the salt air and examined the outline of an empty shore.

There were no lights visible other than the vague urban glow of Dammam, sixty kilometers to the south. A slightly shorter distance to the north was Al-Jubail, the city this vessel would soon set sail for in order to unload its legitimate cargo. Until then, the captain stood near the bow, looking nervously to the horizon.

Azarov finally put on a well-used dive mask and followed the men into the water. Even rudimentary scuba gear had been impossible to bring. It would have been discovered by the Coast Guard boarding party and might have raised suspicions.

He dipped beneath the swells and kicked toward the two similarly equipped men working beneath the hull. A single glow stick cast a green haze over their effort to open the container attached near the keel. They worked with impressive efficiency, something Krupin had assured him would be the case. Both men had trained on an exact replica of the dhow's hull submerged in a Russian lake.

Azarov surfaced, turning again toward shore. His mask fogged and he lifted it, making out the shadow of a small fishing boat approaching from the west. As instructed, it was equipped with an electric motor that made far less noise than a conventional outboard.

Something bobbed to the surface to his right and he glanced briefly at what would be the first of six black balloons. The men in the fishing boat were equipped with night-vision gear, making it a simple matter for them to intercept.

Azarov maintained his distance, watching them pull the crate dangling beneath the waves onto their craft. Once safely aboard, a knife was used to deflate the balloon and send it to the bottom of the Gulf. This process continued for another ten minutes. A float would splash to the surface, the men would collect the attached crate, and then the evidence would disappear. When the last crate had been retrieved, Azarov pulled himself over the side of the small vessel.

After confirming that their cargo was adequately hidden beneath a stack of fishing nets, he threw his wet clothes overboard and changed into baggy pants and a sweatshirt similar to those worn by the man steering the skiff toward shore.

Behind, he heard the engines of the dhow as it started toward deeper water. Job done, they would go back to their lives as traders and petty smugglers, as though none of this had ever happened.

The boat grounded on shore and Azarov jumped out. An SUV with two men standing next to it was visible about fifty meters away and he jogged through the sand toward them.

The vehicle turned out to be an impeccable Range Rover. The two men were equally well appointed, in tailored silk suits and traditional headdresses. In most places, their appearance would be less than subtle, but in the context of Saudi Arabia, it was relatively mundane. In fact, these men really were who they portrayed themselves to be—minor royalty who had enjoyed lives of unimaginable privilege since the day of their birth. Like so many young men with similar backgrounds, though, they had become bored. Now they played at jihad.

"Praise be to Allah that you were delivered to us safely," one of the men said, extending a hand. He had been educated in America and spoke flawless English.

"Indeed," Azarov replied, allowing his still-damp hand to be clamped in the crushing grip of overconfident youth.

While the benefit of using these men was obvious—their station in life made them largely above the law—they were not to be trusted. Creatures of comfort and entitlement, they would turn on him, and the God they professed to serve, at the first sign of danger.

The fisherman approached from behind and loaded the first two crates into the Range Rover. Of course neither of the Saudis made a move to help. Azarov knew from his time working as an energy consultant that it would be pointless to ask. They would be genuinely confused by a request that they participate in physical labor.

He wanted to minimize their time on this empty beach, so he turned and ran back down toward the boat. With his participation, they could be loaded and on the road to Al-Hofuf in less than five minutes.

Chapter 45

Al-Shirqat
Iraq

Rapp was sitting on the floor of the tiny bedroom with his back against the wall. He'd removed the makeshift shade from the apartment's only window and the morning sun was casting a dim glow over Laleh as she squinted in his direction. Her wrists were free and she was curled up beneath the covers with her dark hair tossed across her face.

"Why are you looking at me that way?" she said. "What are you thinking?"

He was thinking about the panicked girls running past him at the school. About the ones on stage being sold off to the highest bidder. About the ones still in hiding, praying to Allah to keep them safe. But most of all, he was thinking about her.

In a few hours, he would leave for Saudi Arabia to try to stop whatever attack Ali Mustafa was planning. That was his responsibility, he told himself. His only responsibility. Laleh and the thousands like her weren't a priority. They couldn't be.

"You've never told me your name," she said when he didn't answer.

"No, I didn't."

"You're Mitch Rapp, aren't you?"

Lying came easily to him, particularly on the subject of his identity. But she deserved better than that.

"Yes."

She nodded but didn't otherwise react. "You'll leave with them tonight, then. You'll stop them. Kill them."

"If I can."

"Good."

They sat in silence for a long time, the intensity of the light in the room growing with an uncomfortable inevitability.

"There's going to be no way for me to get back here, Laleh. Assuming I even survive."

"I know."

"Get dressed. I'll take you to your brothers."

"And how would you explain my absence to the men who come for you?"

"Let me worry about that."

"Thank you, Mitch. But it's impossible. My brothers are good men, but they're not like you. They're not strong enough to protect me."

"They'd want the chance to try."

"Of course. But they would fail and I would be the cause of their deaths. For what? To delay my fate another week? No. Without me, they have a chance. With me, they're dead men."

Rapp was surprised when Laleh pulled back

the blankets covering her. She was still wearing only the panties and bra he'd insisted on so as not to raise the suspicions of Mustafa and his men.

"Now come back to bed."

The chime was barely audible, but still caused Rapp to jerk awake. It was the first electronic sound he could remember hearing in days. He would have assumed it was just a dream if it weren't for the elated shouts filtering in from the street.

Rapp eased himself out of bed, careful not to wake Laleh, and walked naked into the outer room. The torn blackout shade was on the floor, so he skirted the wall and slipped up alongside the cracked glass. Below, he saw two men talking excitedly. They seemed consumed with something the one on the right had cupped in his hands.

Eric Jesem's cell phone was still charging in the window and Rapp picked it up. The screen showed three bars and a weak data signal.

Irene Kennedy making it rain. He would love to have been a fly on the wall when she asked Jimmy Templeton to pull the plug on his beloved jamming program.

Rapp punched in the U.S. country code and dialed Kennedy's private number. He didn't really expect it to go through and was surprised when an echoing ring started.

"Hello?"

"Irene! Can you hear me?"

The delay was infuriating, but she finally responded. "Mitch. Thank God. Where are you?"

"Al-Shirqat."

"Al— Suspected . . . region."

"Irene! This connection sucks. We may not have much time. What have you been able to figure out?"

When she came back on, the signal had stabilized a bit. "Not much, Mitch. We've run scenarios for the potential use of the fissile material and I've prioritized them in order of probability. But we're working more with hunches than data."

"Okay, listen. Here's what I can tell you. This thing's being run from here by one of Saddam's former Generals. Ali Mustafa. The six com-promised warheads we know about are all they have. And when I said that the CIA thought ISIS was building nukes to smuggle into the U.S., Mustafa made it clear that wasn't the plan."

"What *is* the plan?"

"I don't know, but it's starting tonight and it sounds like it's about Saudi Arabia."

"Have you seen the fissile material? We could bring teams in."

"No. And my gut says it isn't here."

"Mine, too. If it's coming from Pakistan for use in Saudi Arabia, why move it into Iraq? More likely they'd transport it up the Gulf."

"I've gotten myself in on the operation, Irene. I'm on the backup team and I leave sometime tonight."

"Understood. Everything you've told me confirms my suspicions. I don't think we're looking at nuclear explosions, Mitch."

Rapp nodded in silent agreement. If the goal was to take out Saudi Arabia, six nukes was overkill.

"The evidence that Maxim Krupin is involved keeps getting stronger," she continued. "If we add the intelligence you've managed to gather, I think the most likely scenario is a dirty bomb attack."

"So Riyadh, Jeddah, and Medina. Are you thinking they'd hit Mecca?"

"Not the cities, Mitch. The oil fields. It would destabilize Saudi Arabia to the point that they'd become vulnerable to ISIS. And after that—"

Her voice dropped before she could finish the sentence, but it didn't matter. He knew what she was going to say. After that, Kuwait, Bahrain, and the UAE would fall. Oil prices would shoot through the roof and Maxim Krupin would go from clinging to power in that shithole he called a country to master of the universe.

"Irene? Are you there? Irene!"

The line was dead.

He looked out the window and saw that the

men on the street were having the same problem. As more people discovered the network was back online, more people logged on. The system was overloaded and there was a good chance it would stay that way.

Chapter 46

Langley, Virginia
U.S.A.

Irene Kennedy sat motionless, lost in the split-screen image on her computer. To the left was a public webcam showing a swath of desert southeast of Riyadh. According to the Agency's weather forecasters, the wind was blowing north at an average of almost thirty knots, with gusts exceeding fifty. Based on the disorienting swirl of dust and sand that made up the video feed, she saw no reason to doubt them.

The other side of the monitor depicted a map of Saudi Arabia's main oil fields, with six markers spread strategically across it. Her analysts had placed them based on their best guess as to the most likely deployment of Pakistan's missing nuclear fuel. Taking into account the amount of fissile material in ISIS's hands, the prevailing winds, and the distribution of Saudi oil reserves, the markers depicted optimal release points. The current theory was that the radioactive material would be wrapped around six explosive charges powerful enough to blow it into the sky and prevailing winds would then irradiate the world's most productive oil fields.

If Maxim Krupin was directing this operation—and she was increasingly convinced he was—his people would have provided him with similar data. Was he sitting in the Kremlin at that moment examining an identical map?

Her phone buzzed and her assistant's voice came on. "I have Prince Khaled bin Abdullah on the line for you, Dr. Kennedy."

Ten minutes late, as usual. She didn't immediately reach for the handset, instead taking a moment to steel herself for the conversation. Abdullah was both extremely conservative in his religious beliefs and utterly incompetent. While he understood that Saudi Arabia needed the U.S. as an ally, he despised Christians in general and American Christians in particular. To make matters worse, he was misogynistic to the point that it made it difficult to have a coherent conversation with him.

Mitch had offered to quietly dispose of the man on a number of occasions, which was tempting. Unfortunately, the line of succession was full of even worse men. While Abdullah was an anti-American religious hardliner, at least he was a predictable anti-American religious hardliner.

Finally, she picked up the phone and spoke smoothly into it. "Your Highness. Thank you so much for taking the time to return my call."

"I have a full schedule today, Dr. Kennedy.

What is it you want that my assistant couldn't provide?"

"I recently received a disturbing report about a potential threat to your country."

"We live in a dangerous world. There's no need to become hysterical about every report that comes across your desk."

Kennedy smiled at the use of the word "hysterical." While she understood the importance of keeping Saudi Arabia's oil flowing, it was hard not to fantasize about leaving its dysfunctional royal family at the mercy of the radicals it had created.

"Of course you're right, Your Highness. But this threat seems credible and President Alexander requested that you be informed."

Predictably, Abdullah perked up a bit. By bringing up the president, she became just a messenger—something less offensive to his values.

"What are the president's concerns?"

"ISIS has obtained the nuclear fuel from six warheads and it appears that they're attempting to smuggle it into your country."

"What?" he shouted. "Why am I only hearing about this now?"

"So this is something you'd like to pursue?"

"Don't be a—" he started, but then managed to catch himself before another insult escaped. Perhaps the man wasn't as dim as she thought.

"Do they have a way to detonate it?" he asked, struggling to keep his voice even.

"We think it's unlikely."

"A dirty bomb, then."

"Our analysts give that scenario the highest probability."

"What are they targeting?" he said, his words coming in a panicked jumble. "Riyadh? Jeddah? Where are they entering our country? How many are there? Do you—"

"Your Highness! Please. Try to be calm."

"You're giving me no information I can act on!" he protested. "You tell me my country is under a catastrophic threat and you don't have even rudimentary intelligence. How can I be calm in the face of this kind of incompetence?"

The fact that his organization didn't know anything at all about it seemed to escape him. And, of course, she did have actionable intelligence. She just had no intention of sharing it with him. The moment she did, he would send patrols into the desert, likely spooking the ISIS teams and scattering them. At that point it would be virtually impossible to track them or to discover their secondary targets. Once Krupin lost control, ISIS would be free to act on its own, potentially striking Israel, Europe, or the United States.

"Confidentially, we have an informant inside

ISIS and he's working to provide us with details of their plans."

"I demand that you contact him immediately so that I can speak with him."

"I'm afraid that we don't currently have that capability, Your Highness."

"Who is this man? Where in ISIS territory is he?"

She ignored his questions. Abdullah wouldn't hesitate to contact ISIS leadership and expose Rapp if he thought it might be to his benefit.

"I assure you that we're doing everything possible to reestablish contact with him and that you'll be the first to know when we do. In the meantime, may I suggest you put your special forces on alert? When my man resurfaces, it's likely that we'll have to move quickly."

Chapter 47

Al-Shirqat
Iraq

"Shit!" Rapp said, staring down at the phone's screen. He'd never reestablished contact with Kennedy and now the signal had disappeared. By his calculation exactly eight hours after it came on.

"Is everything all right?" Laleh asked, coming out of the kitchen. She had spent the last hours cooking every MRE in Eric Jesem's collection, sampling each with infuriatingly fatalistic pleasure.

"The jamming's started again."

"Oh, that," she said dismissively. "I've just made jambalaya. It's not as good as the chicken and rice, but you should have some."

Her expression was impossible to read. The apartment had turned gloomy with the setting of the sun, putting her face in the shadow of her dark hair.

"I wanted to set up an extraction for you, Laleh. But it's not going to be possible."

"No. Of course not."

"It's time for you to get out of here," he said, holding out the phone. "Go to your brothers and tell them to take you east toward the Iranian border. That's your best bet for a signal. When you can, dial the last number in the registry and tell the woman who you are. She'll help you."

"My brothers won't leave. They're not as strong as you, but they can still fight for their home."

"Then go there and stay with them."

"I told you, my presence would be too dangerous."

"It will be worse if you don't. They'll try to rescue you again. And take it from me, they're not cut out for that kind of work."

"I'm twenty-two years old and no longer a virgin. I doubt I'm worth much more than a pack of cigarettes. But even if I was, I don't think that will be my fate. No. There will be no attempt to rescue me this time."

Rapp knew she was right. The auctioneer she'd partially blinded would take her and immediately put her to death by the most painful means possible.

"Then just leave. Better to die trying to save yourself than waiting for death to walk through the door."

She had a beautiful smile, even in the semi-darkness. "A woman alone? You know this place as well as I do, Mitch. It's impossible."

"Nothing's impossible, Laleh."

"And how would you explain my absence?"

"I'll come up with something."

"You could say I escaped but Mustafa wouldn't believe you. And if he did, he would begin to question his decision to allow you to go on this mission. Your only other alternative would be to say that you sold me, but I think he would be interested in to whom, no? He might kill you. Then the people you're trying to save will be lost. And for what? The small chance that I can make it hundreds of miles through ISIS territory and call your friend to be rescued? I don't want your blood on my hands. Or my brothers'. Or anyone else's."

Rapp was accustomed to being in charge. To solving problems quickly and permanently. Now he found himself standing in front of this girl with no solution to offer.

"Come," Laleh said. "The jambalaya is getting cold."

She disappeared back into the kitchen but Rapp remained motionless, trying to find a way out for her. Finally, he followed and sat at the table, watching her eat. When the inevitable sound of a fist against the door finally started, she didn't even seem to notice.

He walked into the outer room and opened it, taking a step back as three men entered. Mustafa had come personally, something Eric Jesem would have seen as a great honor if he hadn't been rotting in a Pakistani garbage chute.

"It's time," the general said.

Gaffar hadn't asked for his gun back and Rapp hadn't offered. It was now stuffed into his waistband near the small of his back. He could put all three men down in less than a second, get supplies from Laleh's brothers, and steal a truck. Let Saudi Arabia and the world deal with their own problems.

"Where's the girl?" Mustafa asked.

"I'm here," Laleh said, appearing from the kitchen. She still had a bit of what Rapp suspected was chili on the side of her mouth.

Mustafa indicated toward one of his men, who grabbed her by the arm. She didn't resist when he began dragging her toward the door.

"I've negotiated a very good price for you from Zaid Salib—the man she blinded. There was no amount of money he wasn't willing to part with in order to once again possess—"

"Pig!" Laleh shouted as she was dragged past the general. Something flashed in her hand and Mustafa suddenly fell silent. An expression of confusion crossed his face as he looked down at the knife hilt protruding from his stomach.

The man holding Laleh jerked her back with a startled shout, while the other lowered the general to the floor. Despite the considerable width of the chef's knife and the depth it had penetrated, Mustafa was still capable of speech. His voice was barely a whisper, but Rapp could make out enough to know that he was ordering the man kneeling over him to get someone named Najjar. Likely a doctor they had imprisoned somewhere.

Rapp looked up and focused on the girl. She met his gaze and fought to keep it as she was wrestled through the door. For the first time in their short relationship, her eyes were full of fear. Rapp pulled the Smith & Wesson from his waistband and when he took aim, that fear turned to tranquility.

The round struck her directly in the heart and she crumpled to the ground with an arm still gripped in her captor's hand.

Expressionless, Rapp looked down at her body for what was probably too long. It had always bothered his late wife that he could sleep so well after everything he'd done. She would be happy to know that those days were likely over.

The man next to Mustafa leapt to his feet and Rapp shoved him roughly back. Weakness was not an admired trait in this part of the world. Mustafa's injury at the hands of a woman and his pathetic demands for medical attention were undermining what little authority he had left. That created a power vacuum Rapp could use.

"The general has been martyred. Leave him. We have God's work to do."

The man still holding Laleh's arm gave a short nod and translated for his companion. A moment later both were retreating down the stairs. Before Rapp followed, he knelt next to the man now begging for help in breathless English.

Leaning into the Iraqi's ear, he spoke quietly. "How do you like spirited women now?"

Chapter 48

Al-Hofuf
Saudi Arabia

Grisha Azarov sat in a chair next to the apartment's dirty windows. It was a small two-bedroom, crammed with brightly colored rugs and a mishmash of peeling furniture. Hardly what he'd grown accustomed to, but unquestionably more anonymous than his normal suite at the Intercontinental. The street below, which had been bustling only an hour ago, was now largely deserted. Night was falling and the wind that was such an integral part of Maxim Krupin's plan was gaining power again.

He wiped away some of the grime from the glass and peered out at the world's most poignant reminder of America's reach: the golden arches of a McDonald's. The sign's lights flickered on, pushing his thoughts from the task at hand to Mitch Rapp.

Krupin would tell him that he was suffering from paranoia with regard to the man. That even if the CIA had managed to piece together a picture of his plan, it would be impossible for them to drill down to the level of detail necessary to lead Rapp to Saudi Arabia. The Geiger

the corner. One of them apparently spoke English, but there was no need for conversation. They had been fully briefed on the operation's protocols and already possessed the GPS that would lead them to the place where they were to detonate the bomb—in their case, a nondescript and uninhabited swath of desert more than six hundred kilometers to the southwest.

In the unlikely event that they were stopped by authorities, they would be indistinguishable from the myriad Aramco geologists exploring the area for new drill sites. Authorities would never think to examine the toolbox thoroughly enough to find its false bottom. If they did, though, they would find a powerful C-4 charge next to a container full of Pakistani fissile material. And be rewarded with a bullet in the back of the head.

"May Allah smile on you," Azarov said as they hefted the toolbox and started back to the door. One nodded his understanding and Azarov closed the door behind them.

Both men would happily die for the bizarre illusion that God cared about their brutal and pointless enterprise. That the creator of biology and the laws of physics was reliant on humans to enforce His archaic laws. If God did exist, Azarov was confident that mankind lived and died out-side His gaze.

Reminding himself that philosophizing about

the Almighty had little bearing on his survival over the next twenty-four hours, Azarov unwrapped a medium-size package that had been delivered just over an hour ago. The detonator inside was designed to his specifications by an eminently reliable Spaniard with whom he had worked in the past.

Kneeling next to another of the toolboxes lined up along the wall, he removed the false bottom and looked down at the explosive charge inside. The detonator connected to it didn't look substantially different than the one in his hands, and maybe it wasn't.

It was possible that Krupin was telling the truth; that the men Azarov was to lead into the desert would activate the bomb only after he reached a safe distance. It was a longer leap of faith than he was willing to take, though.

After replacing the existing detonator with his own, he went to his phone and replaced the software Krupin's people had installed with an application created by his Spanish associate.

Azarov watched it go through its diagnostic cycle, locating the detonator and confirming that all systems were functional. When he had green lights in all categories, he shut down the app and replaced the box's false bottom.

He had considered sending the Russian-made detonator to Madrid for examination, but then decided there would be no profit in it. Whether

Krupin intended for him to die in this operation or not was of no importance. He had no intention of doing so. Should the Russian president attempt to press the matter, Azarov would deal with him in the same way he had dealt with so many others.

Chapter 49

Northeast of Riyadh
Saudi Arabia

The sun was up, but visibility was only about a hundred yards due to the swirling sand. The SUV Rapp was driving had been modified to handle the terrain but was still struggling where the unpaved roadbed had softened or drifted over.

They'd crossed into Saudi Arabia about five hours ago at a checkpoint manned by guards sympathetic to ISIS's mission. Rapp's best guess was that they were now somewhere east of Hafar Al-Batin, headed south.

He glanced in the rearview mirror at the four men crammed into the backseat and then at the man next to him—Mihran. Rapp hadn't caught the names of the others and it was hard to ask because he assumed that Eric Jesem had trained with them at the girls' school. In fact, he was fairly certain that the one sitting directly behind him had been there the night he'd attacked the facility.

"I'm losing the road," Rapp said in English.

"Shut up and keep going straight," Mihran responded. He was staring at the screen of a Toughbook attached to a satellite link.

"It would help if I had a sense of where I'm going," Rapp probed.

"You're going south, idiot! Now find the road again and drive on it."

It was clear that he and Mihran were never going to be friends. The man had been clear from the beginning that he despised Americans—even radicalized ones. And while he spoke English quite well, he seemed embarrassed by the fact. His education at the hands of a "godless British female" had been forced on him by moderate Muslim parents and he was determined to make the world pay.

"The weapons reached al-Hofuf and are in the process of being distributed," Mihran said, switching to Arabic in an unsuccessful effort to isolate Rapp. "The operation has begun."

Excited conversation erupted in the backseat but Mihran quickly put a stop to it. "We will continue for another half hour and then hold and wait to see if we're needed. Pray to Allah that we are not."

"What's happening?" Rapp asked, as would be expected.

"Drive the car. Don't speak again unless I address you directly."

Rapp nodded submissively. It looked like Irene and her people had guessed right. If he had to put money down, he'd bet that they smuggled the weapons up the Gulf in a dhow.

After landing it on an uninhabited beach, they'd transport them by truck to al-Hofuf, which would put them within striking distance of the Saudi's most productive oil fields.

Rapp glanced over at the computer on Mihran's lap and saw their position marked in red on an empty section of map. More interesting was a similar dot moving southwest from al-Hofuf. He assumed that it depicted the position of one of the primary teams.

It was something he hadn't considered and he mentally kicked himself for the lapse. His initial reaction had been to try to convince the Iraqi general to put him on one of the attack teams, but now he realized that would have been a fatal mistake. If Krupin was behind this, he'd keep everyone on a need-to-know basis. No individual team would be aware of the status or destination of the other teams. That kind of secrecy wasn't possible for the backup, though. They would need a view of the entire game board.

"Go left here," Mihran said, pointing through the windshield at a barely visible fork in the dirt road. Rapp did as he was told and they soon arrived at a cliff band tall enough that the top disappeared into the dusty air.

"Pull in."

Rapp gunned the vehicle into a hollowed-out section of rock probably thirty feet deep and the sound of sand blasting the paint off the vehicle's exterior subsided.

They all piled out, Mihran immediately taking his laptop to the mouth of the shallow cave in order to maintain satellite reception. The others went around to the rear gate to get water. Three grabbed bottles and went for the cliff wall to maximize shelter from the wind. The fourth grabbed the last water jug and put it to his lips, taking a long pull before replacing the cap. Rapp pointed, but the young man just pulled back with a cruel smile.

He was probably no more than eighteen, with a scrawny body and scraggly beard. He'd obviously picked up on Mihran's dislike for their American comrade and was going to take a run at asserting a little authority of his own.

Rapp pretended to search the back of the vehicle for more water, but was really taking stock of what was there: primarily a zipped bag of weapons and a well-thought-out assortment of replacement engine parts. Food was minimal, suggesting that the operation wasn't expected to go on for long. Other than that, there was little more than a couple of five-gallon gas cans and some wooden stakes in case they needed to use the winch to pull themselves out of the sand.

The kid behind him took the top off the water container and started drinking again, glugging loudly in an effort to regain his attention.

Teenagers. They were the same the world over.

Rapp glanced through the windshield, confirming that he couldn't be seen by the men who had taken shelter at the back of the cave. Behind him, Mihran was in clear view but completely consumed by his computer screen, waiting for a signal that one of the primary teams was in trouble.

The boy tapped him on the shoulder, holding up the water and making a show of putting the lid back on. In response, Rapp grabbed the handle of a jack and swung it full force into the side of his head. His lifeless body hit the sand with a muffled thud and Rapp stuffed it under the vehicle before picking up the fallen container and draining a third of it.

A quick search of the weapons bag turned up several handguns and a collection of spare magazines. Rapp passed over a Kel-Tec P11 and a Ruger SR9—neither was a weapon he favored, particularly in these conditions. The Sig Sauer P226 he found at the bottom, though, was another matter.

He started around the front of the vehicle and after a few moments spotted the three men huddled at the back of the cave. He would have preferred to get in close, but without a silencer, there was no way to make this stealthy. Mihran would hear it and Rapp wasn't sure how he'd react. Better to not be too far away.

By the time he'd closed to within fifteen yards, all eyes were on him. Over the endless hours in the car, he'd become reasonably satisfied that Mihran wasn't armed but had no idea whether these men were. Now he was going to get a chance to find out.

Rapp slid the P226 from his waistband and extended it, watching the men's reactions carefully. The one on the far left dove to the ground while the one next to him crouched and began sprinting along the back of the cave. The remaining one stood his ground and reached behind him with his right hand. Rapp put him down first, hitting him in the side of the head and sending him toppling backward into the rock face. Next was the running man. His head was hidden by the angle so Rapp went for his lower back, severing his spine and dropping him into the sand. He wasn't dead, instead screaming in pain while trying to drag himself away, paralyzed below the waist.

The last man was still just lying on the ground, frozen by a combination of terror and confusion. He was staring up with wide eyes and Rapp put a bullet between them before running toward the mouth of the cave.

As he'd expected, Mihran was in a full sprint, angling toward the truck and the weapons it contained. When he saw Rapp on an intercept path, he reversed course, scooping up his laptop and heading out into the desert.

The Arab wasn't particularly fast and Rapp was content to give chase, closing from behind. When Mihran tried to open the laptop, though, Rapp stopped and lined up the P226's sights. He squeezed off a round, hitting the man in the ass and sending him rolling down a short slope to his right. The Toughbook flew from his grip and landed a few yards away. Hopefully, it would live up to its branding.

"What are you doing?" he yelled as Rapp approached. "You swore your allegiance to God!"

"Changed my mind," Rapp said, crouching next to the laptop and opening it. Still running and still logged in.

He stood and walked over to the man, aiming the pistol at his terrified face.

"Stop! What do you want? Information? I can give it to you."

"Go ahead."

"If I do, will you let me go?"

"No."

These ISIS pricks were fundamentally different than the al Qaeda operatives he'd spent much of his life fighting. Beyond having somewhat hazy goals, they lacked a consistent level of personal commitment. They fed off each other, working themselves into a frenzy using the energy of the mob. Cut off from that, many seemed small and weak.

"I want—" he started but then went silent when Rapp slammed a foot into his side.

A number of the man's ribs collapsed and Rapp just stood there watching him writhe in pain. What he really saw, though, was Laleh. The expression of terror when Mustafa's man began dragging her out of Jesem's apartment. And the relief when Rapp leveled his weapon at her.

He was only vaguely aware of the man's screams and couldn't be certain when they finally stopped. Eventually, Rapp took a step back, breathing hard and looking down at Mihran's broken neck, shattered skull, and open eyes caked with sand.

Finally, Rapp returned to the laptop, kneeling next to it and starting the process of linking to the CIA's mainframe. The security was extensive and the connection was spotty—probably due to dust interfering with the satellite connection. After a solid ten minutes, he managed to initiate a software download and route a call to Kennedy's office.

"Hello?"

"Jamie!" Rapp shouted. "Can you hear me?"

There was a long delay before she came back on. "Mitch? Is that you?"

"Connect me to Irene."

"Trans"—she dropped out for a moment—"now."

Kennedy's voice came on a moment later. "Mitch! Are you all right? Where are you?"

"Fine. About a hundred miles east of Riyadh."

"That puts you right in the middle of the Saudi's main oil-producing region," she said, though her words were difficult to decipher. "We were right."

"Yeah. Look, I'm downloading software that will allow Marcus to take control of this computer. At a minimum, it's tracking one of the teams that ISIS has in Saudi Arabia. I'm guessing it will have the capability of tracking all six once they go active."

"Marcus is on his way to my office now."

"What do the Saudis know, Irene?"

"I told them I had a man inside ISIS and that there was a potential nuclear threat, but I didn't give them any more details than that. Their special operations group is on alert and waiting for a target."

"Do they have anyone who can get to me?"

No answer.

"Irene!"

"I can do you one better," she said, coming back on. "I sent Fred Mason to Riyadh in case you needed an extraction. He and his copilot have been sleeping in their helicopter since they got there. Give me your coordinates. The weather looks bad, but I'll see if I can get him in the air."

Chapter 50

Riyadh
Saudi Arabia

A violent gust slammed into the chopper when it was only ten feet off the ground, sending it toward a series of aircraft lined up on the tarmac. Rapp braced himself as the pilot barely missed some Saudi asshole's Learjet and set the bird down with a surprising lack of drama.

"Thanks for the ride, Fred," Rapp said before removing his helmet and going for the open door.

"No problem," Mason shouted over the sound of the rotors. "Between this and Pakistan, Irene's gonna send my daughter to grad school."

Rapp jumped out, clutching the Toughbook he'd taken from Mihran. Ahead, a white SUV was barreling toward him on the runway.

It lurched to a stop a few yards away and a young man in the uniform of a spec ops officer exited. He took a few steps but then stopped short. The abruptness of it seemed odd, but then Rapp remembered what he must look like. The battered face had been bad enough, but now the bottom of Eric Jesem's pants were splattered with the story of Mihran's last moments on earth. In fact, there was still a dried piece of his scalp, complete with hair, stuck to the top of Rapp's boot. In retrospect, he probably should have scraped that off.

"Mr. Rapp?" the man said, sounding a bit uncertain. Undoubtedly, he'd heard endless stories about the CIA operative and what he saw before him didn't match the image he'd built up in his mind.

"Take me to King Faisal," Rapp said in Arabic, passing by the young officer and climbing into the back of the SUV.

"I'm afraid he's not available," the man said, taking a seat next to Rapp and slamming the door closed behind him. "I'm Captain Bazzi. I've been instructed to take you to your hotel, where you'll be met by the government's representative in this matter."

"Prince Abdullah?" Rapp said. He despised the Saudi security chief with an intensity that he reserved for only world-class scumbags. Every time he got close to the man, he could barely keep himself from snapping his neck.

"No, sir. But one of his most trusted men. My commander, Colonel Wasem."

Rapp examined the young man through swollen eyes. "The royals have all skipped the country, haven't they, Captain?"

"They're busy men, sir. A number of them had important matters to attend to in Europe."

Rapp nodded and looked out the window as the SUV accelerated. No big surprise. They'd be lying around their yachts waiting for him to make the place safe for their pampered asses again. And if he failed, they'd probably never return. Instead, they'd live out their lives in Monaco, Beverly Hills, and London, while their country was overrun.

His hotel suite was predictably gaudy—the product of a Middle Eastern decorator with too much money to spend. Rapp strode across it, his impatience turning to anger when he realized no one was there to meet him.

"We've set up a secure computer and satellite phone on the desk for your use," Bazzi said. "Clean clothing is on the bed."

"Where's Colonel Wasem?"

"My understanding is that he's on his way. He thought that you'd want to contact your people for an update before he arrived."

Rapp didn't bother to hide his contempt. There was little doubt that Wasem was somewhere in the hotel waiting for Rapp to use one of the communication devices he'd been provided. All of which were guaranteed to be compromised.

"There's food on the table. Do you need medical assistance? I can have a doctor—"

"What I need is Wasem. And for you to have five spec ops teams in choppers ready to fly."

"Yes, sir. We have people standing by, waiting for the colonel's orders."

Rapp pointed to the door and Bazzi took the hint, moving quickly toward it. When he was gone, Rapp lifted the sterling silver cover off a plate set up on a rolling cart. Underneath, he found a bacon-wrapped filet with all the trimmings. Not something you saw every day in a Muslim country. He grabbed it in one hand and carefully gnawed an end off with his undamaged teeth, chewing painfully as he used the Saudi computer to start a download from an innocuous commercial website Marcus Dumond had set up.

Next up was Mihran's Toughbook. It came to life when he opened it, but now there was just a black screen requesting a password. Dumond had already gotten control and locked it out.

Rapp sat on the desk with his back to the wall in order to thwart the cameras that were undoubtedly watching. His main Agency password was rejected, as were a number of secondary passwords he used for access to CIA front companies. It took almost ten tries, but he finally made it past the security screen. Dumond had used the password to Rapp's personal bank account. Little hacker punk.

The screen refreshed and Rapp looked down at four dots floating across a map of Saudi Arabia. All were west of Al Hofuf, spreading out through the country's main oil-producing region. The ISIS teams were staying off main thoroughfares and even appeared to be avoiding secondary unpaved roads used by Aramco, sacrificing speed for the anonymity of the open desert.

Rapp locked down the Toughbook again and checked the progress of his download on the Saudi laptop. Six minutes left to finish. Just enough time.

He grabbed a few potatoes and headed for the bathroom. Before stripping, he turned on the shower and piled the food in the empty soap-dish. His face was obviously on the mend, because the hot water hitting it produced little more than an intense sting. He lathered up his sweat-matted hair, occasionally retrieving food from the soap dish and cramming it in his mouth. As near as he could tell, the teeth he was going to lose were already gone. A few borderline ones had tightened up enough to make the potatoes no problem. The steak was going down in partially chewed chunks.

Rapp allowed himself four minutes before stepping out and going for the suite's main bedroom. A meticulously pressed desert camo uniform had been laid out for him along with a Glock 19, shoulder holster, and a few extra mags. No silencer, but still, the young captain was starting to grow on him.

The download was complete when he came back out, and he rebooted the Saudi computer. Dumond's program would disable the operating system and replace it with one he'd designed for one purpose only: security.

Rapp slid up on the desk again, pulling a wired headset over his ear and connecting the computer to the hotel's Wi-Fi. Everything coming in and out of it was now heavily encrypted and bouncing all over the world. Further, Dumond's operating system had no ability to save anything. If you received an email and needed information from it, the only recourse was to take a picture of the screen or copy it down on a piece of paper.

Rapp launched a phone app and dialed Kennedy's private number. Not surprisingly, she picked up on the first ring.

"Hello?"

"It's Mitch."

"My understanding is that you've arrived in Riyadh."

"Yeah. What's Marcus been able to find on the Toughbook?"

"Not much more than you did, I'm afraid. Its only real capability appears to be to track the ISIS teams—three more of which have come online since you've been out of contact."

"So no information on the teams' final destinations?" Rapp asked.

"None. We do have projections from our people, though, and I think they're going to be fairly close. Krupin would be working off the same weather and geological data we have. Marcus is almost done integrating all that information into the map on the Toughbook. In the meantime, I'm sending overhead photos of the areas we think they'll target. We can't reliably narrow it down to anything much less than a one-mile radius, but we're fairly confident at that resolution."

A moment later one of the photos she'd promised flashed onscreen. It depicted a nondescript area of desert with a longitude and latitude printed at the bottom. He scrolled through four similar pictures before landing on one depicting a massive tangle of gleaming pipes and tanks.

"Is this an oil refinery?"

"Abandoned production facility. It's right in the middle of those targets."

Rapp nodded silently. "Have you found the man who attacked Scott?"

"We know he's a former Russian soldier who goes by the name Grisha Azarov. Have you heard of him?"

The name rang a bell, but he couldn't put his finger on why. After a few seconds it came to him. "That Russian mobster in Africa. Before he died he said something. That Grisha was going to come for me."

"I don't know if that's true, but what I can tell you is that we don't have a current location on him."

"He's there," Rapp said. "At the production facility."

"It's a possibility we've considered. Our people agree that it would be an ideal command post. It's centrally located and provides shelter from the wind as well as a place to set up equipment. The question is whether Krupin would send his man personally."

"My gut says he would. This operation is too important and has too many moving parts to trust it to a bunch of ISIS idiots."

"I tend to agree." She paused for a moment. "Mitch, Scott's going to make a full recovery and my understanding is that Joe injured you fairly seriously."

"Your point?"

"I don't want you going up against this man. Not now."

"Yeah, me neither."

"Don't patronize me, Mitch. I'm serious about—"

As Rapp had been expecting, the door at the far end of the suite suddenly burst open. He disconnected the call as four armed men rushed him. Two aimed their U.S.-supplied weapons at his head while the others snatched the laptop from his hands and the Toughbook from the desk next to him.

Once the room was secured, a man wearing the uniform of a Saudi army colonel strode through the door. Bazzi was right behind, with an even younger man who had the unmistakable look of a computer tech.

"What took you so long?" Rapp said.

Bazzi gave a weak smile but Wasem just pointed to the computers now sitting next to what was left of Rapp's lunch. The hacker knelt and went to work on the Saudi-supplied laptop.

"The operating system has been bypassed, Colonel. There is a telephone application on-screen but the call has been disconnected."

"Who was the recipient of the call?" Wasem asked.

"There is no record."

"What do you mean no record?"

"This operating system appears to be exclusive to the CIA. I assume that all information is permanently wiped the moment it's no longer necessary."

The young man moved to the Toughbook and woke the screen. "This computer is password-protected, sir."

Wasem turned his attention to Rapp. "What's the password?"

"Don't waste my time, Colonel."

"I don't think you understand your position," Wasem said, pulling his sidearm and aiming it at Rapp. "My country is under nuclear threat and you're withholding the information I need to protect it."

Rapp slid off the desk and walked over to the table containing the computers. Instead of reaching for one, he grabbed a stalk of asparagus and took a bite off the end. "Am I supposed to be afraid?"

"Colonel," Bazzi intervened, "the Americans are our closest allies. Surely, Mr. Rapp is going to do everything in his power to help us. He wouldn't be here otherwise."

Rapp finished the asparagus and reached for another, using it to point at Wasem. "Here's how this is going to work, Colonel. You're going to get five attack choppers in the air. No missiles. Just guns. The people we're going after are carrying dirty bombs and I don't need you doing their work for them. When your men are in the air, I'll give them targets. But no one attacks until I give the order."

"So you'll be here, directing things from the safety of your hotel suite?" Wasem mocked.

"No, I'll be in a helicopter of my own on my way to take out the man running the operation."

"Out of the question. You're to give me all the intelligence you have, immediately. I will handle this personally."

"Colonel," Bazzi interjected again, "perhaps we could go with Mr. Rapp and supervise the operation from the field? That would—"

"Shut up, Captain! If I want your opinion, I'll ask for it."

"You should listen to your man," Rapp said. "Because if those birds aren't in the air soon, you're going to spend the rest of your short life explaining to King Faisal why he doesn't have a country anymore."

Chapter 51

East of Riyadh
Saudi Arabia

Azarov ignored both the GPS on the dashboard and the man driving, instead looking out the side window at the blowing sand. They'd abandoned Saudi Arabia's well-maintained road system about two hours ago and were now surrounded on all sides by nothing but empty desert and desolation.

The SUV's powerful engine roared as they crested a large dune and dropped over the other side, fishtailing down the steep slope. For a moment, Azarov thought the vehicle might roll, but the driver regained control and accelerated through the bottom. His skill was admirable. Suspiciously so.

Perhaps it wasn't the bomb that Krupin would use against him. Perhaps it was these two men. Did they have special forces backgrounds? What were their orders? Certainly, to ensure that the mission was carried out. But was there more?

"You can see it," the man in the backseat said, speaking for the first time since their initial meeting. "Just ahead."

He was right. A web of pipes and containment

tanks began to separate itself from the dust. As they closed in, Azarov could see that sand had partially reclaimed the south side of the facility. The Saudi Aramco logo on the largest of the tanks was still clearly legible, though.

He continued to study the structure as it grew in the windshield, mentally comparing it to the 3-D simulation he'd trained on. Everything appeared to be as anticipated and there was no sign of any recent human activity. Having said that, the weather system enveloping the region would obscure tracks almost as they were made. In a few minutes, evidence of even their own approach would fade from existence.

"In there," Azarov said, pointing to a gap between a vertical cylinder used to burn off natural gas and a horizontal storage tank the size of an attack submarine. The driver did as he was told, continuing forward until the drifts beneath the facility became impossible to negotiate.

"One of you take the northeast side," Azarov said, opening the door and stepping out. "The other, the southwest."

"Our duty is to protect you," the driver said. "We—"

"The best way for you to perform that duty is to warn me if anyone approaches."

Azarov hefted the backpack containing Krupin's bomb and started toward a staircase.

"Can we at least clear the area?"

Azarov didn't dignify the question with a response. The structure was far too large and complex to be cleared reliably. This was one of the reasons it had been chosen as a command center—it gave the occupying force a significant advantage. If the CIA had managed to arrive first, that advantage would be reversed and they were all dead men.

Azarov drew his weapon, more out of habit than any expectation of necessity. He followed the path laid out in his simulation, minimizing the possibility that anyone could get behind or above him. It took a full half hour, but he finally arrived at the heart of the complex, having found nothing suspicious.

"Report," he said, activating his throat mike.

"North and east clear," came the first reply. It was followed by similar assurances from the southwest.

Azarov bypassed the area that Krupin's people had told him to set up in and descended a ramp to an alternate position. Not as convenient for the operation as a whole, but more advantageous to his personal goal of surviving this fool's errand.

He slid his backpack beneath a massive valve system and took a few moments to pile sand around it. A maze of steel walls surrounded his position, protecting him from the wind but also contributing to the deafening drone of vibrating metal. He retrieved his phone and pulled up the feeds from his teams. Three were red, indicating that they were still on the move. The dot representing him had turned green, indicating that he was in position. The other two teams hadn't started their relatively short journeys yet and therefore weren't represented.

Azarov found himself forced to move to a less easily defended position in order to utilize the transmission system that had been integrated into the structure. While communications with the two men who had accompanied him could be easily handled with commercial walkie-talkies connected to throat mikes, getting a reliable signal to the other teams necessitated something encrypted and far more powerful.

Once connected, he sent Maxim Krupin a coded text informing him that all was well.

The sun was a hazy disk in the west, inflicting slightly less heat than it had the day before. Azarov sat down behind a disused oil tank, mindful that the metal was still too hot to touch with bare skin. The teams were projected to arrive at their targets simultaneously in just over four hours. They would deploy their weapons and then it would be done.

He would return to Al-Hofuf and meet with the private contractors he'd hired to get him out of Saudi Arabia. Then he would begin his circuitous route back to Central America. And that would be the last the world ever heard of Grisha Azarov.

Chapter 52

Even with Fred Mason at the controls, the helicopter felt like a toy in the jaws of a rabid dog. A violent downdraft caused them to plunge a good fifty feet, and Captain Bazzi finally looked like he was going to lose the fight to keep his lunch down.

The young officer bent at the waist and put his hands over his headphones as though to drown out the sound of the engines struggling to keep them aloft. Rapp moved his boots out of range and Colonel Wasem watched his assistant with undisguised contempt. The older man's years in Saudi Arabia's special forces allowed him to remain unaffected by the rough ride and to forget what it was like to be new at this game.

The chatter coming over the comm had gone from nervous to near panicked. Five similar choppers were hunting the scattered ISIS teams depicted on Rapp's Toughbook. The last two had finally come online only fifteen minutes ago, flashing to life and joining the other teams closing in on their targets. The one he was being carried toward had arrived at the abandoned oil facility over an hour ago and hadn't moved since. The leader.

"This is Scout Four," a voice said in Arabic.

"Winds in this sector are becoming too strong for me to safely control my aircraft. Recommend that we abort."

"Negative," Wasem said. "Continue on target."

Rapp squinted through the dust at the computer propped on his knees. Marcus Dumond had once again done his magic. Target positions were being updated in real time, with the assist of a number of military, intelligence, and hijacked commercial satellites. Their CIA-projected destinations showed up as hazy orange circles and the red dots depicting ISIS teams now included ETA countdown clocks. Blue icons tracked the chasing Saudi Air Force choppers, along with their projected time to intercept. Scout Four was southeast of their position with thirty-three minutes to intercept.

"This is Scout Five," another static-ridden voice said. "I have a visual on my target."

"How's your weather, Scout Five?" Rapp said.

"Manageable."

"Stay out of sight and keep tracking."

"Disregard," Colonel Wasem barked into his headset. "Engage the target immediately."

"Belay that," Rapp said, and then isolated his mike to include only the men with him in the helicopter. "We talked about this before we lifted off, Colonel. We wait until we've acquired all the targets and take them out at the same time."

"The plan has changed," Wasem said. "This is

not America and your CIA has no authority here. King Faisal has made it clear that I am in command of this operation. You're here only as an observer. And as such, you'll remain silent. Is that clear?"

Rapp tried to keep his voice even. This situation was too complex to let it devolve into a pissing contest. "If you take that target, their central command is going to know. And if they think they're compromised, they'll order the rest of their teams to detonate. Even if most of them are outside of their optimal position, that's going to cause a hell of a mess, Colonel."

"You have no idea what they'll do and I won't be lectured by an American about terrorists. These ISIS men are little more than goat tenders and children. They have no operational discipline and their command structure is virtually non-existent. If you don't have the courage to act, I will."

Rapp considered pointing out that the sophisticated, satellite-linked Toughbook on his knees was part of that nonexistent command structure, but it seemed like too obvious a point to bother with.

Everyone at Langley agreed that the ISIS teams would act simultaneously. There was no reason for them to risk tipping off the Saudi military before all their people were in position.

"Colonel," Rapp said, deciding to try reason

Dumond finally came back on. "If he turns pretty much right now, he might make it. But it's going to be tight. We go from having a forty-minute cushion to more like a three-minute cushion."

"Mitch," Mason said over his headset, "keep in mind that if I take that detour, I won't have enough fuel to get back to base."

"Then you'll have to do a little walking."

"Have I mentioned my ditching fee?"

Rapp picked up the laptop and held it out to Bazzi. "This is your op now, Captain. Do you understand your responsibilities?"

"Yes, sir."

"You're certain? Because if you don't, you better hope I never make it back."

The young Saudi officer nodded convincingly. "Wasem was an arrogant fool. Your strategy is the only logical one."

Rapp leaned back in his seat again, more or less satisfied. The kid was a little green but he wasn't stupid. And he seemed anxious to stay inside the chopper.

"What's the story?" Mason said over Rapp's headset. "You getting out or not?"

"Yeah."

"Then I've got some bad news for you."

"You charge extra."

"Goes without saying. But that's not the worst of it."

"What is?"

"I can land this bird, but with the wind I can't guarantee that I'll ever be able to get her back up again."

"Do we have rappelling gear?"

"That's a negative."

"So I'm jumping?"

"Yeah."

"How far?"

"Well, the way—"

"How far, Fred?"

"I can probably get you to within thirty feet. You know. Roughly."

Rapp unstrapped from his seat and moved to the chopper's open door. Dangling his legs out the side, he squinted at the desert floor flashing by. The temperature was hovering at just over a hundred, and he could feel the sun burning into the thin fabric covering his legs. There was a one-liter water bottle strapped to the side of the seat next to him and he started chugging it.

This part of the operation had always been a long shot. The hope was that he could get to the abandoned oil facility in time to neutralize ISIS's command structure before the Saudi aircraft attacked. It would significantly reduce the chances of a detonation, but it wasn't as simple as taking out a couple of guys driving through the open desert. The facility was immense, compli-cated, and hiding a force of unknown strength. Now he was going to have to cover a lot of ground on foot with no practical way to carry water and armed only with a Glock that might or might not shoot straight.

Fred Mason's voice came over the comm as they slowed to an unsteady hover above the southern face of a massive dune. "This is about the best I can do, Mitch."

"You've got to be kidding."

"What are you complaining about? I don't see any rocks."

Rapp removed his headset and put his feet onto the skids, leaning out over the desert. A gust caused the helicopter's nose to dip and he let go, falling for what felt like way too long before hitting the sand and plummeting down the slope. He didn't fight it, staying relaxed and letting gravity do its work until he bogged down twenty feet from the bottom.

Chapter 53

Rapp lay on his stomach in the sand, completely motionless. There was no sign of life in the oil-production facility intermittently visible four hundred yards away. But that was expected. His gut told him the ISIS men were there. The question was how many, how well armed, and in which of a thousand tactically viable positions?

A particularly strong gust tore across the landscape and Rapp leapt to his feet, running almost fifty yards before being forced down again by the clearing air.

While waiting for another opportunity to advance, he examined the details of the structure. At this range, the size and complexity of it made a serious impression. Countless thousands of tons of steel had been fashioned into a maze of pipes, ladders, and walkways. The sand was drifted up beneath one end but otherwise the facility looked like it could still be in operation.

His earpiece started to crackle, but the bulky radio clipped to his belt wasn't enough to fully pick up the signal. He maxed out the volume and a few intelligible words emerged from the static. Bazzi checking in with his men. Responses were spotty due to the limitations of Rapp's equipment, but the Saudi officer's calm tone suggested that the remaining choppers were all still in the air.

"This is Scout Six," Rapp said into his throat mike. "Come in, command."

"Go ahe—" Static drowned out Bazzi's voice. "I repeat. Go ahead, Scout Six."

"I've got too much ground to cover and not enough time, Captain. If I move fast, I'm going to risk being spotted and blowing this whole thing to shit."

"Copy that, Scout Six. I understand that you're going to hold your position until I give the attack order. Please confirm."

"That's an affirmative, command. Good luck."

"May Allah be with you, Scout Six."

"How much longer?" Captain Bazzi said into his headset.

"The ETA on your screen's about right," Mason responded. "A little less than five minutes."

"That's cutting it very close, Mr. Mason."

"I'm dealing with the laws of aerodynamics up here, Captain. Unless God owes you a serious favor, this is as fast as we go."

Bazzi saw no reason to question the man further. He had flown with Saudi Arabia's best pilots and none were even remotely as skilled.

The engines were pushed to—or perhaps past—their limit and no compromises were being made in the interest of safety. Outside the door to his left, the desert floor was speeding by far too close for the conditions and visibility had gone from poor to disastrous.

On the laptop screen, the dots continued to glow, indifferent to his situation. The CIA was constantly updating the data and as of now they were projecting the soonest possible detonation at approximately seven minutes.

"Status report," he said into his headset.

Every one of his men responded that they were in position and holding, one minute out from their target.

Bazzi wiped the gritty sweat from his forehead and continued to stare at the screen. In the end, there was only one realistic option—to follow Mitch Rapp's orders to the letter. The man had more experience in these kinds of operations than anyone alive and his list of failures was shockingly short. Further, if the worst happened, his reputation suggested that he could be counted on to take responsibility and stand in support of a meaningless young Saudi captain. Men like him—and American soldiers in general—were loath to turn their backs on people loyal to them.

"Hold your position and await my orders," Bazzi said, realizing that those were likely the most critical words he would ever speak. "We will be going in approximately two minutes."

Those one hundred twenty seconds seemed to stretch into infinity as he stared blankly at the seat that he wished Mitch Rapp still occupied. Finally, Mason's voice came over his headset.

"We're one minute out, Captain."

Bazzi activated his own microphone. "Attack. I repeat. Attack."

He took a position at the helicopter's door gun as his teams confirmed his orders.

A few moments later, Mason came back on the comm. "I have a visual. Northwest about a kick. Hold on to your ass."

Bazzi was slammed into the bulkhead and then into the gun as the pilot fought to put them into an attack posture. The helicopter circled east and Bazzi saw the target vehicle's trajectory turn evasive. They'd been spotted.

Mason came to the same realization and immediately rotated the aircraft to bring the door gun to bear. The wind was now hitting them broadside and the chopper pitched wildly as Bazzi depressed the trigger.

The first rounds stitched across the SUV's hood and he fought to adjust his aim to its passenger compartment. The CIA's best guess was that the terrorists would be using military-grade C-4, a stable explosive that was unlikely to detonate even if it took a direct hit. The danger was that one of the men in the vehicle had the detonator in hand and at the ready.

The helicopter rocked back and Bazzi struggled to stay on target, ripping a line of gaping holes down the center of the vehicle before the rounds started slamming into the sand behind.

"Down!" he shouted. "Bring us lower!"

Mason did as he was told and Bazzi managed to realign his sights on the vehicle's front windshield. When he opened fire, it swerved right and overturned, rolling down a steep slope to the east.

Mason tried to pull up, but it was impossible. The rotors were kicking up a dense cloud of sand now, blinding Bazzi as he tried to back away from the door.

"That's it, Captain! Hang on! We're going in!"

He braced himself as Mason tried to control their descent. The soft sand absorbed some of the impact but also created an unpredictable surface that was impossible to compensate for. Bazzi was thrown backward as one side of the chopper sank and the rotors dug in.

When he struggled back to his feet, he registered that his right arm was broken. Not so badly that he couldn't use it to escape, though. He climbed out of the open door, ignoring the pain, and running toward the SUV lying on its side fifty meters away.

The man in the passenger seat was still belted in place but most of the right side of his head was missing. The driver had been thrown from the vehicle and was laying facedown ten meters away.

While neither of them appeared to be capable of detonating the weapon, the danger of a remote activation was still very real. The SUV's doors and rear gate were still shut and Bazzi was unable to get them open. Instead, he used his good hand to push out the spiderwebbed rear window and then began dragging a large toolbox through the opening.

It was an agonizingly slow process, but he managed to get it halfway out before a gun sounded behind him. Pain flared in the back of his right thigh and his leg collapsed beneath him. From his position on the ground, he could see that the driver was on his feet, staggering in his direction with a pistol. The next round hit the side of the car only a few inches from Bazzi's head as he tried to draw his own sidearm with his injured arm.

A rapid burst of shots erupted before he could get his pistol clear of its holster and Bazzi flattened himself in the sand. When the sound faded he looked up, confused by the fact that he was still alive. That confusion was amplified when he saw the driver motionless in the sand. Finally, he glanced back and saw Fred Mason collapse to his knees with an assault rifle in his hands.

Bazzi limped back to the window and wrestled the toolbox the rest of the way out of the vehicle. It took what seemed like a lifetime, but he managed to empty its contents and find evidence of a false bottom. Aware that it could explode at any moment, he fought to keep his hands from shaking.

The release for the bottom was relatively easy to locate and he was relieved to see that the explosive was less complex than he'd anticipated—nothing more than a digital keypad connected to a block of C-4. Next to it was a sizable sheet metal box that he assumed contained the radioactive material.

Bazzi removed the detonator probe and let out a long breath before clamping a hand over his leg wound and lurching toward Fred Mason. The pilot gave him a weak thumbs-up from his position lying in the sand, so the Saudi officer went to the chopper instead. He put on a headset and tried to get a situation report, but the comm was dead.

After a few pointless attempts to get it working, he went forward to check on Mason's unconscious copilot. Their role in this was done. The rest was in God's hands.

"Command," Rapp said into his comm. "This is Scout Six. Come in."

Once again, no response.

He'd been able to make out two confirmed kills but the rest of the chatter was too garbled to understand. Had Bazzi and the others achieved their missions? Or was there a massive radioactive cloud drifting north across Saudi Arabia?

In the end, it made little difference. One way or another, the other scouts were finished with their mission. His was just beginning.

Rapp was still about three hundred fifty yards out—a distance he had deemed safe. If a couple of ISIS fanatics were running this operation from the interior of the facility, they would immediately detonate when they discovered their comrades were under attack. But that hadn't happened. The complex was still intact and there was still no sign of life. Either the Agency's analysts were full of shit and the facility was empty or the man with his finger on the button had no interest in martyring himself.

Azarov.

Chapter 54

"Please repeat your last."

Grisha Azarov reluctantly pushed an earpiece the rest of the way into his right ear. The left was already taken by a radio link. Combined, they muffled the clang of a loose piece of sheet metal above him, but also isolated him from his environment in a way that was always dangerous.

"I am showing all teams moving into position," Maxim Krupin said. "ETA is eight minutes. Confirm."

It seemed pointless since they were looking at the same satellite data, but the Russian president would leave nothing to chance. Azarov used a hand to shade his cell phone and examined the washed-out map image.

"Eight minutes confirmed."

"You have my authorization to carry out the operation. When all teams are in position, signal them to detonate."

"Understood."

Azarov sat with his back against the thick steel plate that made up one side of an enclosure that was one of the most defensible in the complex. After that, time started to pass with almost super-natural slowness. He was accustomed to the mind-numbing lulls of combat, but this one was intensified by the fact that it would likely be his last. He allowed his mind to drift forward—to enjoy the luxury of considering something beyond being victorious on the day. What would it be like to wake up in his home and have no mission to prepare for? No training schedule to obsessively follow or physical test to complete?

Would he . . . fish? It was something he hadn't done since sawing through the frozen lakes of Russia with his father. Or perhaps surfing lessons would be in order. Cara had offered a free introduction to the sport on a number of occasions. Was it time to consider accepting that offer?

A shrill alarm sounded in his remaining earpiece and he looked down at his phone. One of the ISIS teams had gone offline. He assumed it was just a communications problem that would quickly correct itself. Instead, a second alarm sounded and another of the tiny onscreen dots flashed out of existence. The intensifying storm? Or something else?

Azarov connected to the operation's open frequency. "All teams report."

Static.

"All teams report," he repeated.

Still no response.

It was more than could be explained by the

storm. The images on his phone were being transmitted by a satellite link, while voice communications were being handled by a radio-based system. The chance that both were failing at the same time was remote in the extreme. Much more likely, the ISIS teams had been discovered and either succumbed to attack or detonated without his authorization.

The next sound that came over his earpiece wasn't an alarm but a notification of another call from Maxim Krupin. He was monitoring the operation from the comfort of his office in the Kremlin and would be concerned by what he was seeing.

Azarov ignored the call. If the other teams had been discovered, then this place would likely be known to the enemy as well. Attacking the large, complex facility, though, would be significantly more difficult. Did he still have time to escape? The storm would provide cover and if necessary he could—

"Contact north."

The English coming over the radio was excellent, tainted only by a moderate Dutch accent. Hassan was the son of Syrians who had settled in Amsterdam—a store clerk who had become bored with his life and joined ISIS.

"Details?"

"It appears to be a single man. Approaching on foot."

Azarov closed his eyes and let out a long breath. The mental image of his home in Costa Rica, so vivid a few minutes before, began to lose focus.

"Did you say a single man? Confirm."

"Affirmative."

"Keep eyes on the target."

The Russian moved from his protected position and navigated the convoluted collection of ladders, catwalks, and ramps that led to the northern edge of the facility. He crawled the last ten meters, setting up in a well-camouflaged position with a gap wide enough to get a spotting scope through.

He had to admit to being impressed by Hassan's attentiveness. With the blowing sand, it took Azarov almost ten seconds to spot the figure running down the back of a dune some one hundred fifty meters away.

The most immediate impression was that the man was extremely fast. While perhaps not as powerful as he himself was, this lone attacker's skill at negotiating the soft desert surface was unquestionably superior.

Finer details became apparent as the distance between them narrowed. He was wearing the uniform of a Saudi soldier but with no visible insignias. Weaponry appeared to be limited to a single handgun holstered on his hip. Much more interesting, though, was his face. At first Azarov assumed it was just heat distortion but he could now see that this assumption was in error. The man's nose was badly broken and both eyes were blackened. Partially hidden by a thick beard, his lips were split and distorted, complementing similarly swollen cheekbones.

In another world, watching this man charging their position alone would have been almost comical. But this wasn't another world and there was only one man with this combination of speed and audacity.

"Rohab," Azarov said, connecting to his men again, "join Hassan on the north end of the facility. Engage and kill the man approaching."

"I understand," came the reply.

If this was indeed Mitch Rapp, the tactical situation presented some interesting opportunities. The American was clearly injured, had run an undetermined distance in the oppressive heat, and was unlikely to be familiar with the structure that he was approaching.

While escaping and luring Rapp to northern Russia still had benefits, it also had a number of drawbacks. Rapp would have the full resources of the CIA behind him while Azarov would be alone. With no urgency on the American's part, he would have significant control over the time of their next meeting and would use that time to heal and plan.

The more Azarov considered the situation, the

more it became obvious that the moment for this confrontation was now. After he killed Rapp, he would contact Irene Kennedy and propose a truce. She had the reputation of being an eminently reasonable woman and would see no profit in risking more of her men in a pointless quest for revenge.

A gust struck from the south, kicking up an opaque cloud of sand that blasted the skin on Azarov's hands and face. When it cleared, the man was gone.

Chapter 55

Rapp dropped to his stomach, ignoring the searing heat of the sand beneath him. There was still no sign of opposition, but he now had a solid view of the north side of the facility. Azarov would hang back—sacrifice any pawns he had in hopes of getting lucky or at the very least wearing Rapp out.

Those pawns would likely be handpicked from ISIS. Even if they had military experience and additional spec ops training, these weren't SAS or Delta. In his experience, they would lack any capacity for subtlety or out-of-the-box thinking. They'd take the most obvious positions and attack at the first opportunity. No matter what the job, jihadists could always be counted on to reach for the hammer.

When the next gust hit, he sprinted through the opaque dust cloud it created. The soft sand gave way to concrete and he slowed, squeezing between two upright pipes and keeping to where the tangle of machinery was most dense. It robbed him of his ability to see much more than five feet in a straight line, but that limitation would go both ways.

Rapp pulled his Glock and started weaving through the steel maze. There was an obvious vantage point on the second level, about fifteen yards to his right. He himself might have been attracted to it in his younger days. The position would provide an unobstructed view north, as well as reasonable protection from the wind. Even more advantageous, practical access from below was blocked by a massive cylindrical tank.

Rapp spotted a drift that went almost to a catwalk ten feet above and began climbing it. At the top, he had to dig to widen the gap between the sand and the metal grid, but managed to get through without making a sound loud enough to rise above the wind.

He inched forward through the dangerously confined space. After a few feet, he spotted a boot protruding from behind a steel plate. Rapp looked at the Glock in his hand and then reluctantly holstered it. Without a silencer, using the gun would be too much of a risk.

He found a broken pipe and quietly dug it from the sand. While not exactly sharp, one end looked jagged enough for his purposes. He kept moving forward, slipping from beneath the catwalk and continuing along the drift as it climbed toward a hard ceiling of electrical conduits.

After about a minute, he had a full view of his target: Middle Eastern male, lying prone, searching the desert through a scope mounted to an AK-47.

The angle of the sun was going to be a problem.

Rapp had it at his back, which was normally an advantage, but in this case it would cause him to throw a shadow. He stayed low to minimize the problem, but there was no way to change the laws of physics. His shadow moved steadily up the man's back and finally entered his peripheral vision when Rapp was still almost ten feet out.

The terrorist rolled, desperately trying to swing the AK with him. The confined space that was slowing Rapp's approach had a similar effect on his target. The rifle's barrel caught on the edge of a drain lever and a moment later Rapp drove the broken end of the pipe into the man's sternum. He threw his full weight behind it and managed to drive the steel down until it hit concrete.

Rapp immediately retreated, suspecting that the dead man was working as part of a two-man team. That suspicion was confirmed when automatic fire erupted from below and rounds began sparking off a storage tank to his right.

Rapp vaulted a railing and sprinted for a set of stairs to the west, unable to see the man firing. The steps were solid steel plate and he could feel the vibration of bullet impacts as he took them three at a time.

The shooter was still invisible below, but it was clear that he was firing from the left. Ahead, the stairs dead-ended into a T. To the right, they continued up and eventually disappeared into the glare of the sun. To the left was a low gate blocking access to a steel mesh catwalk.

When he reached the T, Rapp feinted right and then went left, leaping over the gate and landing on the catwalk. The shooter had anticipated him continuing up the stairs, and the rounds pounded along them as Rapp drew his Glock.

Through the open weave beneath his feet, he immediately spotted his target: a single man in the process of adjusting his aim from the stairs to the American standing above him.

There was no clear angle, so Rapp just aimed through the steel mesh and began firing. He stayed on target, pumping five rounds into the catwalk before a bullet finally got through clean. It hit the man in the collarbone, causing him to lose control of his weapon and spray a girder above him. A moment later, the right side of his head was torn away. He'd been taken out by one of his own ricochets.

Rapp jumped the guardrail and dropped ten feet into the soft sand next to the body. A quick search turned up a throat mike and he removed it, closing it around his own neck and inserting the earpiece. No one was on the comm, so he activated the microphone and jabbered breathlessly in Arabic.

"I killed him! I'm the only survivor, but I won. The man is dead!"

The voice that responded had a distinct Russian inflection. Not unexpected, but the sound of it still made Rapp grip his Glock a little tighter.

"Hassan. Calm down. Speak in English."

Rapp repeated the sentiment in the requested language but with a distinct Arab accent.

There was a good five seconds of silence before the voice came back on. "My compliments on the speed and stealth of your approach, Mr. Rapp. And with how efficiently you were able to deal with my men. But Hassan was Dutch."

"Sometimes you have to play the percentages," Rapp said.

"It's what I would have done."

"You've lost, Grisha. Why not just surrender? You don't owe Maxim Krupin anything. Sure as hell not your life."

"What you say is true. But I suspect that the future you have planned for me isn't one I would enjoy."

"Maybe we can work something out."

"You would never agree to my demands."

"Are you sure?" Rapp said, checking his magazine and starting toward a ladder to the south. "Try me."

This time the silence stretched out even longer. Finally, Azarov responded. "What I want, Mr. Rapp—what I need—is for you to never leave this place."

Chapter 56

Rapp inched forward on the steel mesh catwalk and then swung smoothly around the corner with his Glock stretched out in front of him. The walkway continued through a corridor of pipes before disappearing behind what looked like a small office.

He was near the facility's high point, following a pattern that avoided choke points where Azarov might be waiting. The longer he could put off their inevitable confrontation, the better.

While Rapp had never been particularly good with names or phone numbers, he had a photographic memory for battlefields and tactical situations. He'd won a fair amount of money in college betting people that he could remember the positions of every person on a lacrosse field at any given moment in a game. Now he was using that unusual ability to create a detailed mental map of the facility.

Unfortunately, its size and complexity were taxing even his considerable talents. It was separated into three sections, largely inaccessible to each other—possibly to contain fires or explosions. There were four loosely defined levels accessed via countless ladders, steps, and ramps. Mesh walkways of varying widths snaked in every direction, diving in and out of view as they faded into the dusty air.

He started forward, moving his head back and forth, taking in everything. About halfway to the office, he crouched beneath a small overhang. The boots he'd been provided were good in the sand, but a disaster on the thin steel he was moving across. They were not only heavy, but also caused a dull ring with every footfall. Rapp was reluctant to abandon them, but decided that it was the better of his two bad options.

He covered the remaining length of the walkway in stocking feet, noting that his footfalls were now completely inaudible and that his traction wasn't too badly compromised. On the downside, the steel was hot enough to burn through to his feet.

Rapp slipped through the open door to the office and ducked below an empty window frame. The room was probably only ten feet square and full of debris not worth taking when the facility was abandoned. A spitting image of the place where Azarov had taken out Scott Coleman. Hopefully, not an omen of what was to come.

He pawed through the files, furniture, and tools on the floor, looking for anything useful. No ice-cold Cokes or silencers were on offer, but he did find a pile of old work clothing that was of interest. Like his abandoned boots, the tan uniform had been useful in the sand but was less than optimal in a complex built primarily of unpainted steel. The gray overalls wadded up in the corner would provide better camouflage and had the potential to confuse his opponent's expectations. They even turned out to be his size.

Better yet was a pair of well-used socks that he pulled on over his own. They added just enough insulation to protect his feet from the sun-heated metal and would mitigate any damage should he hit a jagged edge or have to move fast.

Rapp started crawling back toward the door when he spotted a large wrench beneath an Arabic language newspaper. He wrapped it in the pants he'd taken off and shoved it down the back of his overalls. It wasn't the most convenient thing to carry into battle, but he had an idea that might make it worth the weight.

Rapp stayed low as he came back onto the catwalk and turned left. He covered the next fifty yards in a little less than a minute, continuing to mentally map the maze around him. As he was nearing a set of steps connecting two catwalks, his peripheral vision detected motion above and to his right. Instinctively, he threw himself backward and fired in the direction of the movement. Just as he did, a bullet sparked off a pipe directly to the left of where his head had been a split second before.

● ● ●

Grisha Azarov ducked involuntarily when a bullet hissed past him at what he estimated was a distance of less than a meter. His own shot had been perfectly aligned, but Rapp dropped to the ground an instant before it could find its mark.

The Russian immediately began analyzing the rare failure. As expected, Rapp was extremely quick and had razor-sharp battlefield instincts, but these gifts weren't the reasons he was still alive. That was Azarov's own fault. He'd been looking for a man in Saudi army fatigues and the change had caused him to hesitate. A brief sliver of time that against any other opponent would have been meaningless. Against Mitch Rapp, it was the kind of mistake that could prove fatal.

Now there was nowhere for the CIA man to go—he was stranded in the low ground with little overhead cover. Azarov sprinted toward a ladder and climbed halfway up it, leaping onto an immense pipe and landing with a deep ring that resonated through the air. He let his momentum carry him to a three-meter gap that plunged down to the base of the facility. Falling forward onto his stomach, he thrust his pistol over the edge of the narrow platform he'd come to a stop on. Rapp was one level below, running along the only catwalk accessible to him. His back was square to Azarov's position. An easy shot even for a novice.

He lined up, but before he could fire, Rapp vaulted the railing and fell toward the top of a containment tank no more than two meters in diameter. The reason he'd been able to run so silently became evident when he landed. His stocking feet provided no purchase on the smooth steel and he slid out of control toward its edge. A moment later, he was gone. Azarov heard the dull thuds of a body bouncing through the pipes on its way to the ground. While impossible to see from his current position, he knew that it was at least a thirty-meter drop. Impossible even for the storied Mitch Rapp to survive.

The Russian continued to aim over the top of the platform, his heart rate higher than it had been on an operation in years. It was difficult to conclude anything but that the man had fallen. Removing his boots had been a reasonable risk to take, but in this case the strategy had failed. Mitch Rapp was either dead or dying, his broken body bleeding into the sand.

Then why was he still afraid of the American? It seemed inconceivable that Rapp had survived, but until Azarov saw the body, the possibility existed. As much as he wanted to retreat to the SUV and escape across the desert, he couldn't bring himself to do it. Not until he was certain of the CIA man's fate.

• • •

Rapp threw himself to the catwalk, already certain that the Hail Mary shot he'd taken at the Russian had gone wide. He immediately rolled to his feet and began sprinting toward a series of tanks about ten feet from the edge of the right hand railing.

If he were Azarov, he'd climb halfway up the ladder to his left and then use a large pipe to gain a platform that jutted out over open air. It would provide a perfect position to fire down on Rapp's unprotected position.

He was only about halfway to the tanks when the ring of someone landing on that very overhead pipe sounded—a full second sooner than Rapp thought possible. He pushed himself to a speed that felt like it was going to shatter his bad knee with every stride.

The second ring reached him when he was still ten feet out from the section of railing he was he was going for. Azarov would be lining up and this time he wouldn't miss.

Rapp leapt the rail earlier than planned but still managed to clear the gap, landing on top of a tank and going into an uncontrolled slide toward the opposite edge. He tumbled over and dropped five feet before grabbing a steel grid that, thank God, was right where he remembered it. The Glock was still in his left hand and stopping his momentum with only his right

risk. However, there was an open pipe
ix feet in diameter ahead of him and only
 four feet were visible from Rapp's
. It was Azarov's only option, and it
a bad one. He undoubtedly knew where
hile Rapp had no idea.

ongated shadow appeared at the entrance
pipe and Rapp unloaded his entire clip
 confined space, firing a wide, random
He pulled back and slammed in his last
gazine before rising again. The shadow
e but there was something near the edge
 pipe that he didn't remember seeing
Rapp thought it might be rust, but when
ed to a better vantage point, the dark
 took on a familiar color.

.

kept moving through the pipe, not
 until it took a hard bend to the right.
en did he pull up his soaked sleeve to
 the neat hole in his biceps. It was
 badly but the ricochet had passed
 without hitting bone. He pulled off
 and tied it around the wound, sitting
he curved wall to catch his breath.
had Rapp survived the fall from that
nd more important, how had he crossed
barrier without using the high catwalk?
y answer was that somehow the CIA

demanded a graceless maneuver that nearly dislocated his shoulder.

Once he got his feet under him, he yanked the wrench from his overalls and threw it down at the pipes below. The fact that it was wrapped in cloth kept it from ringing against the metal, instead giving it a muted thud that would be fairly convincing mixed with the howl of the wind.

The Russian was in an adjacent section of the facility and there was no easy way for him to cross over. That made it possible for Rapp to take his time climbing down and gaining a walkway twenty feet below. What would Azarov do now? Was he trusting enough to go for his vehicle and run? Or would he want to confirm that his adversary was dead?

Probably the latter, Rapp decided. The question was what to do about it. Though he and Azarov couldn't easily get to each other, the Russian did have access to a vantage point that would allow him to see that his opponent's corpse was conspicuously absent. That left Rapp with a short window where he could use the element of surprise. The problem was that the only way he knew of to cross to Azarov's sector was an open catwalk on the top level. By the time he reached it, the Russian would know his opponent was alive and would be looking for the move.

Rapp traversed the walkway, protected by a

man understood this complex better than he himself did. If that was the case, then he knew where this pipe let out and that there was only one vantage point that would allow him to see both ends simultaneously. Was he currently making the difficult climb to get there, or would he risk chasing his injured quarry?

Speculation was pointless. Azarov had failed to predict the man's actions at every turn. The question that had existed for so long in the recesses of his mind was now answered. Rapp was the better man. The weaker, older American was going to kill him.

No.

Not now. Not when he was on the verge of escaping Maxim Krupin's orbit and pursuing a life of his own. An identity of his own.

Azarov unwrapped his wound and used the back of the shirt to sop up the blood flowing from his arm. When the cloth was well impregnated, he tore off part of the left sleeve and used it to rebandage his arm. Finally, he put the shirt back on. The blood on the back would make him appear more badly injured than he really was. Hopefully it would be enough to lull Rapp into a moment of carelessness.

Azarov started moving along the interior of the pipe again, forced into a slight crouch by the confined space. Even if Rapp did know the facility better than he did, it would be difficult for the man to reach the far end of the pipe in time to line up a reliable shot.

Azarov told himself that if he remained focused, if he timed everything to perfection, there was still a chance that he would be the one who survived.

Rapp stayed high, moving from catwalk to catwalk as he tried to figure out where the pipe Azarov was hiding in led. After a few minutes it became clear that he wasn't going to be able to keep the entrance in view if he went much farther. For all he knew, the pipe didn't go anywhere and the Russian was sitting a few feet inside, waiting to attempt an escape. Or he could be dead. Or—as likely as the first two scenarios—he could be running along it looking for a way out.

Rapp stopped, suffering a rare moment of indecision. The only thing he was sure of was that he didn't want to go in after the man—it was too confined a space. So forward or back? His gut said forward and he decided to listen. While his battlefield intuition had failed him more than a few times, it was right more often than it was wrong.

He dropped onto a tightly packed series of pipes before crossing to an adjacent catwalk. When he lost sight of the pipe entrance, he increased his pace to a point that it would be impossible for Azarov to come up behind him. Even at that speed, it took him almost five minutes to reach the place where the pipe disappeared into a large storage tank. A hatch on top was open and Rapp slowed, aiming his Glock upward when he spotted movement.

Azarov had cleared the tank and was lurching along a catwalk more than fifty yards away. Based on his awkward gait and the amount of blood that had soaked through his shirt, he looked to be in pretty bad shape.

Rapp moved into a position behind the man, initially hanging back to reduce the chance of being spotted. Eventually, he started to close the gap, lifting his pace only when he had a clear understanding of his surroundings and a solid view of his still-dangerous opponent.

Azarov was bleeding enough to leave a visible trail and his movements were becoming increasingly labored. Further, he was heading into territory that would put him at a significant tactical disadvantage. The terrain got physically more demanding and he was going to hit the edge of the facility in a position that would make it easy for Rapp to get above him. Pain, blood loss, and desperation could do terrible things to a man's judgment—particularly one so talented that he might never have been faced with those challenges. He was checkmating himself.

Or was he? Rapp stopped at the bottom of a set of steps.

While it looked like Azarov was barely putting one foot in front of the other now, he'd made pretty good time in that pipe. And the blood trail was heavy enough to follow but not heavy enough to suggest the man was bleeding out.

The Russian had wanted to force this confrontation when he believed he had the tactical advantage. Now, though, that advantage had been lost. He was smart enough to know that. And if that was the case, he was probably also smart enough to be looking for a way out.

Rapp spun and started sprinting in the opposite direction, dropping his weapon and launching across a ten-foot gap to a ladder. He gripped the sides with his hands and feet, dropping down it in a near free fall before hitting the catwalk below. The east edge of the facility was visible ahead and he ran toward it, taking every opportunity to drop down to lower levels. He was only a few yards away when the blast hit him.

The force of it threw him over the guardrail and he didn't bother fighting it. The sand and sky looked pretty much identical as he went end over end through the air, making it necessary for him to use the rising flames to orient himself. He cleared the concrete slab and landed feetfirst in the sand, immediately pitching forward and trying to roll with the impact.

Dazed, it took him a few seconds to realize that his hair was on fire. Once he'd patted it out, he just lay there staring up at the debris arcing through the sky. Azarov would have dropped off the north side before triggering the explosion and would now be following the wind into a radioactive no-man's-land intended to discourage a chase.

Rapp considered defying the man's expectations and going after him, but the idea faded quickly. He'd had enough of Grisha Azarov for one day.

Chapter 57

"Just keep holding the ice bag to it," the camouflage-clad nurse said.

"That's it?" Rapp responded. "That's your expert advice?"

His nose had started bleeding again after the explosion and despite every effort by him and the army's medical team, it wouldn't stop.

"I've seen a lot of stuff, sir. But that nose . . . how did it happen?"

"Angry woman."

She let out a hesitant laugh but then fell silent when he didn't smile. "Sir, I'd suggest you get stateside as soon as possible and find the best plastic surgeon you can."

Since no one in the medical tent seemed to be in danger of telling him anything he didn't know, Rapp wandered out into the night.

Lights had been set up to illuminate the temporary American base, their powerful beams extending into the desert well past the two-hundred-yard perimeter. He stopped to let a truck carrying hazmat suits roll by and then crossed a section of compacted sand that functioned as road.

Two choppers passed overhead, angling north toward the radiation zone Grisha Azarov had created. Surprisingly, it was the only one. Bazzi and his men had managed to take out all the ISIS teams without giving any of them time to detonate. That left Rapp owning the only failure.

When he got home, Kennedy would casually mention—repeatedly—that backing Azarov into a corner had been a mistake. Of course, Rapp would passionately defend his actions and there would be no clear winner. There never was. In this case, though, she was more right than wrong. In the heat of the moment he hadn't been able to see that it was a contest that could only have losers. Chalk it up to too many years of examining problems through a set of gun sights.

"Mitch!"

Rapp turned and saw Mike Nash jogging toward him. When he pulled alongside, he was noticeably out of breath. The muscle weight he'd added apparently helped his back but wasn't doing much for his stamina.

"I know I've already told you this today but I want to make sure I drive home the point. You really look like shit."

"Thanks."

"Can't they get that thing to stop bleeding?"

"They tell me I should see a doctor."

"Your tax dollars at work."

"Where do we stand?"

Nash shoved his hands in his pockets against the cool desert evening. "So far the Saudis are letting us take the lead. The royals are still cowering in Europe and it's thrown a wrench into their chain of command."

"Probably better for us."

"No doubt. And I have even more good news. We found Colonel Wasem's body and Bazzi's backing up our story that it was an accident. Apparently, he couldn't stand that asshole."

"And the bad news?"

"That's a longer list. One of the fissile material containers was breached by a door gun. Not ideal, but nothing that can't be taken care of by removing and disposing of a few thousand tons of sand. The main site is a whole other story. We're still trying to figure out how far the radioactivity has spread, but because of the wind it's going to be pretty bad. Best-case scenario, the cleanup is going to cost three quarters of a billion dollars and reduce the area's oil production by ten percent for the better part of five years."

"Tell the Saudis to write a check. What about—"

"Hold on. I'm not done. The Team Four chopper that went down had no survivors and the Pakistanis are already up our asses to get what's left of their fissile material back."

"Now are you done?"

"Yes."

"What about Azarov?"

"Nothing yet. We're only using choppers if we

have to because of the weather and we're only using ground patrols if we have to because of the radiation. You said the guy looked like he was bleeding pretty badly and that's a whole lot of desert out there. My guess is that he's dead and buried in the sand by now."

Rapp didn't respond other than to adjust the ice pack on what had once been the bridge of his nose.

"But, if I'm wrong, don't worry. We've got other lines on the guy and after this clusterfuck we're pretty confident he's not going back to Russia. We'll find him."

Rapp turned and started toward a line of military vehicles near the west end of the compound.

"Where are you going?" Nash said. "We've got a meeting with the Saudis in five minutes."

"Handle it."

"They're expecting you. What do you want me to tell them?"

"Tell them to go fuck themselves. I'm heading home."

Chapter 58

Fairfax, Virginia
U.S.A.

Rapp gunned the Charger, barely making it through the dark intersection before the light turned red. He'd hopped a military transport out of Riyadh and spent the last fifteen hours lying on top of a bunch of flak jackets in the back. Now that he was finally in the last five minutes of his trip home, those minutes seemed to be stretching out forever.

His phone rang and he patched it through the car's anemic sound system.

"Hello, Irene."

"I hear you're back in the States."

"Yeah. About a mile from my apartment."

"Oh," she said. "That's gone, Mitch."

"What's gone?"

"The apartment. We emptied it and it's been rented. You need to turn around and go *home*."

The inflection was impossible to miss. "My house is done?"

"I think Claudia's still working on the punch list, but yes. It's done."

For some reason the news hit him with a force that he wasn't prepared for. He glanced at the clock in his dashboard. A little after nineteen thirty.

"Maybe we should get together and debrief," he heard himself say. "Are you at the office?"

"I am, but it's completely out of the question. Claudia's holding dinner for you."

That hit even harder. Why? Why did he suddenly want to put the Dodge on a random highway and floor it? Was this fear? After everything he'd just been through, was this what scared him?

"First thing tomorrow morning, then?" Rapp said before he could stop himself.

"No. Tomorrow morning you're going to sleep in and have a nice breakfast. Then, at eleven, you have an appointment with a plastic surgeon. Claudia has the details."

"Fine. I'll swing by after—"

"Actually, you won't. Because you'll be on your way to your appointment with a reconstructive dentist. Claudia has—"

"The details," he finished.

"Exactly. The Middle East and Russia will still be there day after tomorrow, Mitch. Now go have a nice, quiet evening."

The line went dead and Rapp kept driving straight for another mile before finally summoning the courage to make a U-turn.

The narrow road wound through dense trees and intermittent farmland before climbing to a flat summit overlooking all of it. Rapp's twenty-acre lot was along the south edge of what was supposed to be an airy subdivision with ten home sites. That is, until his brother, an obscenely wealthy money manager, purchased the other nine. In case he ever needed a vacation home, he'd explained.

Rapp pulled up to the empty neighborhood's gate and found that the keypad had been replaced by a thumbprint reader. Not sure what else to do, he pressed his left one against the screen. The steel barrier obediently swung back.

All markers and other clues that the unused lots existed were gone. There was nothing but natural landscaping, pristine asphalt, and dark sky. A traditional red barn appeared on his left, glowing dully in the moonlight. Originally intended to keep the residents' horses, it now contained what was left of his contractor's equipment.

The white stucco wall surrounding his house appeared as he crested a small rise, glowing a little brighter with the help of a few hazy spotlights. The copper gate was already taking on a green patina, visible as he pulled up next to the call box. There was a padded envelope on top of it addressed in a childlike scrawl.

4 Mich

Tearing it open, he found a single remote. A

push of the button caused the heavy gate to slide smoothly out of sight.

The garage doors were closed, so he parked next to a modern sculpture that looked a little like debris from a plane crash painted with blue Rust-Oleum. It probably symbolized something deep and he made a mental note to tell Claudia how much he liked it.

The house itself was admittedly a bit unusual. It consisted of a single floor with a half basement and had no exterior windows at all. His late wife and the architect had done everything they could with textures, shapes, and roofline to keep it from looking like a prison and they'd largely succeeded. It might have been the most aesthetic bunker ever built.

There was no one to greet him when he came through the front door, so he took a moment to admire the warm lighting and sparsely arranged Asian furniture. A bold painting of a flower to his right looked almost as expensive as the downed Cessna out front.

At the end of the entryway, the left wall transformed into floor-to-ceiling glass looking onto a beautifully landscaped interior courtyard. The house's living space ringed the courtyard, with virtually every room having access to that central garden. Through the newly planted trees, he could just make out the elegant lines of an industrial kitchen and the raven-haired woman moving through it.

He found a sliding door and stepped outside, crossing to the kitchen on a flagstone pathway. When he entered a similar door on the other side, Claudia yanked a spoon from the pot she was stirring and spun to face him. Clearly, she'd been coached and her reaction to his face consisted of nothing more than a brief flash in her dark eyes.

"Mitch!" she said, tossing the spoon on the counter and throwing her arms around him. The hug was more than a little painful, but he found that he didn't mind at all.

"I'm sorry I didn't meet you at the door, but I didn't want anything to burn."

"No problem," he said, immediately wishing he'd come up with something a little more suave.

"Well?" she said, spreading her arms wide. "Do you like it?"

"I do," he said, feeling a little overwhelmed. "Great sculpture out front."

"Isn't it fantastic? It's an Aubarge."

He nodded as though that meant something to him. "Where'd all this furniture come from?"

"Where didn't it come from? Do you like it? It's modern, but not sterile, don't you think?"

"That's exactly what I was going to say."

"You were not," she responded, picking up

her spoon and going to work on one of the pots boiling on the stove. She indicated with an elbow toward an open bottle of wine sitting on the counter. "Have a glass. But be warned, it's a bit cold. I just pulled it from your cellar."

"I have a wine cellar?"

She switched to the French she was more comfortable with. "Of course! Fully stocked!"

He found a glass and examined the label on the bottle. Not surprisingly, he'd never heard of it, but the fact that it had been produced before he'd learned to read worried him a bit. Through a few bizarre twists of fate and his brother's financial genius, Rapp had amassed a fair amount of money. Not this much, though.

"Claudia?"

"Yes?"

"First, let me say that the place is amazing."

"You love it, right?" she said, twisting around to look at him with a broad smile.

"Absolutely. I do. But could I ask you how much it cost?"

"Oh, not much. I was a little overbudget but I just paid for that myself."

"Paid for what?"

"The overbudget part."

"How much are we talking about?"

"Not much."

"Is there some reason I shouldn't know the number?"

"*With* the artwork?"

"Yes. With the artwork."

"But not the wine."

"The artwork, the wine. Everything."

She shrugged at the sheer triviality of the amount, making a show of carrying out the necessary calculations in her head.

"Twoish . . ."

"Two hundred thousand?" Rapp said, deciding to fall off the wagon and pour himself a glass of what was apparently extremely expensive wine. Still, it could have been worse. He could reimburse her for that without too much juggling.

"Million."

The glass stopped a few inches from his mouth but then he decided to just go with it. That number was so big, it didn't bear worrying about.

"Now go away," she said. "I need to concentrate. Go see Scott and Anna."

"Scott?"

"Well, I couldn't leave him in that horrible hospital and he didn't have anyone else to take care of him. They're in the guest bedroom playing LEGOs."

Rapp started for the hallway but then stopped after a few steps. "Where is that?"

"Directly opposite of where we are now. You can't miss it."

●●●

Anna had been coached, too, but it didn't help. She let out a high-pitched shriek when he walked through the open door.

"It's okay! It's me. Mitch."

The young girl slid off the bed where she and Scott Coleman were attempting to build something that may have been the Eiffel Tower. "Mom said you were in a car accident. Were you wearing your seat belt?"

"I wasn't."

"You know that's illegal. You *have* to!"

"You're right. I'm sorry."

"Anna," Coleman said, "your mom probably could use some help. Why don't you go see."

"When are we going to finish?" She pointed to the LEGOs. "Maybe Mitch wants to play."

"I'm sure he does, but we should save the rest for tomorrow."

She nodded and went for the door, giving Rapp's leg a quick hug before starting down the hallway.

"Anna?" Mitch called after her.

She stopped and turned.

"Maybe you could ask your mom to put my food through the blender."

The request obviously confused her but she gave a quick nod before tearing down the hallway.

Coleman waited until she was out of earshot

before he spoke. "Jeez . . . Mas said he worked you over, but I had no idea."

"You don't look so great yourself."

Rapp was happy to note that his retort wasn't entirely accurate. While Coleman had lost a lot of weight and his skin was pasty white, his eyes were clear and his voice had regained its strength. Most of all, though, he was above-ground.

"I hear you're going to make a full recovery," Rapp continued.

"Yeah. But at the end of a long road."

"No problem. Take a couple of weeks."

Coleman managed to produce the Boy Scout grin his friends had become so familiar with. "The docs say that I should be dead. That if it weren't for you, the infection I got would've been fatal."

"Me? What do I have to do with that?"

"Turns out you dragging me through every third-world shithole on the planet has given me a pretty good immune system."

They fell silent for a few moments and Rapp ran through the Pakistan op in his head—the trashed motorcycle, going for position instead of entering the warehouse . . .

"I'm sorry, Scott. That should have been me in there."

"Fortunes of war, man. What'll you do?"

Rapp nodded. "When you're done with your rehab are you coming back?"

"Hell yeah," Coleman said, pointing a shaky finger at Rapp's damaged face. "You obviously don't do too well without me there to watch out for you."

Claudia's voice floated down the hall toward them. Dinner was ready.

Rapp noticed a walker in the corner. "You need some help?"

"No. I think I'm going to sit this one out. Maybe get some sleep."

Rapp turned toward the door but stopped when Coleman spoke again.

"Can you do me a favor, Mitch?"

"Sure."

"If Azarov is still alive, don't go after him. It won't change what happened."

Rapp ran his hand along the rim of a Chinese vase that he hoped was a reproduction. "Sure, Scott. Whatever you want."

Epilogue

Near Dominical
Costa Rica

"Are you making those fried plantains with it?"

"Do you want them?"

Cara popped the top off her third beer and frowned theatrically. "Come on, Grisha. You have to ask?"

He selected a ripe one from a bowl on the counter. "You chop."

The evening was unusually warm and she was still in a bikini top and surf shorts, padding around his tile floors in the thrift-store flip-flops she favored.

"Be careful," he said when she reached toward the knife block. "Those are sharp."

"You and your knives. I swear you stay up all night grinding them on a big rock in your basement."

"Not *all* night."

She was the most vibrant person he'd ever met. A blinding light in the darkness that had swallowed him so many years ago. Having said that, he had to acknowledge that in the kitchen, she was a danger to herself and everyone around her.

It had been six months since he'd escaped Saudi Arabia. ISIS had taken full credit for the attack and there was no reason for the world to look any further. The cleanup was already well under way and the effect on oil prices had been relatively minor. Maxim Krupin was still in control, but of an increasingly angry populace and dissatisfied oligarchy.

For a time, Azarov had run. He'd used his network of clandestine bank accounts and underworld contacts to disappear into the empty corners of the earth. It was a strategy designed to produce a long existence but not a long life. One morning he'd woken up in an anonymous hotel room in Namibia, packed his bag, and returned home. It was here he would stay. In peace, if possible. In a bloody last stand if necessary.

To his surprise, the former scenario seemed to be the one playing out. Krupin had been completely silent. No messages, no texts, and most important, no Russian spec ops team at his front door. Similarly, the Americans had been quite conspicuous in their absence from his life. With the political uproar caused by a jihadist detonation of a radioactive weapon, he suspected that they had more important things to deal with than a retired Russian assassin.

After his return, Azarov had resisted the temptation that Cara presented for a time, but his discipline had finally faltered. They'd had dinner at a hotel restaurant on the beach and been together ever since. Each day, she pushed the darkness a little further back.

He picked up the platter with their steaks on it and nodded toward the open doors leading to the patio. "Could you help me with the grill?"

The sky was overcast but, between the pool and the glow from the house, there was plenty of light to work by. Cara held out a hand to test the temperature of the coals. Satisfied that they were ready, she reached for the platter but then paused.

"Is that a spot on your shirt?"

He glanced down just as her hand passed in front of his chest. The red dot jumped from white linen to tanned skin.

Azarov dropped the plate and slammed into her, driving her to the deck and shielding her with his body. She was still lucid enough to scream, so he rolled right, throwing her through the air and into the pool.

By the time the sound of the splash reached him, he had taken cover behind the grill and was reaching for the pistol hidden beneath it. He'd barely wrapped his hand around the grip when the cold metal of a silencer touched the back of his ear.

"Grisha!" He heard Cara cough as she surfaced. "What—"

"Be silent and stay still!"

He had never spoken to her in that tone and it seemed to work. All sound coming from her direction faded. Azarov wanted to turn his head to look at her but decided it would be unwise until he determined who he was dealing with. If it was one of Krupin's men, they would undoubtedly delay killing him until the Russian president could phone him and gloat about the limitlessness of his power. It would inevitably be a long and grandiose speech that would give Azarov time to gain the upper hand. And then he would go to Russia and kill Krupin, his political allies, his family, and everyone he'd ever known.

"Nice and easy, Grisha."

The breath went out of him at the sound of the American accent. He rose with comic slowness, finally turning to face the man aiming a Glock 19 between his eyes.

"You look better than the last time I saw you, Mr. Rapp."

"Three different plastic surgeries and I didn't even bother to keep track of the time in the dentist's chair. How about you? Were you actually hit or was the blood just for show?"

"Biceps. In and out."

"Grisha!" Cara said, unable to contain herself any longer. "Who is he? Do you know him? What does he want?"

Azarov eased his face left until he could see her out of the corner of his eye. The hair had matted across her face but it wasn't enough to obscure the terror etched there. It was unfair. A woman like her should never have to feel fear.

"Please, Cara. It's going to be fine. Just stay in the pool."

Rapp motioned with his gun. "Let's take a walk."

The Russian did as he was told, crossing his large patio and starting up the trail that led to his training facility. In doing so, the tactical advantage swung in his direction. The unseen shooter was undoubtedly Charles Wicker, one of the finest combat snipers alive. The jungle at the edges of the trail was extremely dense, though, making it virtually impossible to maintain an unbroken line of sight. Further, Azarov was intimately familiar with the terrain from years of training there.

It was an advantage similar to the one he'd counted on in Saudi Arabia, the Russian reminded himself. And this wasn't a lone, injured Mitch Rapp fresh off a run through the sweltering desert. The CIA man was healthy, rested, and had backup.

The only relevant question Azarov needed to ask himself was how he wanted to die. On his knees or fighting? Oddly, he found that he didn't care. Instead, his mind wandered to the past few months of his life. The time had been agonizingly short, but a gift nonetheless.

They reached the gym and Azarov stopped in front of the glass doors.

"Inside," Rapp said.

He obeyed and Rapp indicated toward a chair next to the squat rack. Azarov sat while the American slid onto a table just over a meter away.

"I'm surprised you made it so easy, Grisha. You're too comfortable here."

"Isn't that the way you're supposed to feel in your home? Comfortable?"

"Not us."

Azarov nodded. "And so you've come to kill me."

"That was the plan. But now I'm not sure."

"What's changed?"

"You jumped on the surfer girl. The smart money would have been to keep her in front of you when you went for cover. Or at least to just leave her standing there as a distraction. It makes me wonder if Irene Kennedy's right and you're not a complete waste of skin."

"She thinks that?"

Rapp put his gun on table next to him and Azarov focused on it in his peripheral vision. The short distance between them could be easily covered if it had been anyone else. With Rapp, though, it would be suicide.

"We can't find a record of you contacting anyone in Russia since you got back. Even your company doesn't know where you are. They figure you're dead."

"Not dead. Just retired."

"Is that what you told Krupin?"

"Maxim Krupin?" Azarov said, feigning ignorance. "The Russian president?"

"It's a little late to try to play that hand, don't you think, Grisha?"

Azarov leaned back in his chair and stared up at the American for a few seconds. "We have ended our association. Permanently."

"What if he feels differently?"

"Then I'll kill him."

"That's a problem for me."

"I don't understand. Maxim Krupin is a sociopath who causes your country and the world nothing but problems."

"That's true. But now we have him by the balls. That bullshit in Saudi Arabia was all for him and it didn't work. If his involvement were made public, the rest of the world would come down on him like the wrath of God."

"And you can use this," Azarov said, "to exert control over Russia without creating a power vacuum."

"That's what Director Kennedy and the president think. Personally, I'd rather just fly over to Moscow and put a bullet in his head."

"So you want me to tell you everything I know about his involvement in what happened in Saudi Arabia."

"It's one option."

"If I agree, are you offering me protection from him?"

"Not my job."

Azarov adjusted his gaze to the glass that looked out into the night. "I was young when I first met President Krupin. A simple soldier from a poor background. His offer to me was . . . everything. Money, beautiful women, power. All things I no longer value."

"What *do* you value, Grisha?"

He was surprised by the question and even more surprised that he wasn't sure how to answer it.

"Not patriotism," Rapp prompted. "I assume not God. The surfer girl?"

Azarov tensed before he could stop himself. The hope that it hadn't been noticed was dashed when a nearly imperceptible smile crossed the CIA man's lips.

"She doesn't know anything about me. There's no reason to hurt her."

"Who the fuck do you think you're talking to?"

Azarov considered the question for a moment before responding. "My apologies. You understand that I'm accustomed to dealing with a different class of opponent."

493

"So we understand each other?" Rapp said, standing.

"Yes."

"And the business between us is finished?"

"Any questions I might have had about our relative abilities were answered in Saudi Arabia."

The American picked up his Glock and started for the door. "Then enjoy the steaks."